THE WORLD'S GREATEST COMIC
DEADPOOL

GERRY DUGGAN
writer

MIKE HAWTHORNE
penciler

TERRY PALLOT
inker

VC's JOE SABINO
letterer

VAL STAPLES [#1-2] & GURU-eFX [#3-5]
colorist

TONY MOORE [#1-3 & #5] and MIKE HAWTHORNE & JORDIE BELLAIRE [#4]
cover art

HEATHER ANTOS
assistant editor

JORDAN D. WHITE
editor

DEADPOOL created by ROB LIEFELD & FABIAN NICIEZA

collection editor   JENNIFER GRÜNWALD
associate editor   SARAH BRUNSTAD
associate managing editor   ALEX STARBUCK
editor, special projects   MARK D. BEAZLEY
vp, production & special projects   JEFF YOUNGQUIST
svp print, sales & marketing   DAVID GABRIEL
book designer   ADAM DEL RE

editor in chief   AXEL ALONSO
chief creative officer   JOE QUESADA
publisher   DAN BUCKLEY

DEADPOOL: WORLD'S GREATEST VOL. 1 — MILLIONAIRE WITH A MOUTH. Contains material originally published in magazine form as DEADPOOL #1-5. First printing 2016. ISBN 978-0-7851-9617-4. Published by MARVEL WORLDWIDE, INC., a subsidiary of MARVEL ENTERTAINMENT, LLC. OFFICE OF PUBLICATION: 135 West 50th Street, New York, NY 10020. Copyright © 2016 MARVEL No similarity between any of the names, characters, persons, and/or institutions in this magazine with those of any living or dead person or institution is intended, and any such similarity which may exist is purely coincidental. Printed in Canada. DAN BUCKLEY, President, TV, Publishing & Brand Management; JOE QUESADA, Chief Creative Officer; TOM BREVOORT, SVP of Publishing; DAVID BOGART, SVP of Business Affairs & Operations, Publishing & Partnership; C.B. CEBULSKI, VP of Brand Management & Development, Asia; DAVID GABRIEL, SVP of Sales & Marketing, Publishing; JEFF YOUNGQUIST, VP of Production & Special Projects; DAN CARR, Executive Director of Publishing Technology; SUSAN CRESPI, Production Manager; STAN LEE, Chairman Emeritus. For information regarding advertising in Marvel Comics or on Marvel.com, please contact Vit DeBellis, Integrated Sales Manager, at vdebellis@marvel.com. For Marvel subscription inquiries, please call 888-511-5480. Manufactured between 2/26/2016 and 4/4/2016 by SOLISCO PRINTERS, SCOTT, QC, CANADA.

10 9 8 7 6 5 4 3 2 1

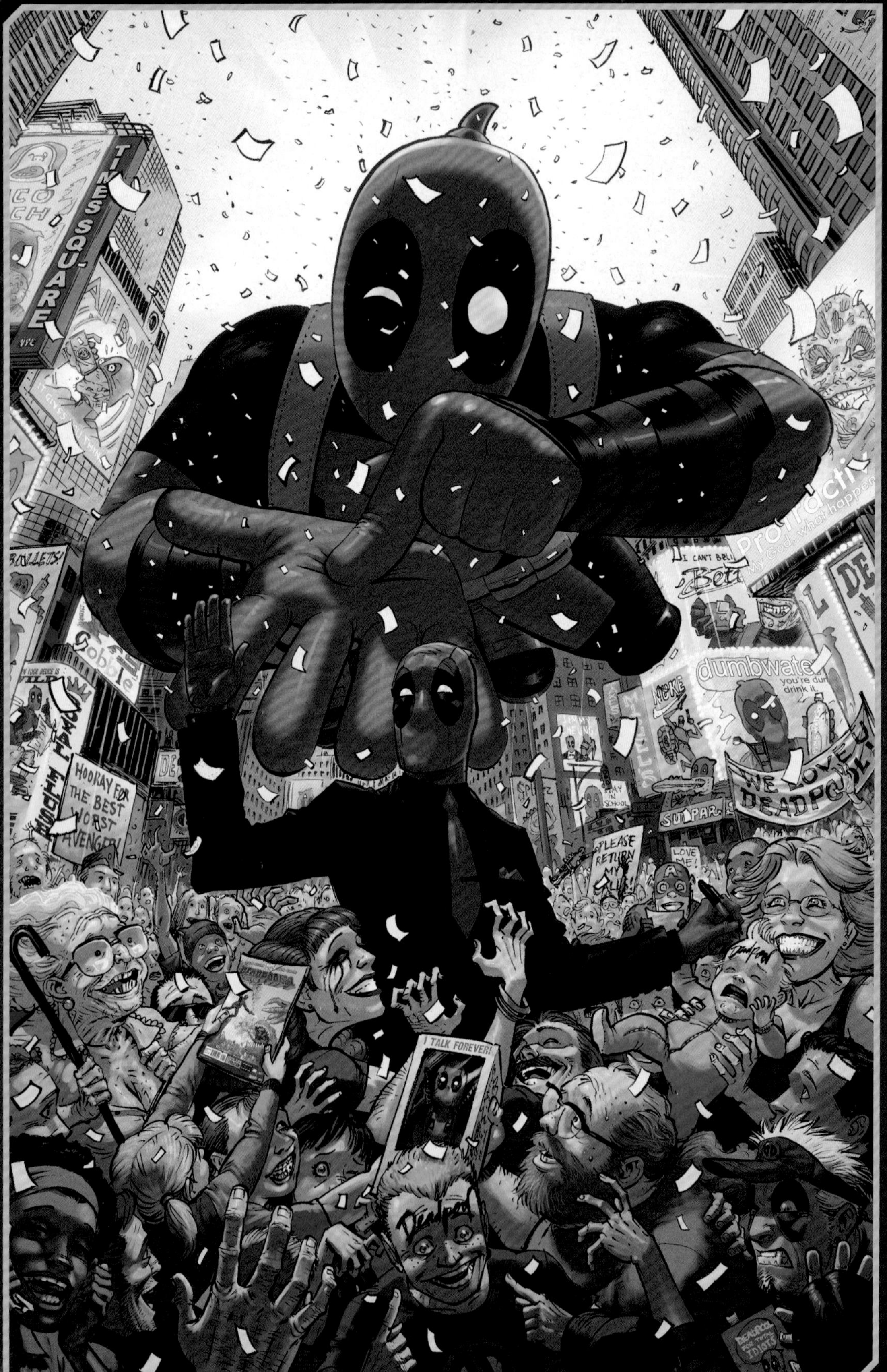
TIMES SQUARE
HOORAY FOR THE BEST WORST AVENGER!
PLEASE RETURN MY
LOVE ME!
I TALK FOREVER!

1 | SUMUS OMNES DEADPOOL

Deadly	Funny
Killer	Hero
Madman	Avenger
Cancerous	Smelly
Irresponsible	Father
Reckless	Husband
Regenerating	Degenerate
Merc	Mouth

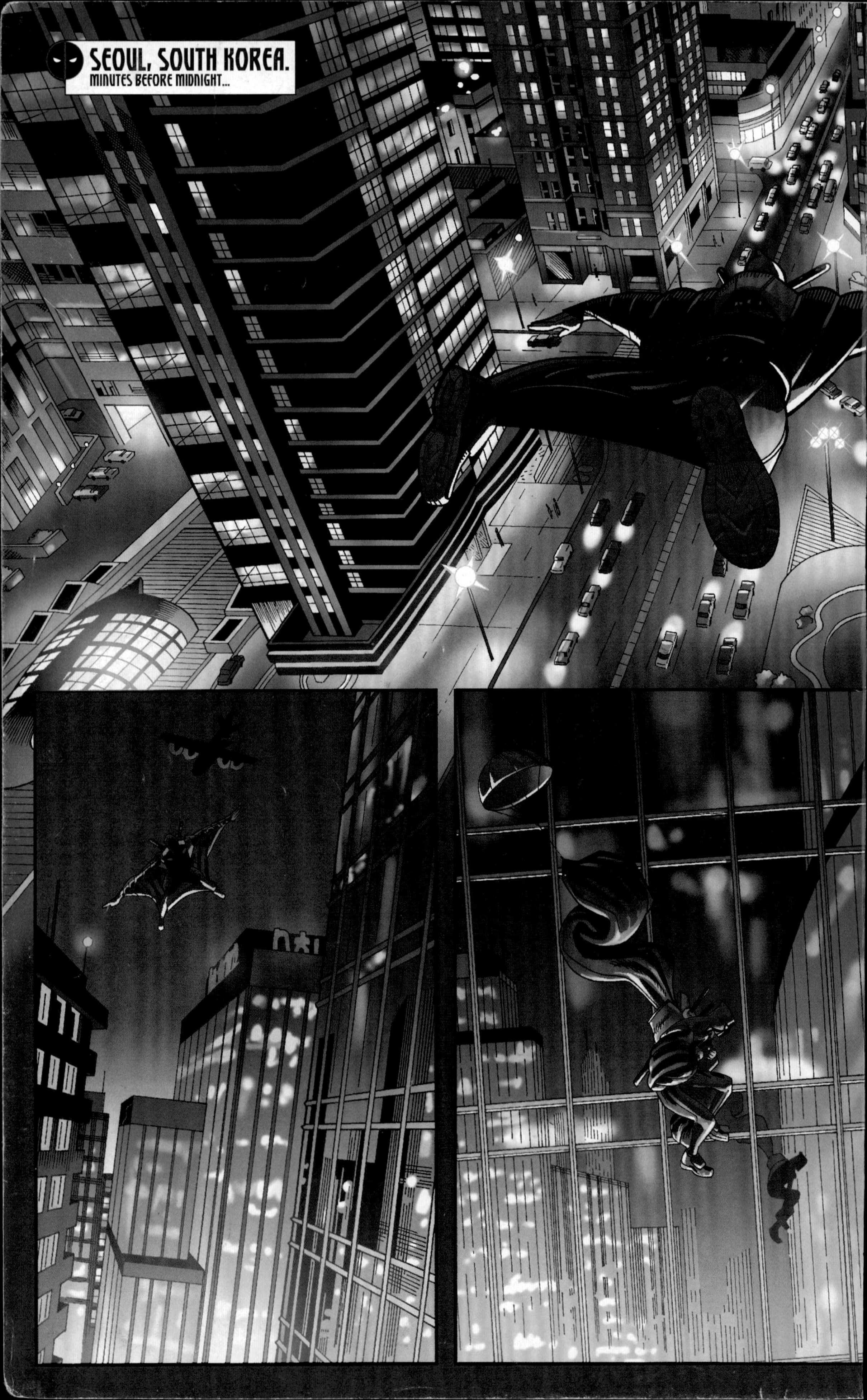
SEOUL, SOUTH KOREA.
MINUTES BEFORE MIDNIGHT...

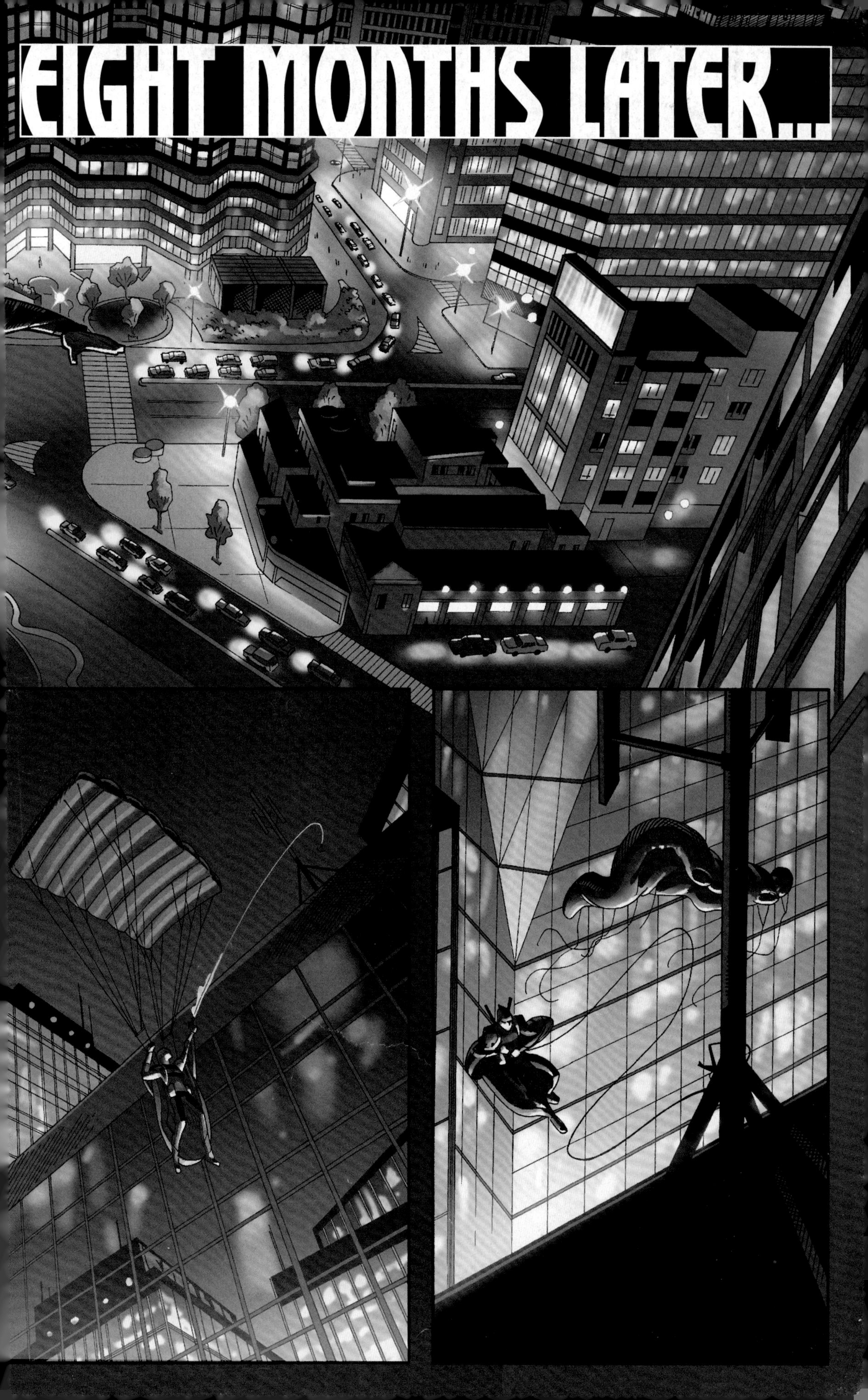
EIGHT MONTHS LATER...

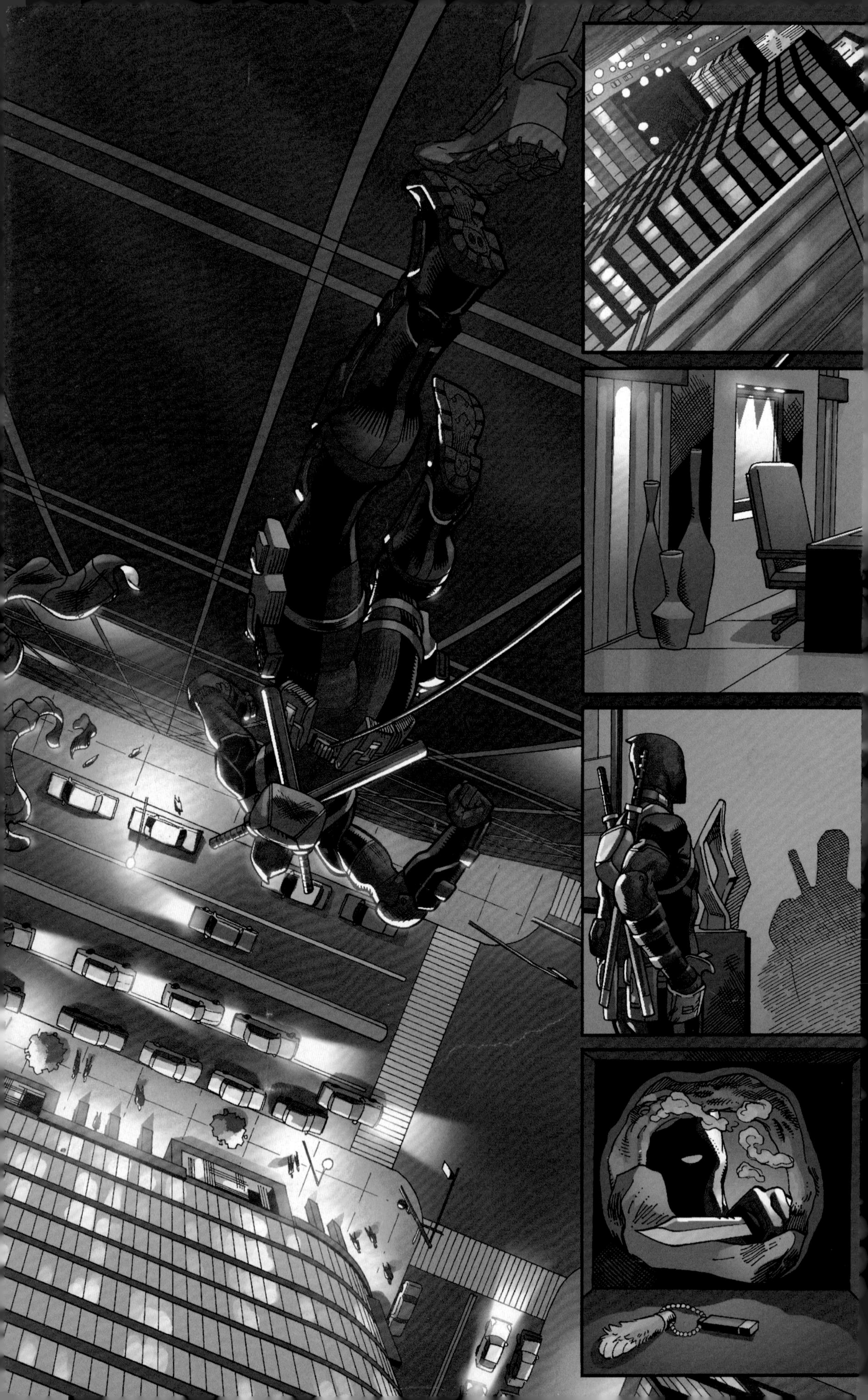

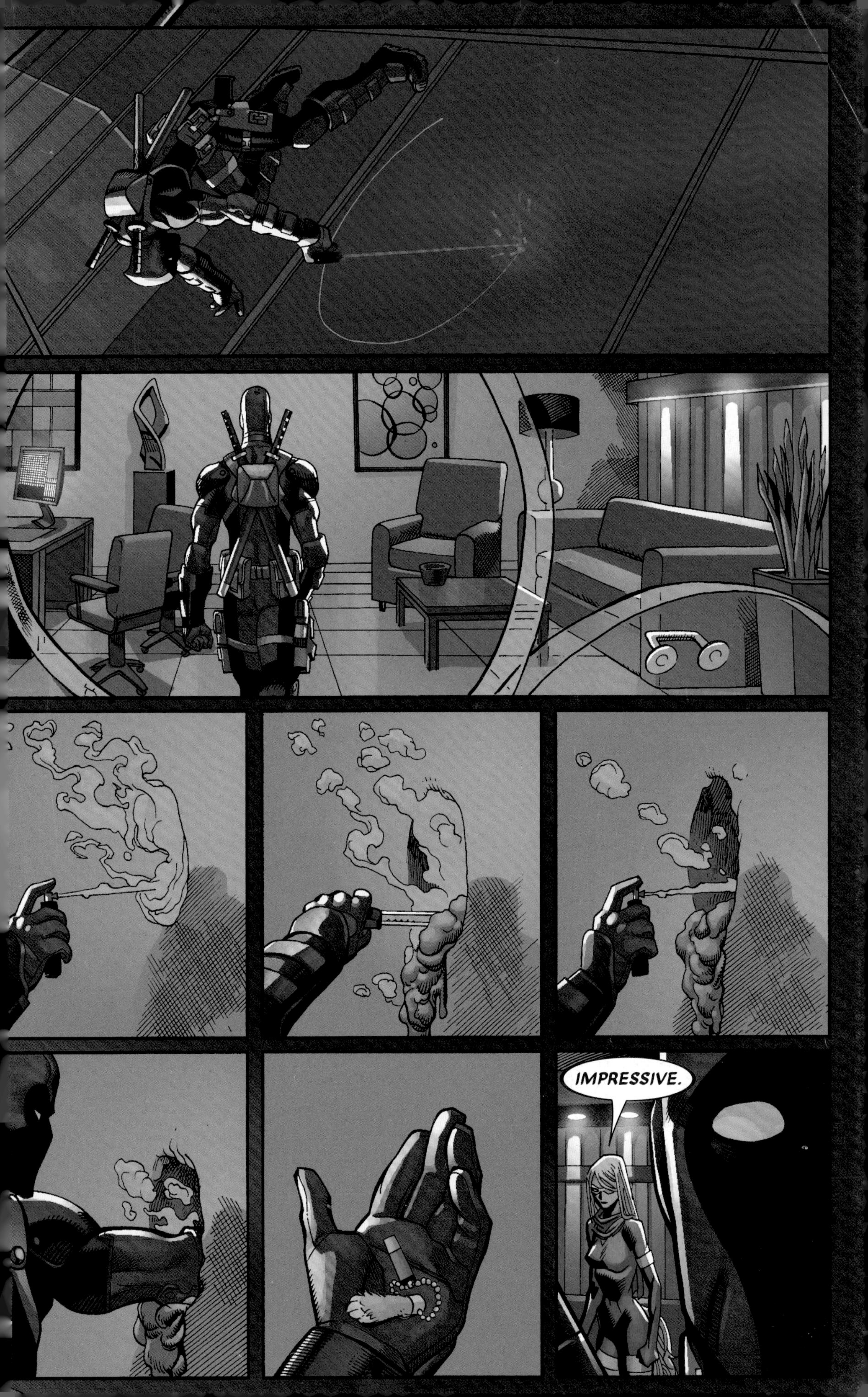
IMPRESSIVE.

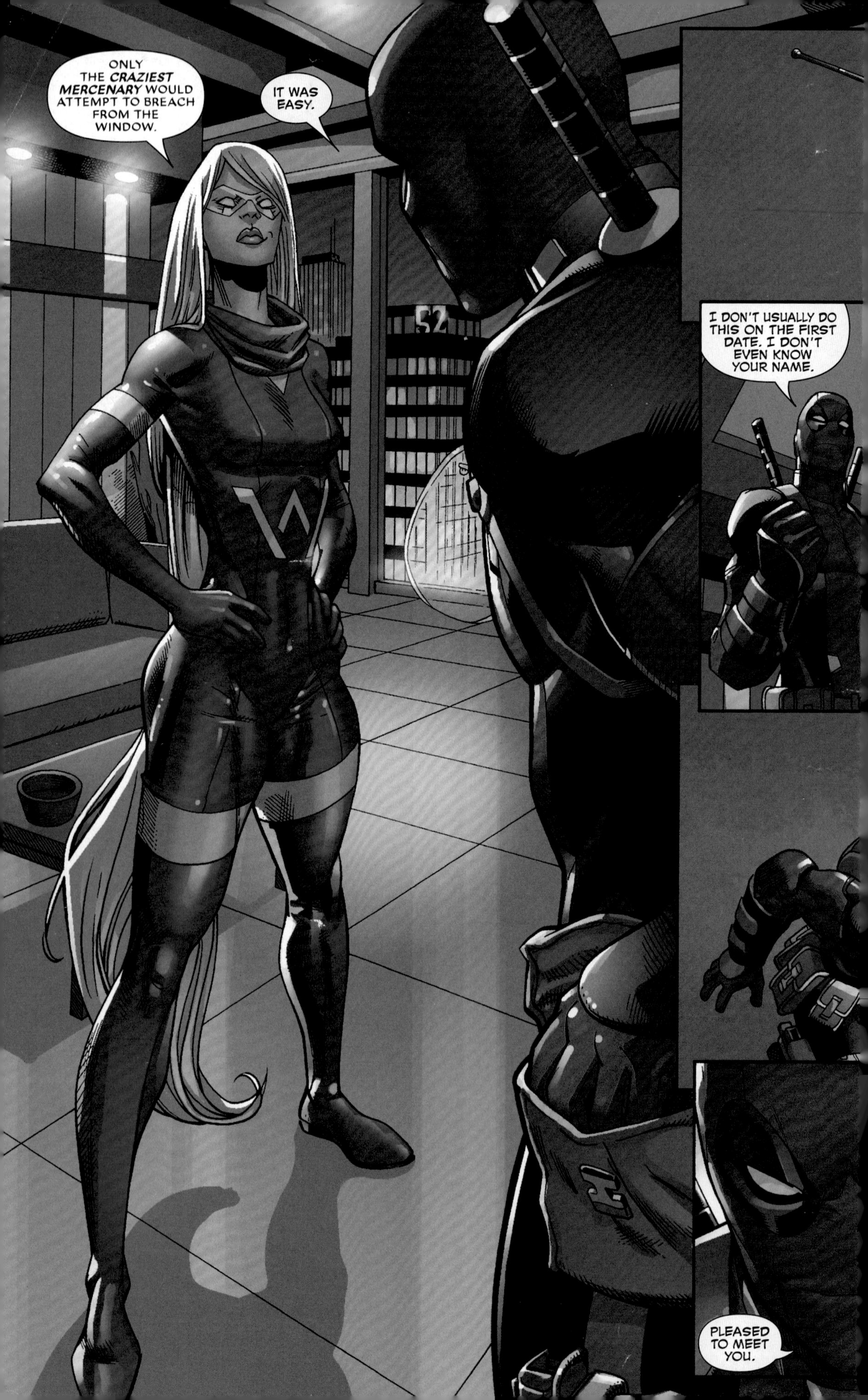

ONLY THE *CRAZIEST MERCENARY* WOULD ATTEMPT TO BREACH FROM THE WINDOW.
IT WAS EASY.
52
I DON'T USUALLY DO THIS ON THE FIRST DATE. I DON'T EVEN KNOW YOUR NAME.
PLEASED TO MEET YOU.

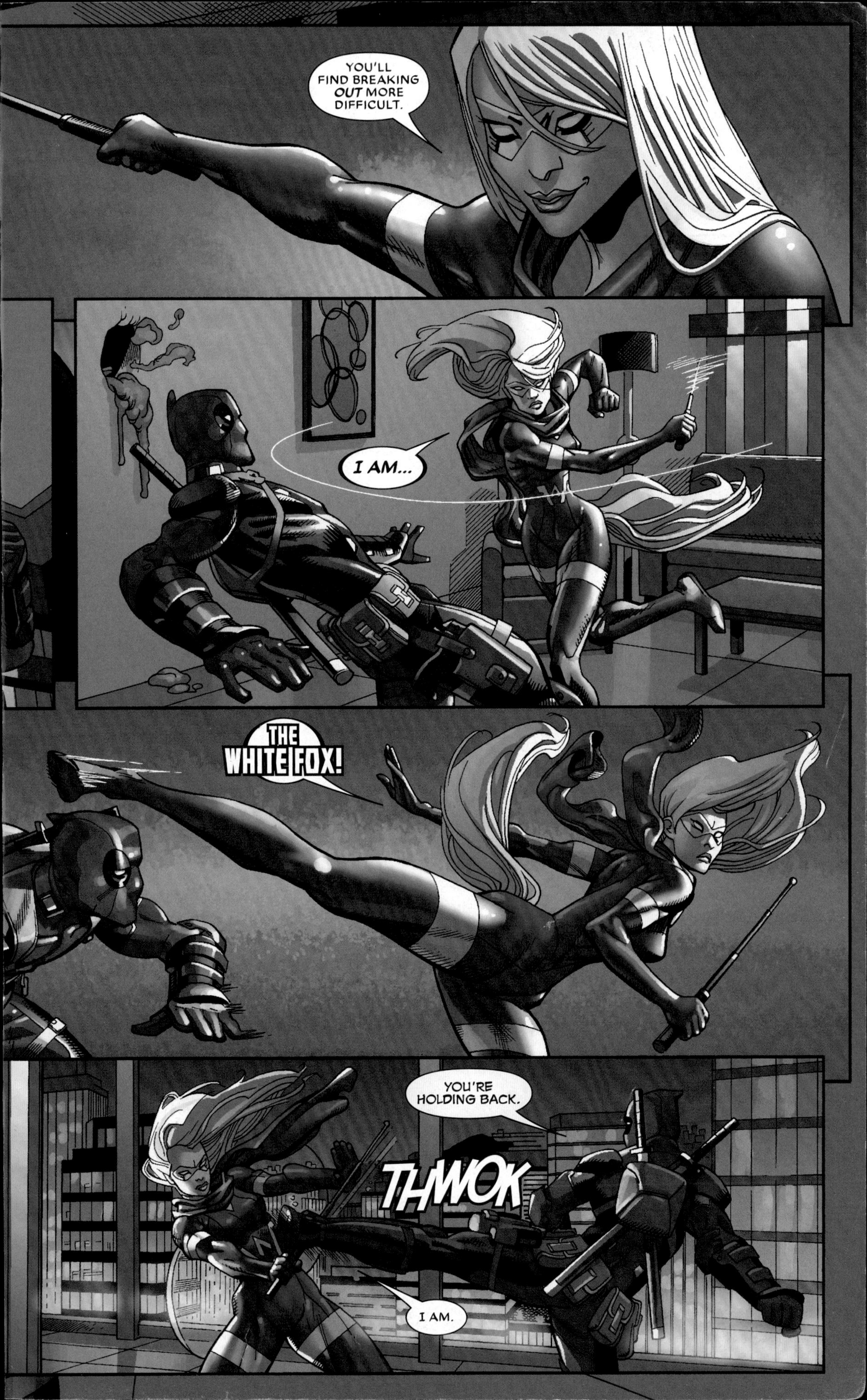
YOU'LL FIND BREAKING OUT MORE DIFFICULT.
I AM...
THE WHITE FOX!
YOU'RE HOLDING BACK.
THWOK
I AM.

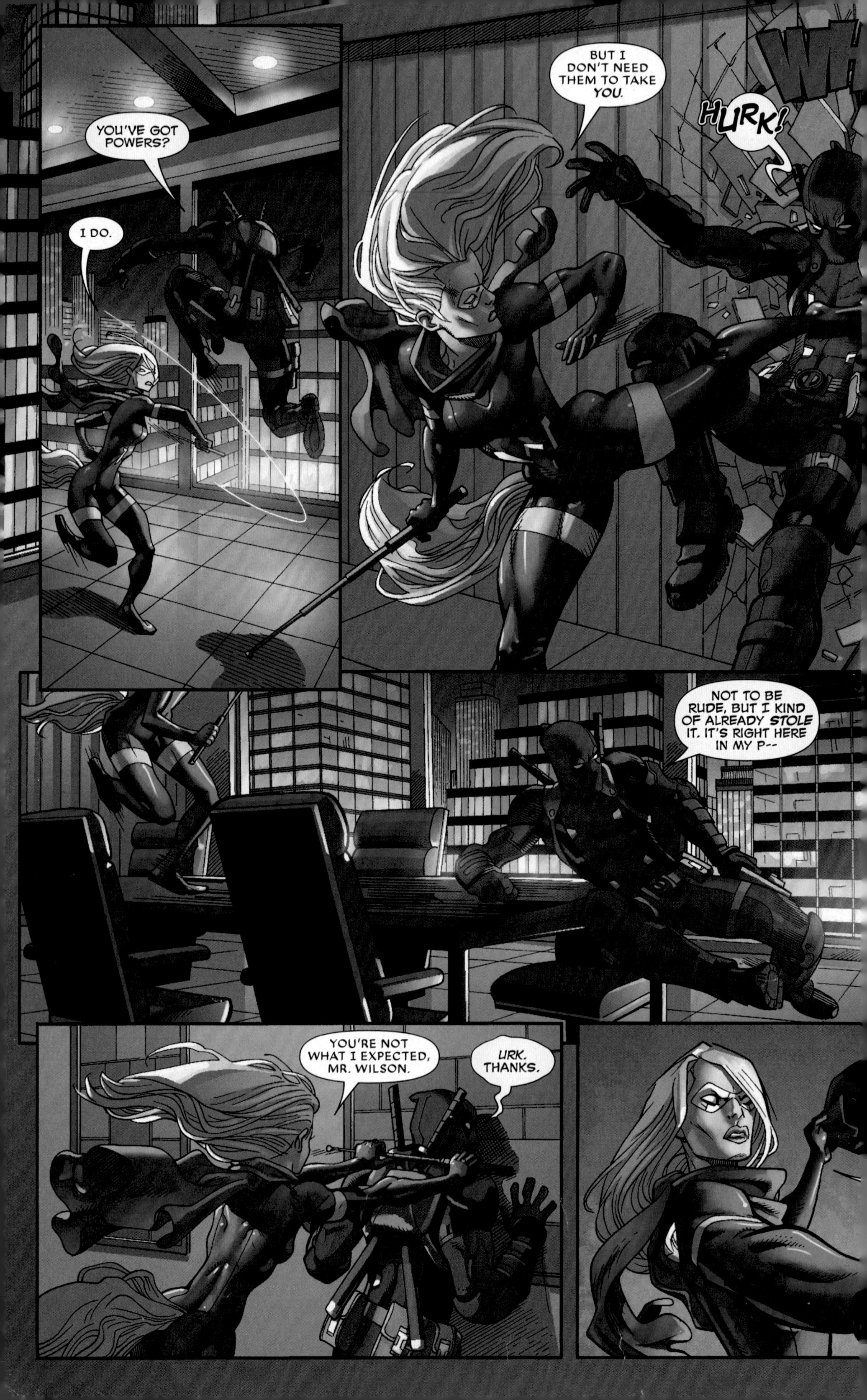
YOU'VE GOT POWERS?
I DO.
BUT I DON'T NEED THEM TO TAKE YOU.
WH
HURK!
NOT TO BE RUDE, BUT I KIND OF ALREADY STOLE IT. IT'S RIGHT HERE IN MY P--
YOU'RE NOT WHAT I EXPECTED, MR. WILSON.
URK. THANKS.

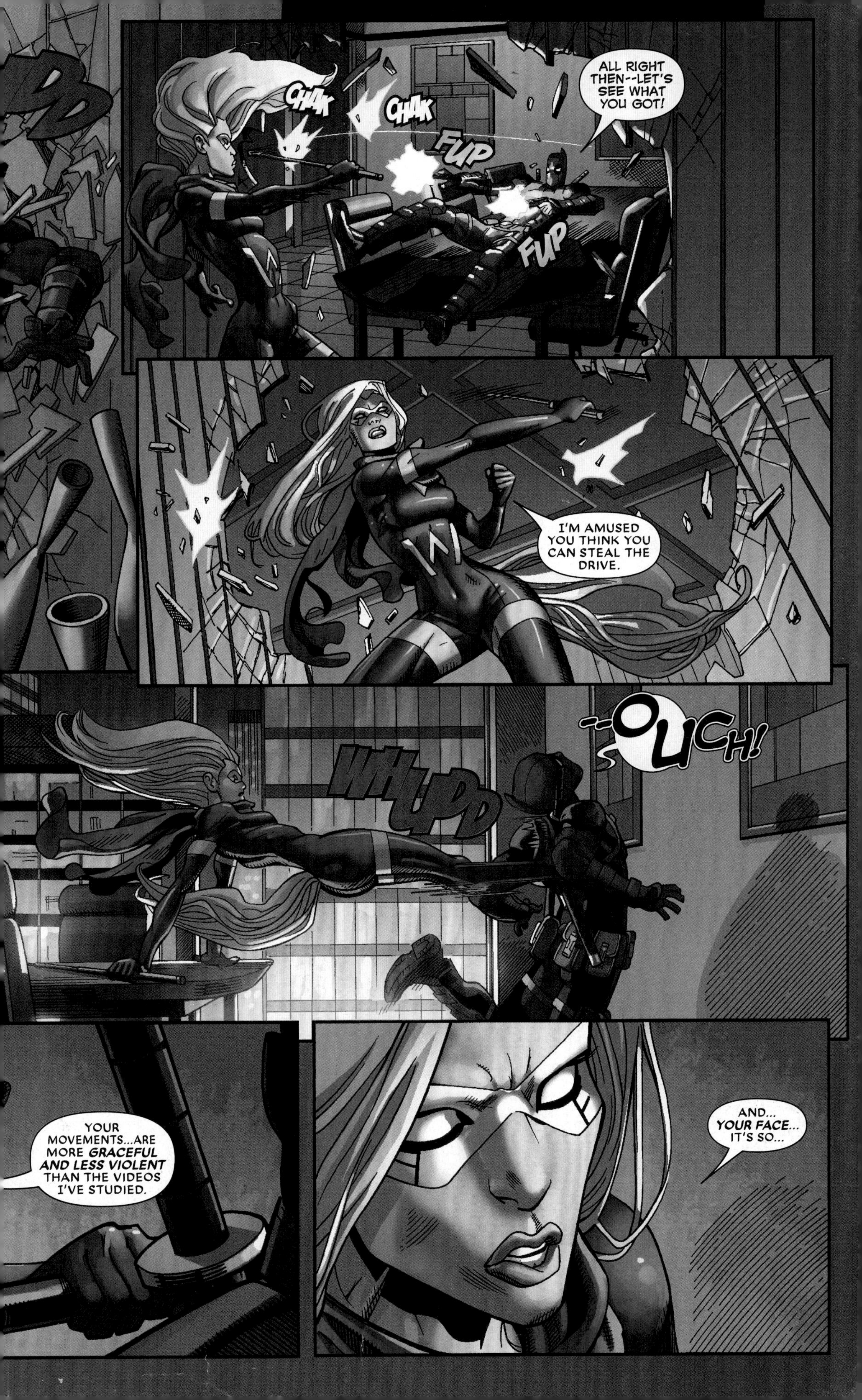
CHAK
CHAK
FUP
ALL RIGHT THEN--LET'S SEE WHAT YOU GOT!
FUP
I'M AMUSED YOU THINK YOU CAN STEAL THE DRIVE.
WHUDD
--OUCH!
YOUR MOVEMENTS...ARE MORE GRACEFUL AND LESS VIOLENT THAN THE VIDEOS I'VE STUDIED.
AND... YOUR FACE... IT'S SO...

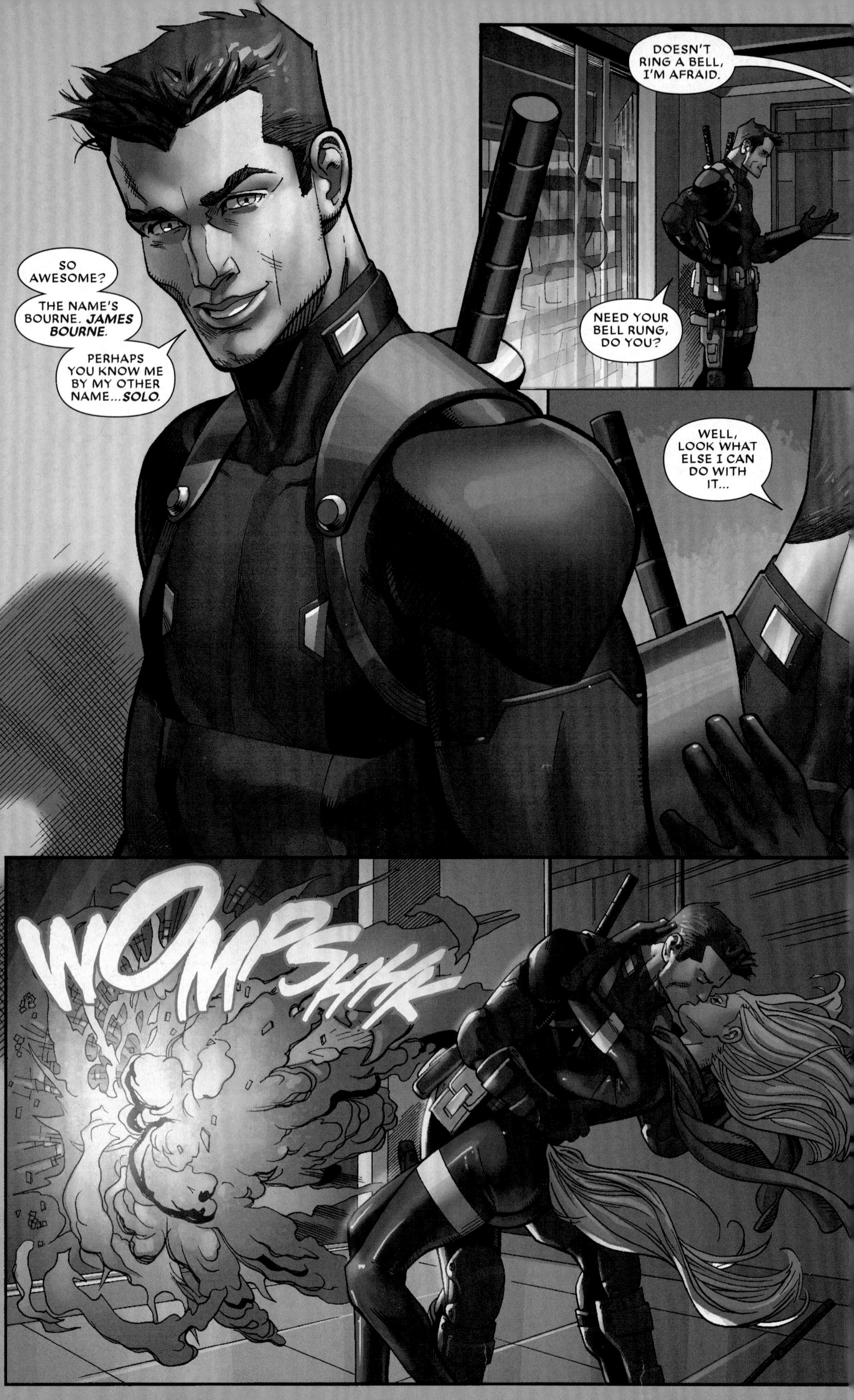
SO AWESOME?
THE NAME'S BOURNE. JAMES BOURNE.
PERHAPS YOU KNOW ME BY MY OTHER NAME...SOLO.
DOESN'T RING A BELL, I'M AFRAID.
NEED YOUR BELL RUNG, DO YOU?
WELL, LOOK WHAT ELSE I CAN DO WITH IT...
WOMPSHKR

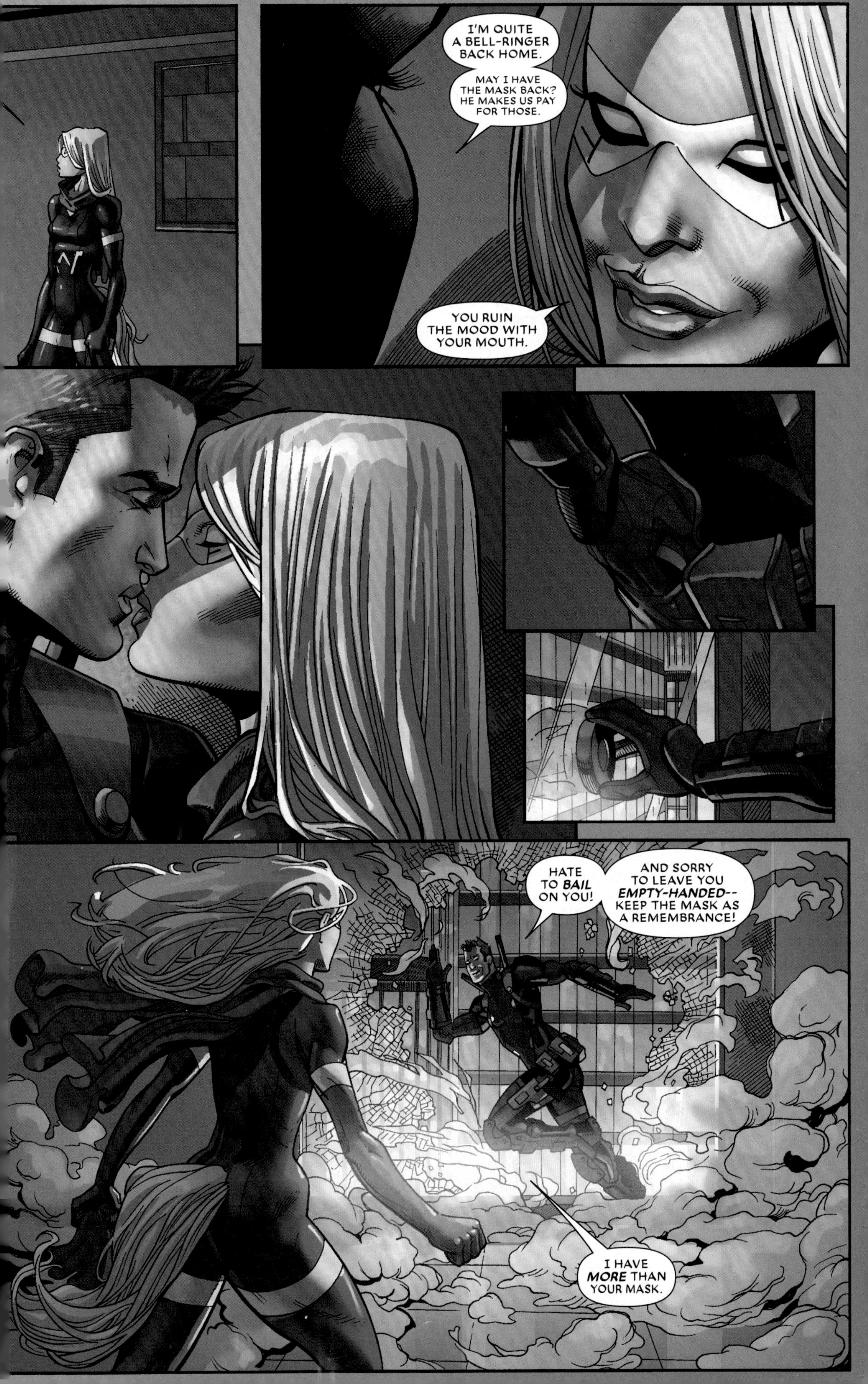
I'M QUITE A BELL-RINGER BACK HOME.
MAY I HAVE THE MASK BACK? HE MAKES US PAY FOR THOSE.
YOU RUIN THE MOOD WITH YOUR MOUTH.
HATE TO *BAIL* ON YOU!
AND SORRY TO LEAVE YOU *EMPTY-HANDED*-- KEEP THE MASK AS A REMEMBRANCE!
I HAVE *MORE* THAN YOUR MASK.

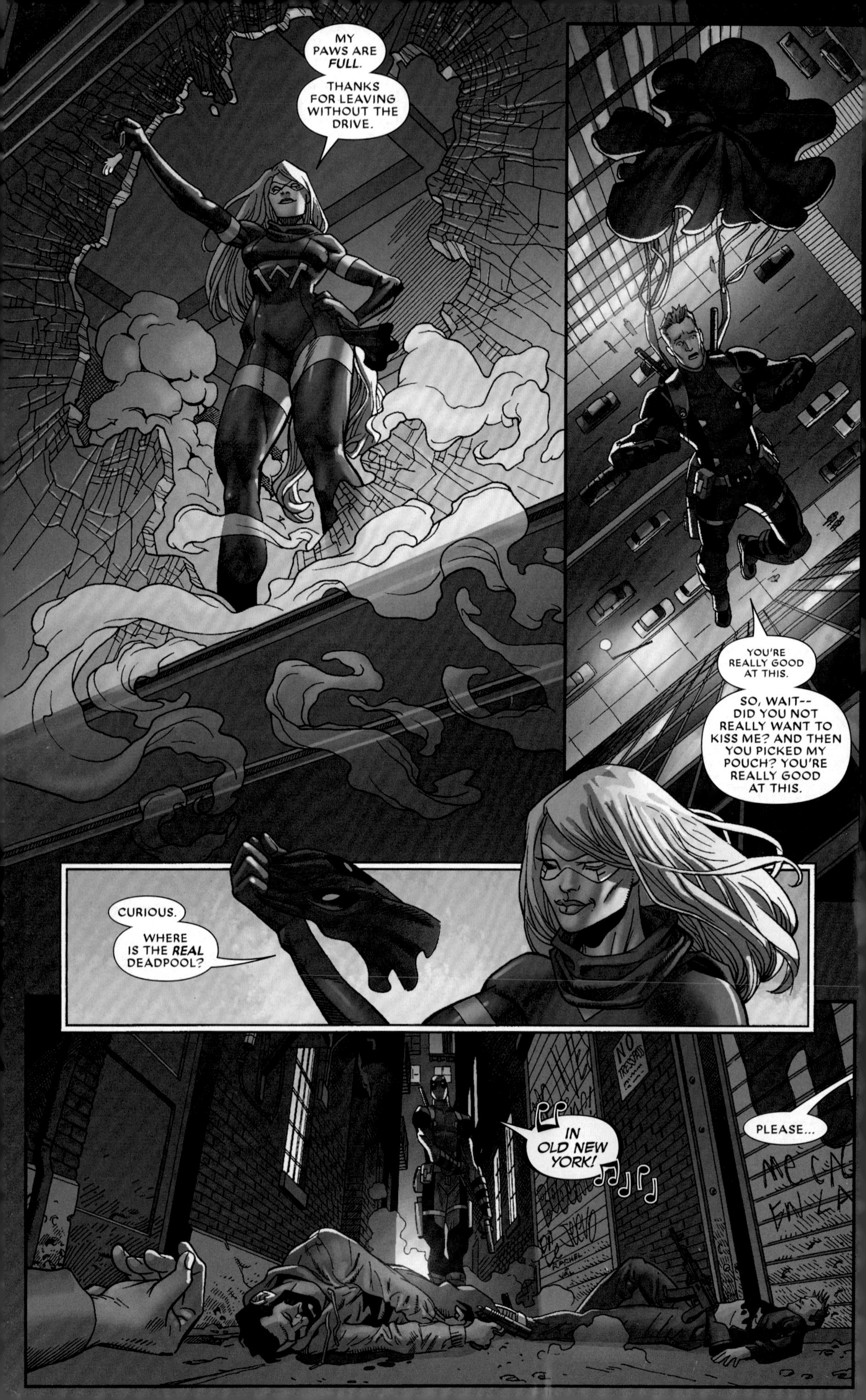

MY PAWS ARE *FULL*.
THANKS FOR LEAVING WITHOUT THE DRIVE.
YOU'RE REALLY GOOD AT THIS.
SO, WAIT-- DID YOU NOT REALLY WANT TO KISS ME? AND THEN YOU PICKED MY POUCH? YOU'RE REALLY GOOD AT THIS.
CURIOUS.
WHERE IS THE *REAL* DEADPOOL?
IN OLD NEW YORK!
PLEASE...

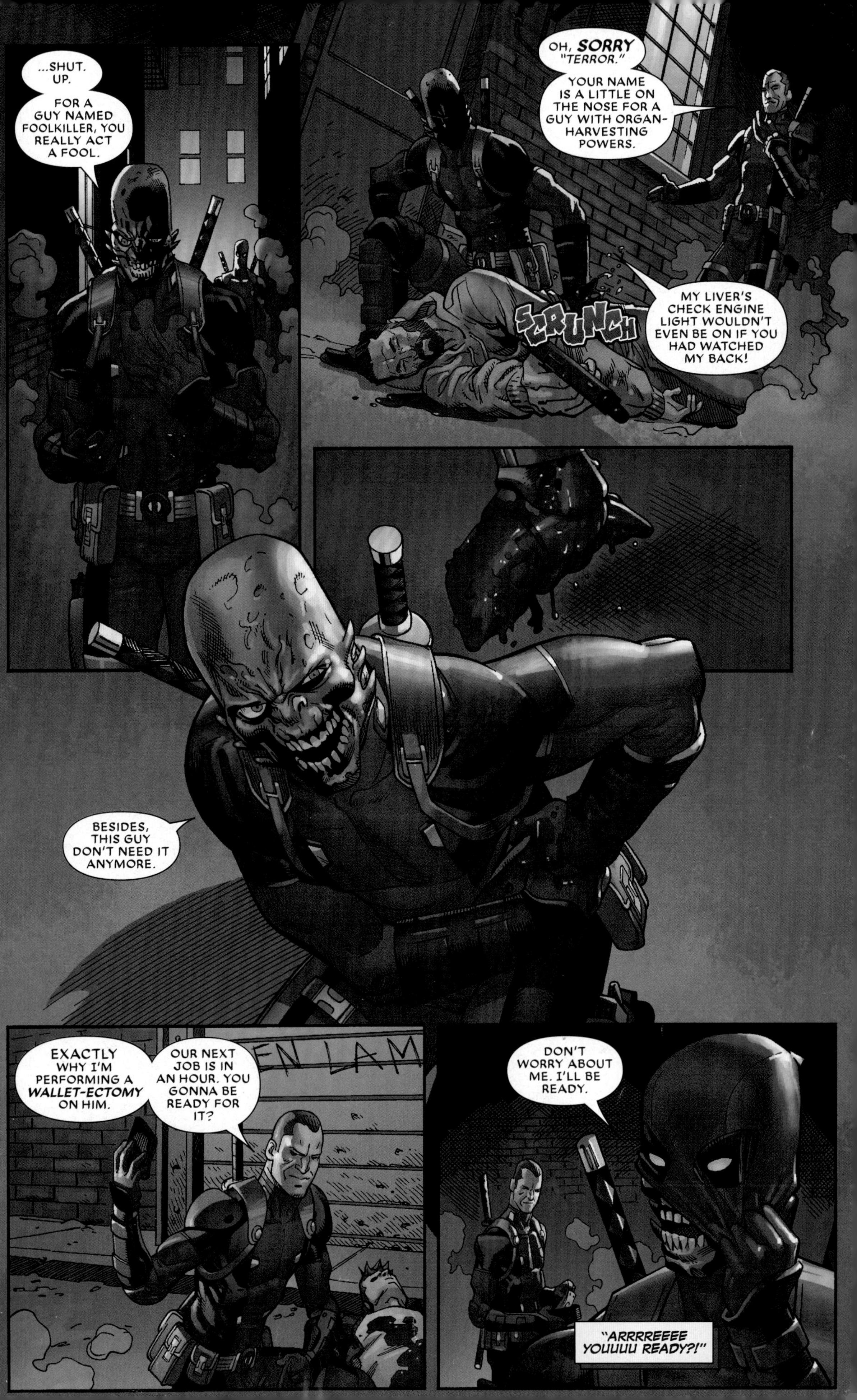

...SHUT. UP.
FOR A GUY NAMED FOOLKILLER, YOU REALLY ACT A FOOL.
OH, SORRY "TERROR."
YOUR NAME IS A LITTLE ON THE NOSE FOR A GUY WITH ORGAN-HARVESTING POWERS.
SCRUNCH
MY LIVER'S CHECK ENGINE LIGHT WOULDN'T EVEN BE ON IF YOU HAD WATCHED MY BACK!
BESIDES, THIS GUY DON'T NEED IT ANYMORE.
EXACTLY WHY I'M PERFORMING A WALLET-ECTOMY ON HIM.
EN LAM
OUR NEXT JOB IS IN AN HOUR. YOU GONNA BE READY FOR IT?
DON'T WORRY ABOUT ME. I'LL BE READY.
"ARRRREEEE YOUUUU READY?!"

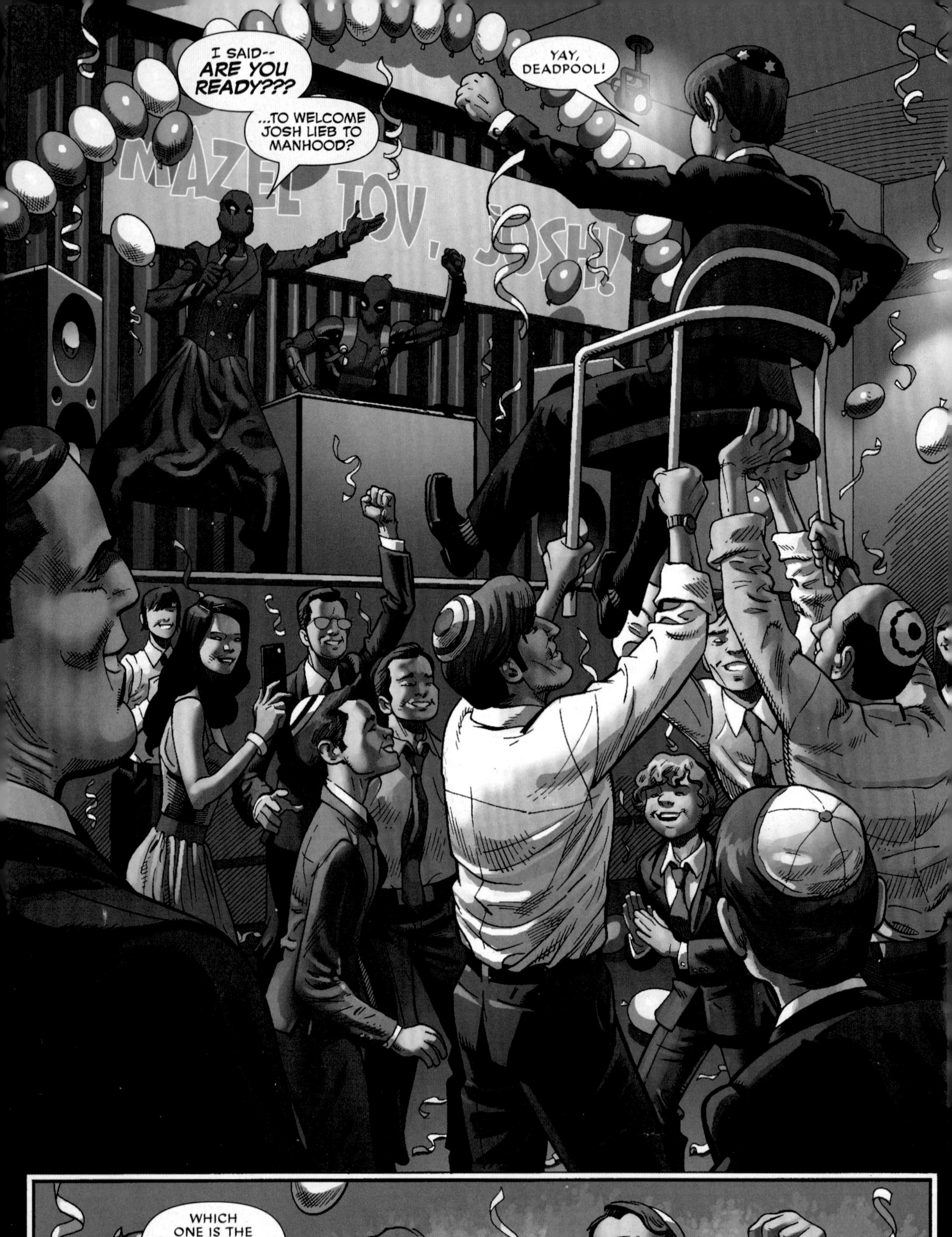
I SAID--
ARE YOU READY???
...TO WELCOME JOSH LIEB TO MANHOOD?
YAY, DEADPOOL!
MAZEL TOV, JOSH!

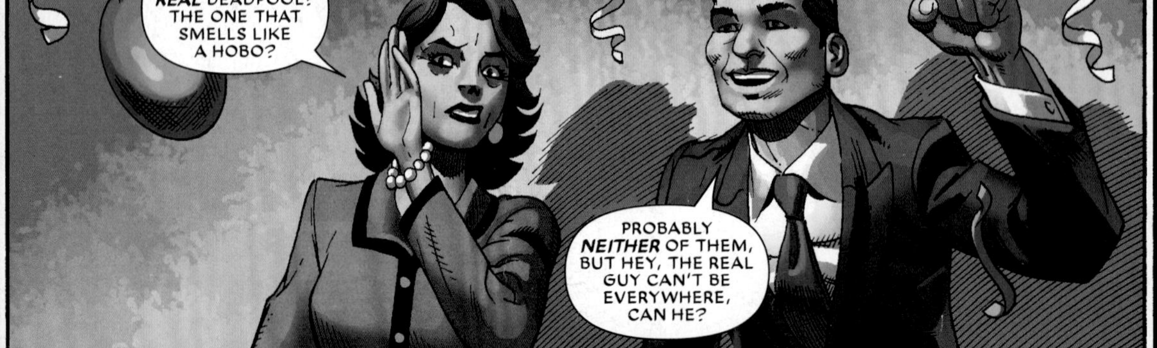
WHICH ONE IS THE REAL DEADPOOL? THE ONE THAT SMELLS LIKE A HOBO?
PROBABLY NEITHER OF THEM, BUT HEY, THE REAL GUY CAN'T BE EVERYWHERE, CAN HE?

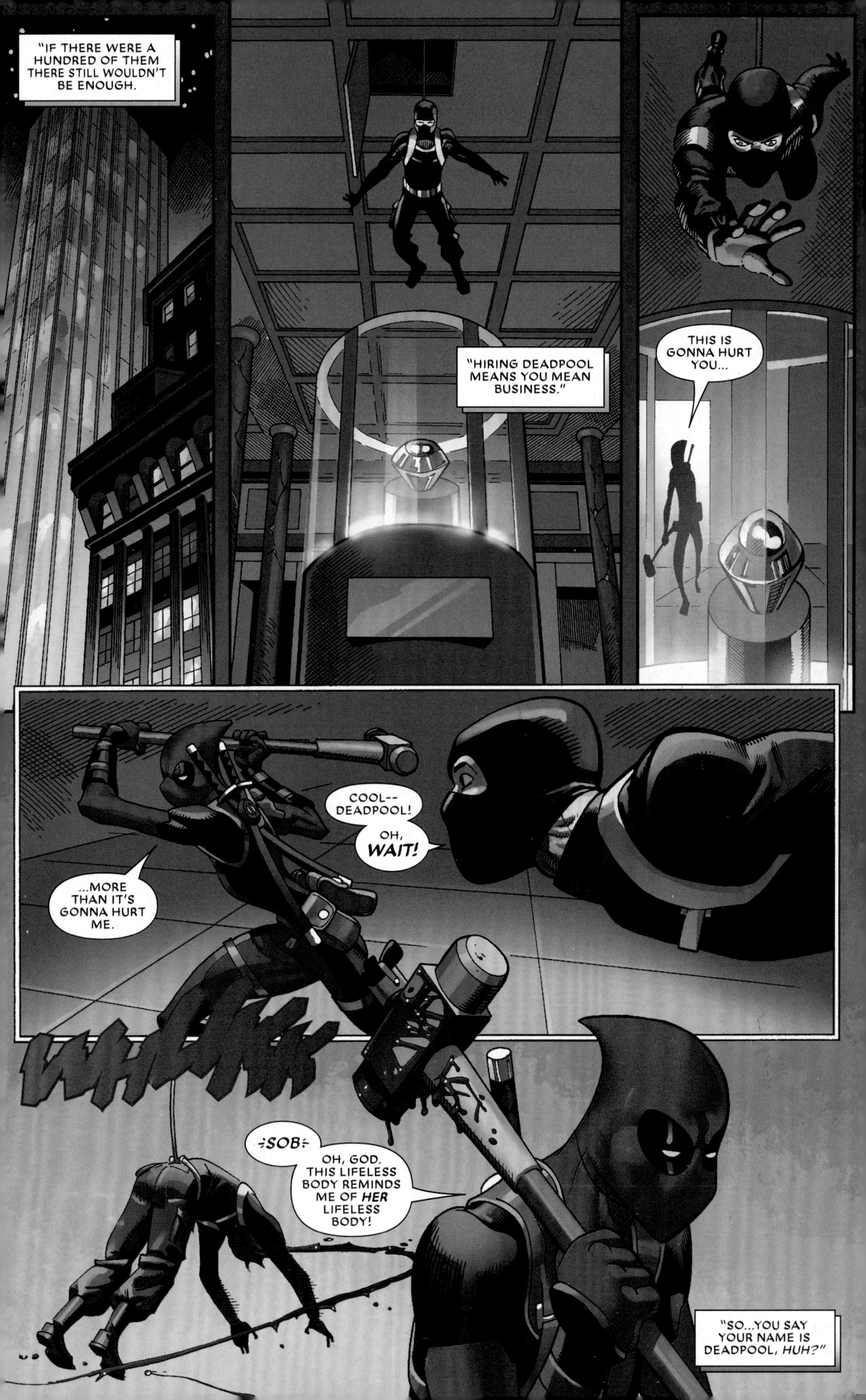
"IF THERE WERE A HUNDRED OF THEM THERE STILL WOULDN'T BE ENOUGH.
"HIRING DEADPOOL MEANS YOU MEAN BUSINESS."
THIS IS GONNA HURT YOU...
...MORE THAN IT'S GONNA HURT ME.
COOL-- DEADPOOL!
OH, *WAIT!*
SOB
OH, GOD. THIS LIFELESS BODY REMINDS ME OF *HER* LIFELESS BODY!
"SO...YOU SAY YOUR NAME IS DEADPOOL, *HUH?"*

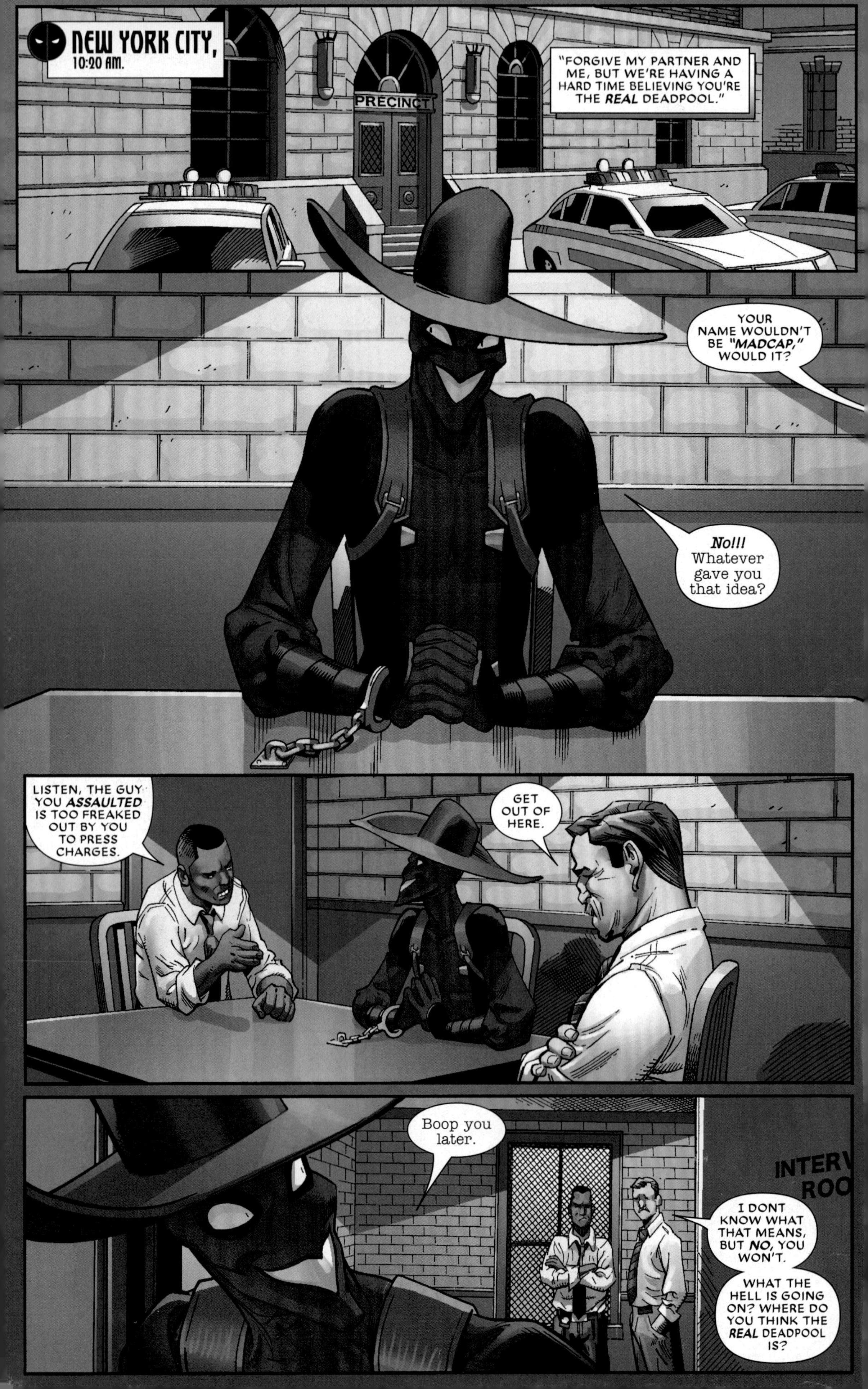
NEW YORK CITY,
10:20 AM.
PRECINCT
"FORGIVE MY PARTNER AND ME, BUT WE'RE HAVING A HARD TIME BELIEVING YOU'RE THE REAL DEADPOOL."
YOUR NAME WOULDN'T BE "MADCAP," WOULD IT?
No!!! Whatever gave you that idea?
LISTEN, THE GUY YOU ASSAULTED IS TOO FREAKED OUT BY YOU TO PRESS CHARGES.
GET OUT OF HERE.
Boop you later.
INTERV
ROO
I DONT KNOW WHAT THAT MEANS, BUT NO, YOU WON'T.
WHAT THE HELL IS GOING ON? WHERE DO YOU THINK THE REAL DEADPOOL IS?

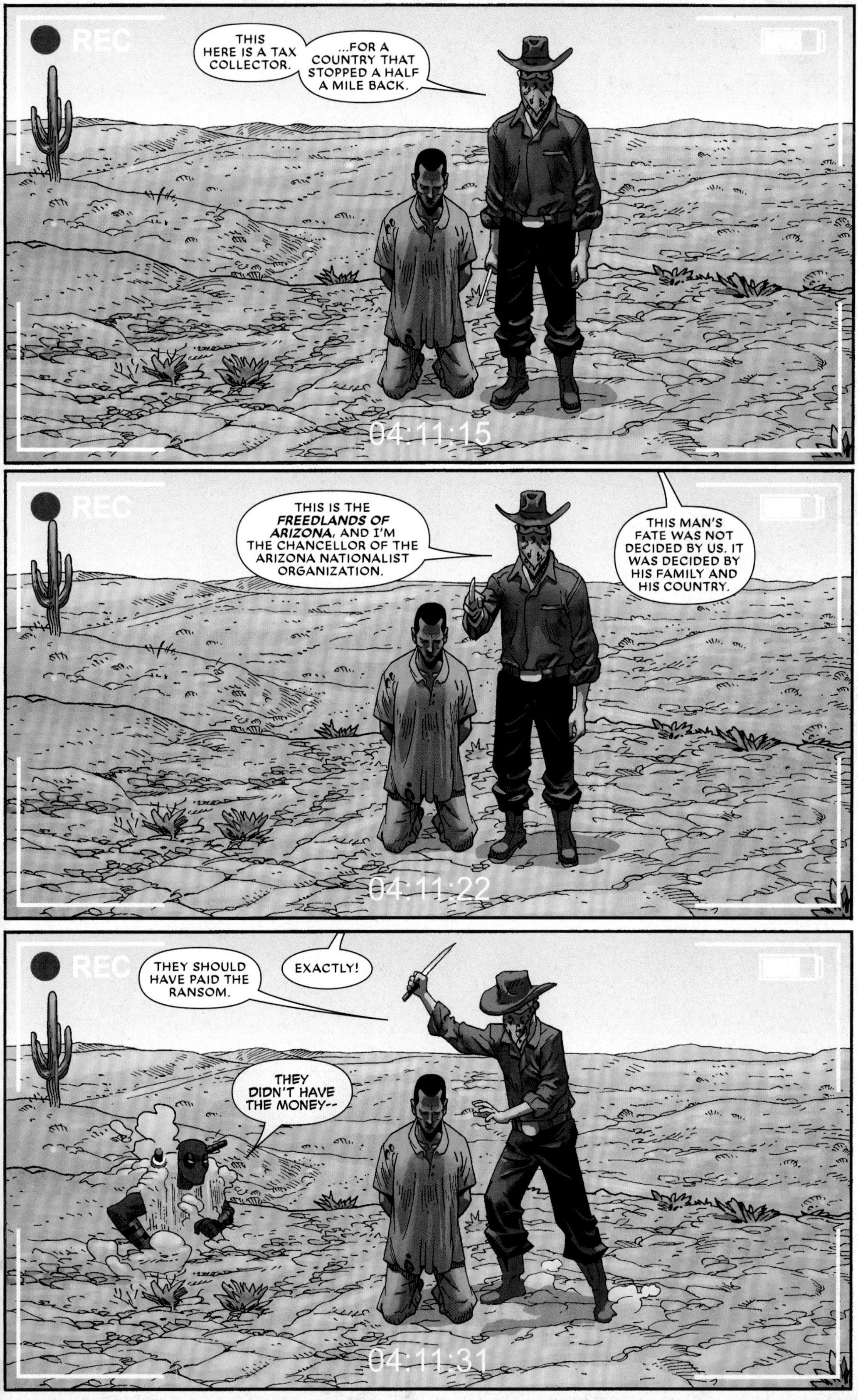
REC
THIS HERE IS A TAX COLLECTOR.
...FOR A COUNTRY THAT STOPPED A HALF A MILE BACK.
04:11:15
REC
THIS IS THE *FREEDLANDS OF ARIZONA*, AND I'M THE CHANCELLOR OF THE ARIZONA NATIONALIST ORGANIZATION.
THIS MAN'S FATE WAS NOT DECIDED BY US. IT WAS DECIDED BY HIS FAMILY AND HIS COUNTRY.
04:11:22
REC
THEY SHOULD HAVE PAID THE RANSOM.
EXACTLY!
THEY DIDN'T HAVE THE MONEY--
04:11:31

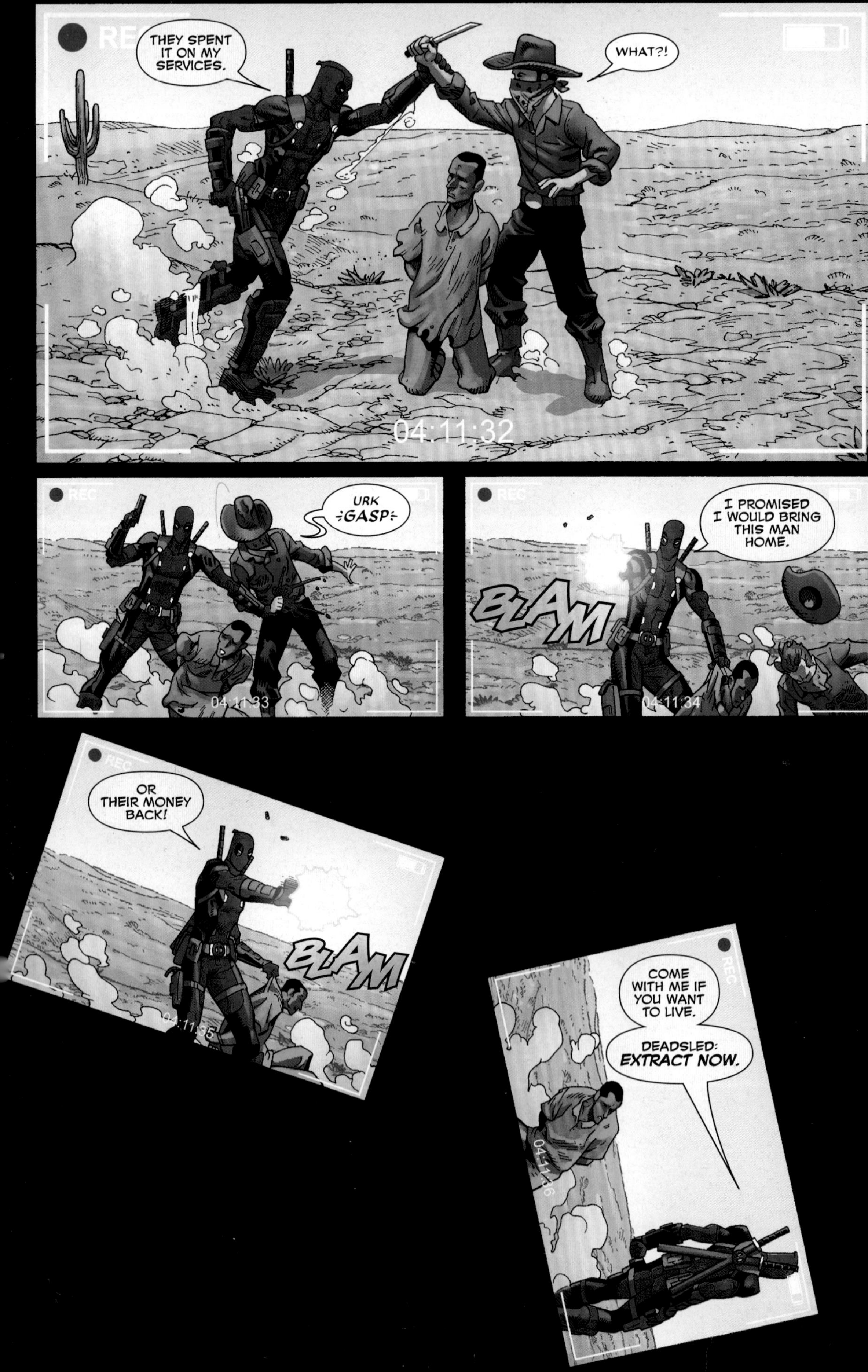
REC
THEY SPENT IT ON MY SERVICES.
WHAT?!
04:11:32
URK
GASP
04:11:33
I PROMISED I WOULD BRING THIS MAN HOME.
BLAM
04:11:34
OR THEIR MONEY BACK!
BLAM
04:11:35
COME WITH ME IF YOU WANT TO LIVE.
DEADSLED: EXTRACT NOW.
04:11:36

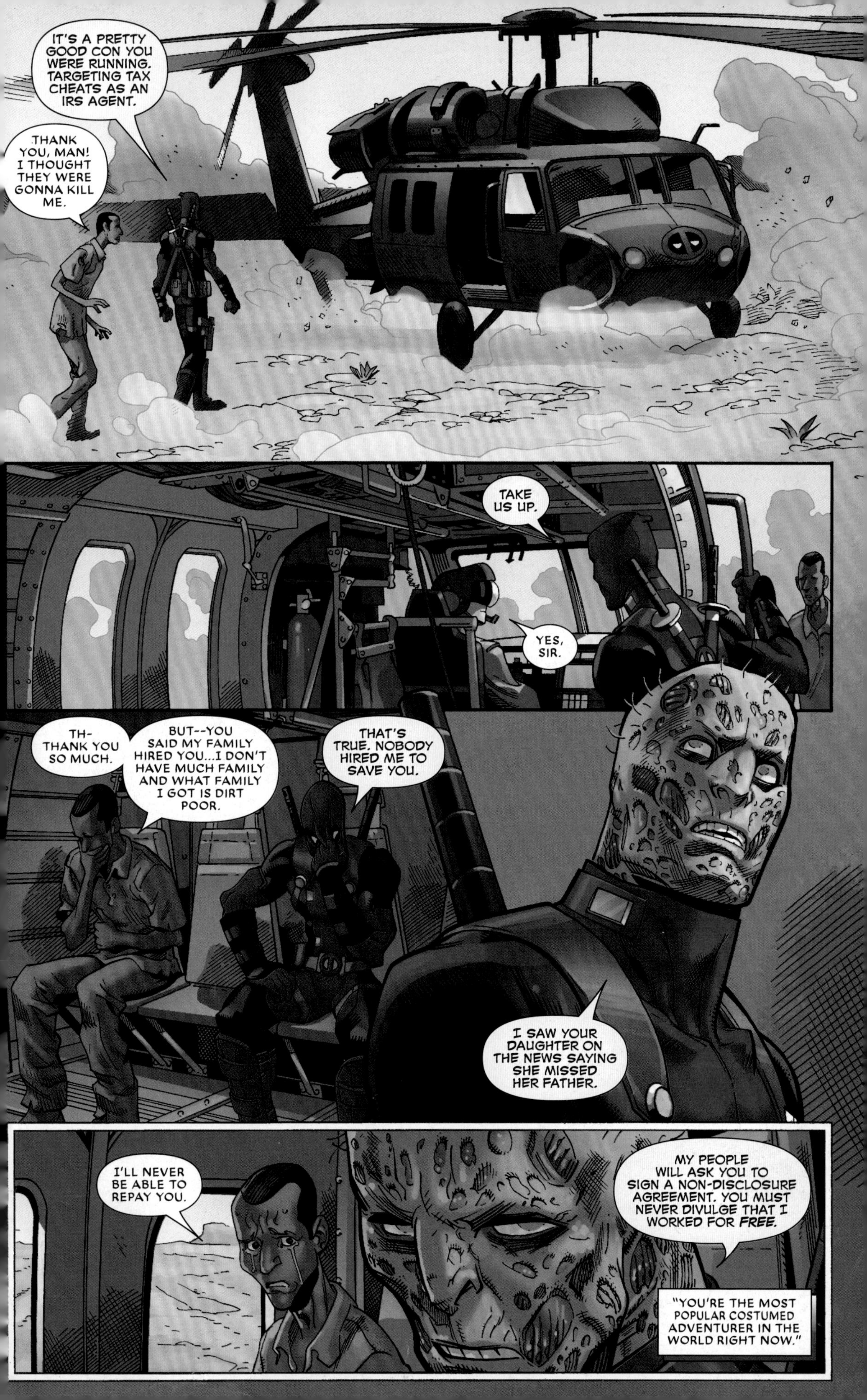
IT'S A PRETTY GOOD CON YOU WERE RUNNING. TARGETING TAX CHEATS AS AN IRS AGENT.
THANK YOU, MAN! I THOUGHT THEY WERE GONNA KILL ME.
TAKE US UP.
YES, SIR.
TH- THANK YOU SO MUCH.
BUT--YOU SAID MY FAMILY HIRED YOU...I DON'T HAVE MUCH FAMILY AND WHAT FAMILY I GOT IS DIRT POOR.
THAT'S TRUE. NOBODY HIRED ME TO SAVE YOU.
I SAW YOUR DAUGHTER ON THE NEWS SAYING SHE MISSED HER FATHER.
I'LL NEVER BE ABLE TO REPAY YOU.
MY PEOPLE WILL ASK YOU TO SIGN A NON-DISCLOSURE AGREEMENT. YOU MUST NEVER DIVULGE THAT I WORKED FOR *FREE*.
"YOU'RE THE MOST POPULAR COSTUMED ADVENTURER IN THE WORLD RIGHT NOW."

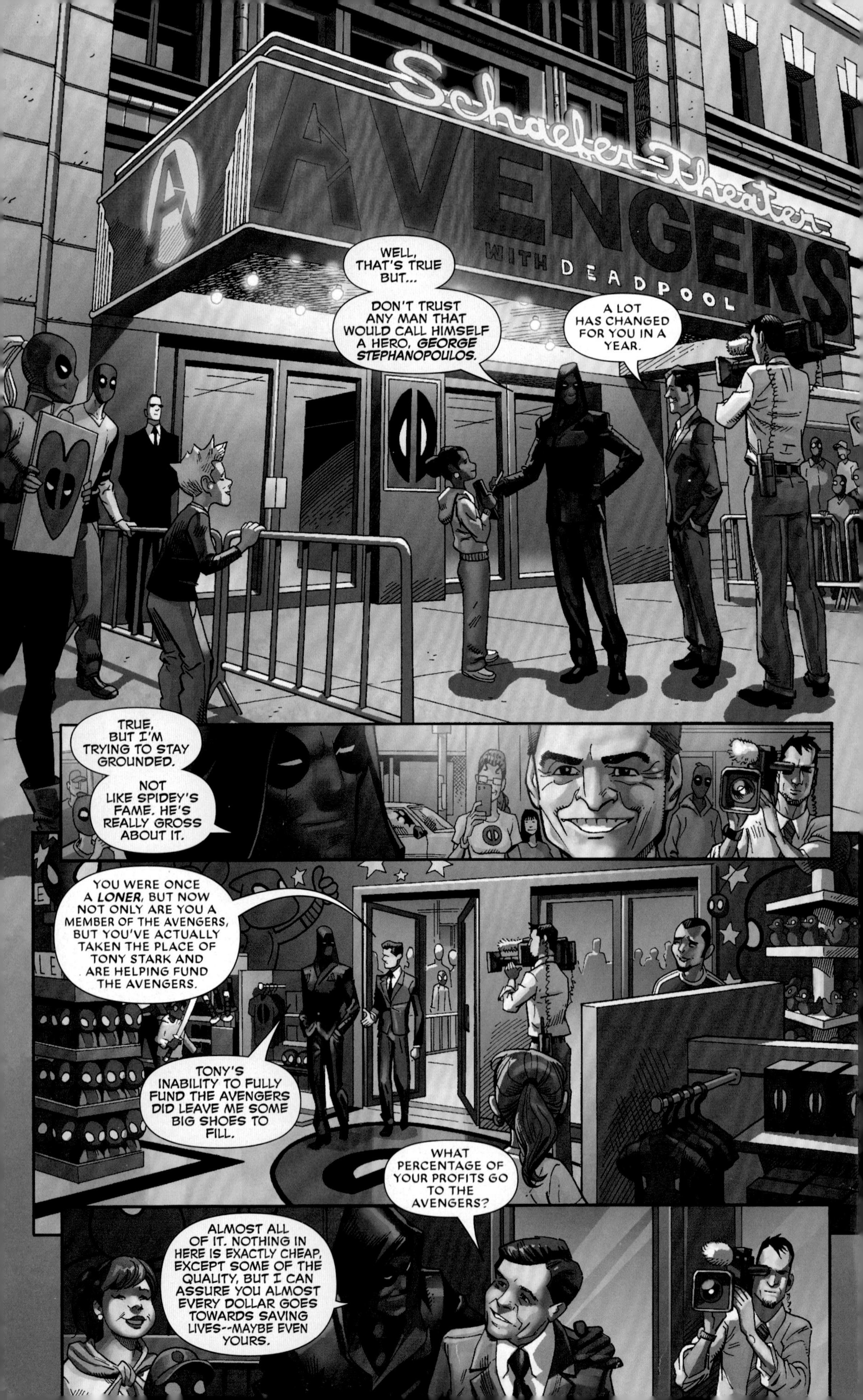
Schaefer Theater
AVENGERS
WITH DEADPOOL
WELL, THAT'S TRUE BUT...
DON'T TRUST ANY MAN THAT WOULD CALL HIMSELF A HERO, GEORGE STEPHANOPOULOS.
A LOT HAS CHANGED FOR YOU IN A YEAR.
TRUE, BUT I'M TRYING TO STAY GROUNDED.
NOT LIKE SPIDEY'S FAME. HE'S REALLY GROSS ABOUT IT.
YOU WERE ONCE A LONER, BUT NOW NOT ONLY ARE YOU A MEMBER OF THE AVENGERS, BUT YOU'VE ACTUALLY TAKEN THE PLACE OF TONY STARK AND ARE HELPING FUND THE AVENGERS.
TONY'S INABILITY TO FULLY FUND THE AVENGERS DID LEAVE ME SOME BIG SHOES TO FILL.
WHAT PERCENTAGE OF YOUR PROFITS GO TO THE AVENGERS?
ALMOST ALL OF IT. NOTHING IN HERE IS EXACTLY CHEAP, EXCEPT SOME OF THE QUALITY, BUT I CAN ASSURE YOU ALMOST EVERY DOLLAR GOES TOWARDS SAVING LIVES--MAYBE EVEN YOURS.

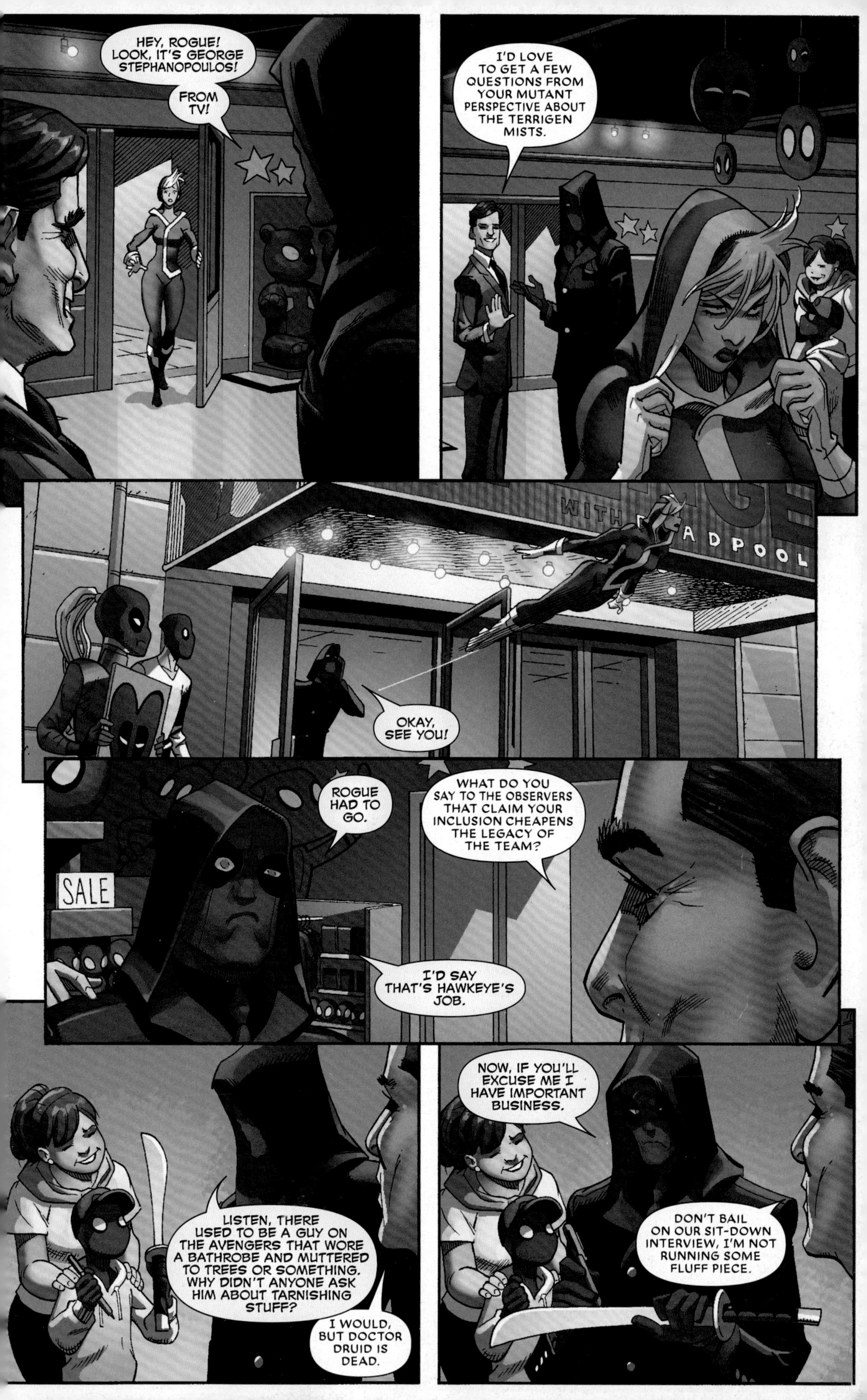
HEY, ROGUE! LOOK, IT'S GEORGE STEPHANOPOULOS!
FROM TV!
I'D LOVE TO GET A FEW QUESTIONS FROM YOUR MUTANT PERSPECTIVE ABOUT THE TERRIGEN MISTS.
WITH ... ADPOOL
OKAY, SEE YOU!
ROGUE HAD TO GO.
WHAT DO YOU SAY TO THE OBSERVERS THAT CLAIM YOUR INCLUSION CHEAPENS THE LEGACY OF THE TEAM?
SALE
I'D SAY THAT'S HAWKEYE'S JOB.
LISTEN, THERE USED TO BE A GUY ON THE AVENGERS THAT WORE A BATHROBE AND MUTTERED TO TREES OR SOMETHING. WHY DIDN'T ANYONE ASK HIM ABOUT TARNISHING STUFF?
I WOULD, BUT DOCTOR DRUID IS DEAD.
NOW, IF YOU'LL EXCUSE ME I HAVE IMPORTANT BUSINESS.
DON'T BAIL ON OUR SIT-DOWN INTERVIEW, I'M NOT RUNNING SOME FLUFF PIECE.

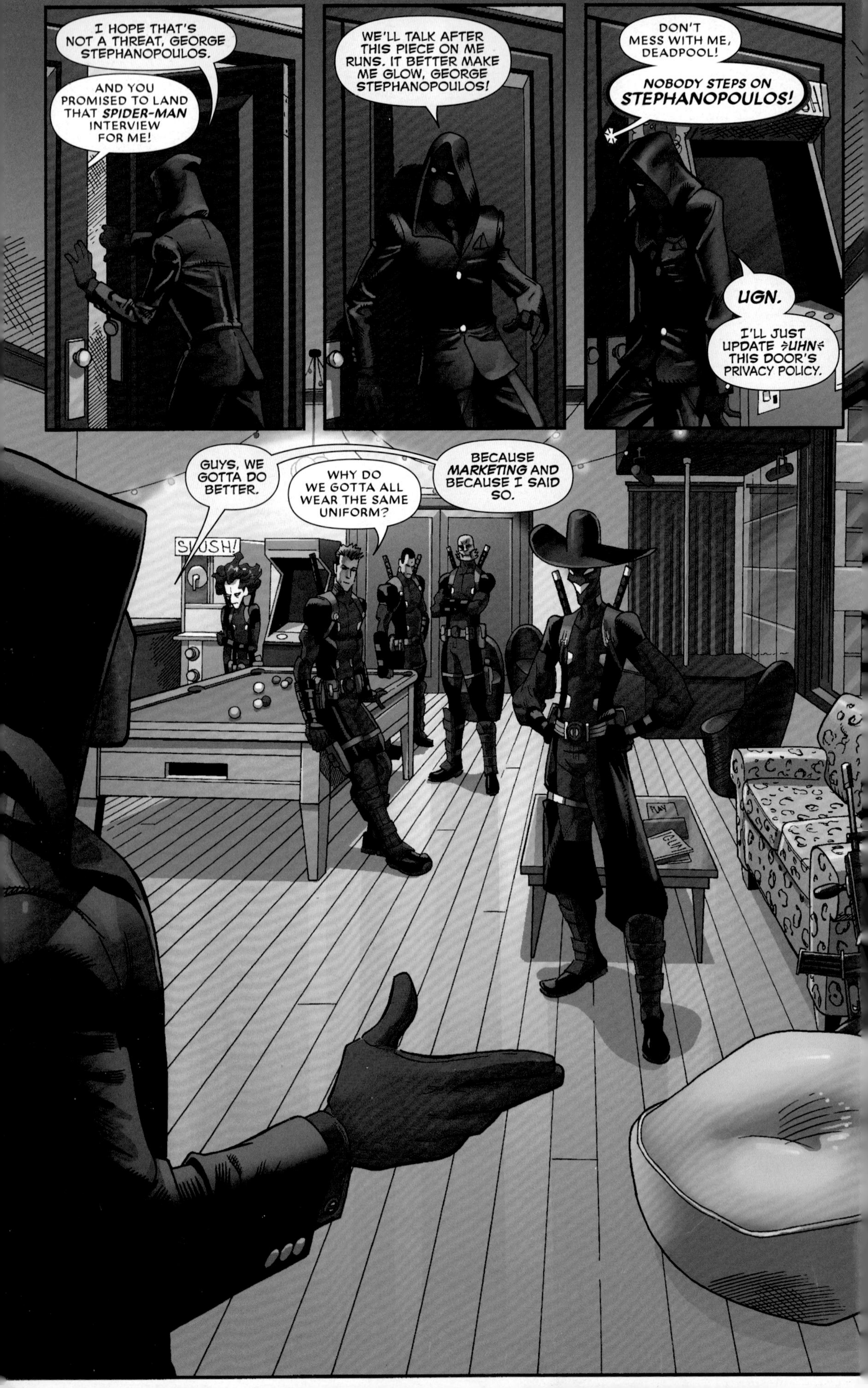
I HOPE THAT'S NOT A THREAT, GEORGE STEPHANOPOULOS.
AND YOU PROMISED TO LAND THAT *SPIDER-MAN* INTERVIEW FOR ME!
WE'LL TALK AFTER THIS PIECE ON ME RUNS. IT BETTER MAKE ME GLOW, GEORGE STEPHANOPOULOS!
DON'T MESS WITH ME, DEADPOOL!
NOBODY STEPS ON **STEPHANOPOULOS!**
UGN.
I'LL JUST UPDATE *UHN* THIS DOOR'S PRIVACY POLICY.
GUYS, WE GOTTA DO BETTER.
WHY DO WE GOTTA ALL WEAR THE SAME UNIFORM?
BECAUSE *MARKETING* AND BECAUSE I SAID SO.
SLUSH!
PLAY

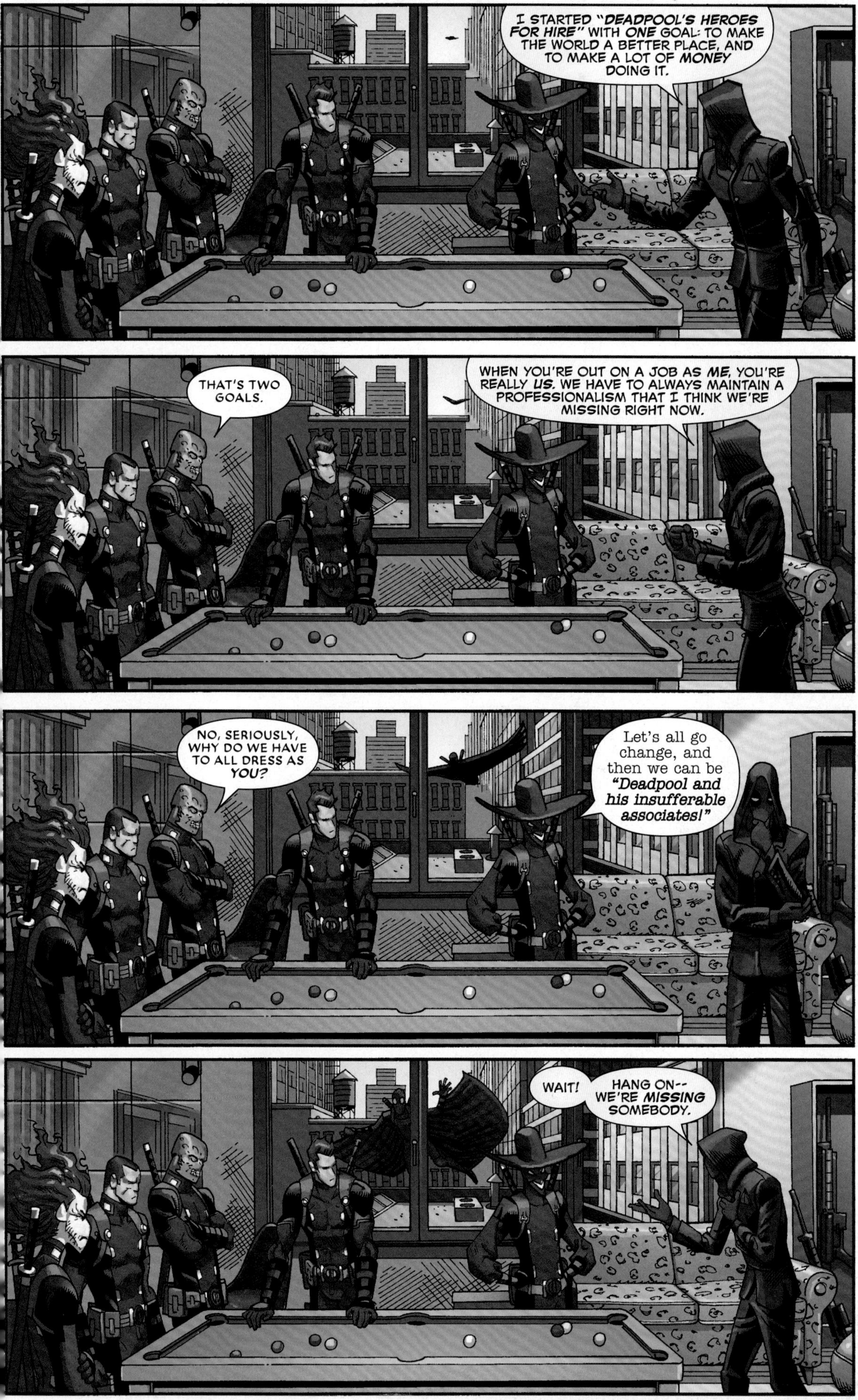
I STARTED "DEADPOOL'S HEROES FOR HIRE" WITH ONE GOAL: TO MAKE THE WORLD A BETTER PLACE, AND TO MAKE A LOT OF MONEY DOING IT.
THAT'S TWO GOALS.
WHEN YOU'RE OUT ON A JOB AS ME, YOU'RE REALLY US. WE HAVE TO ALWAYS MAINTAIN A PROFESSIONALISM THAT I THINK WE'RE MISSING RIGHT NOW.
NO, SERIOUSLY, WHY DO WE HAVE TO ALL DRESS AS YOU?
Let's all go change, and then we can be "Deadpool and his insufferable associates!"
WAIT!
HANG ON-- WE'RE MISSING SOMEBODY.

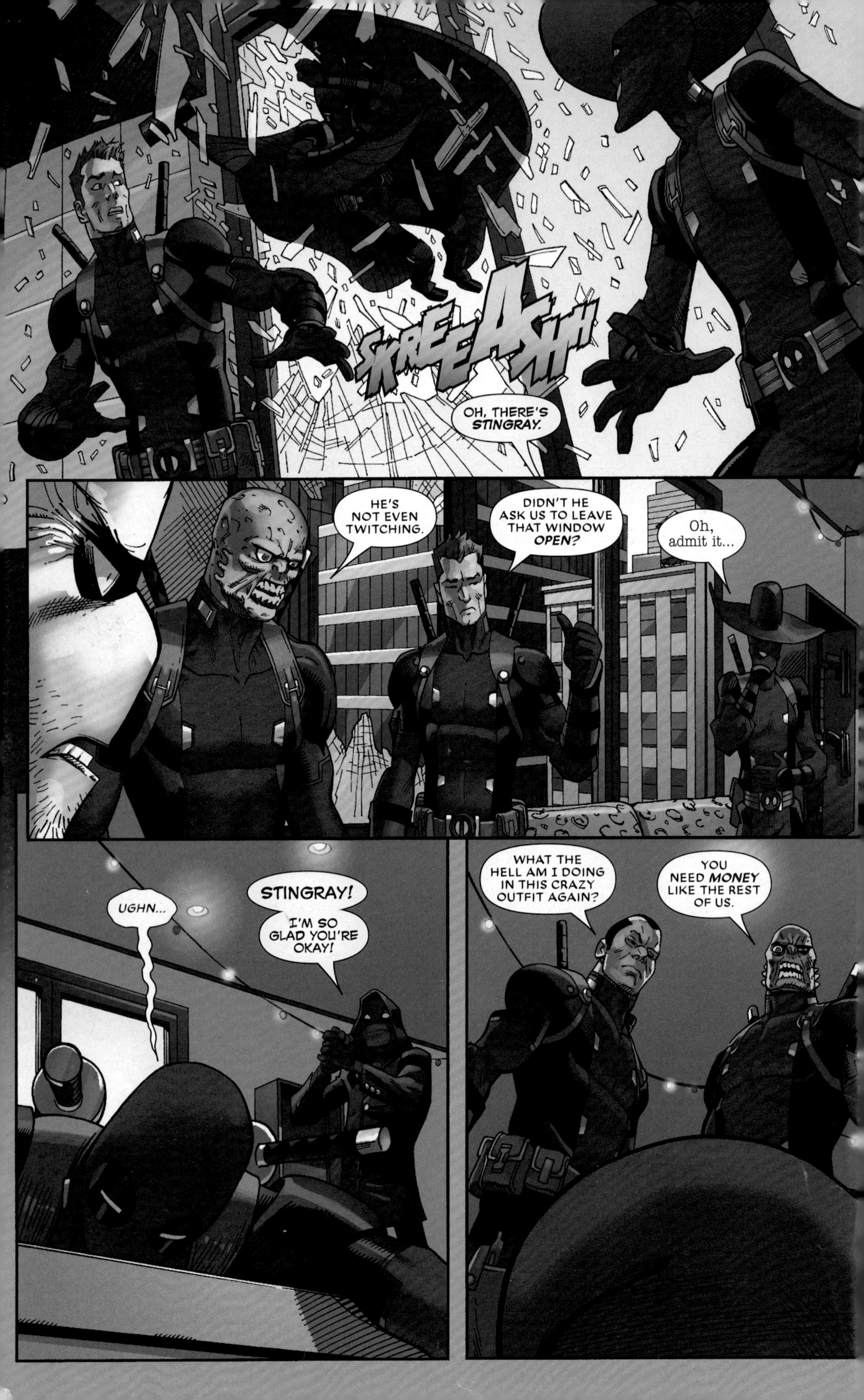
SKREEASHH
OH, THERE'S STINGRAY.
HE'S NOT EVEN TWITCHING.
DIDN'T HE ASK US TO LEAVE THAT WINDOW OPEN?
Oh, admit it...
UGHN...
STINGRAY!
I'M SO GLAD YOU'RE OKAY!
WHAT THE HELL AM I DOING IN THIS CRAZY OUTFIT AGAIN?
YOU NEED MONEY LIKE THE REST OF US.

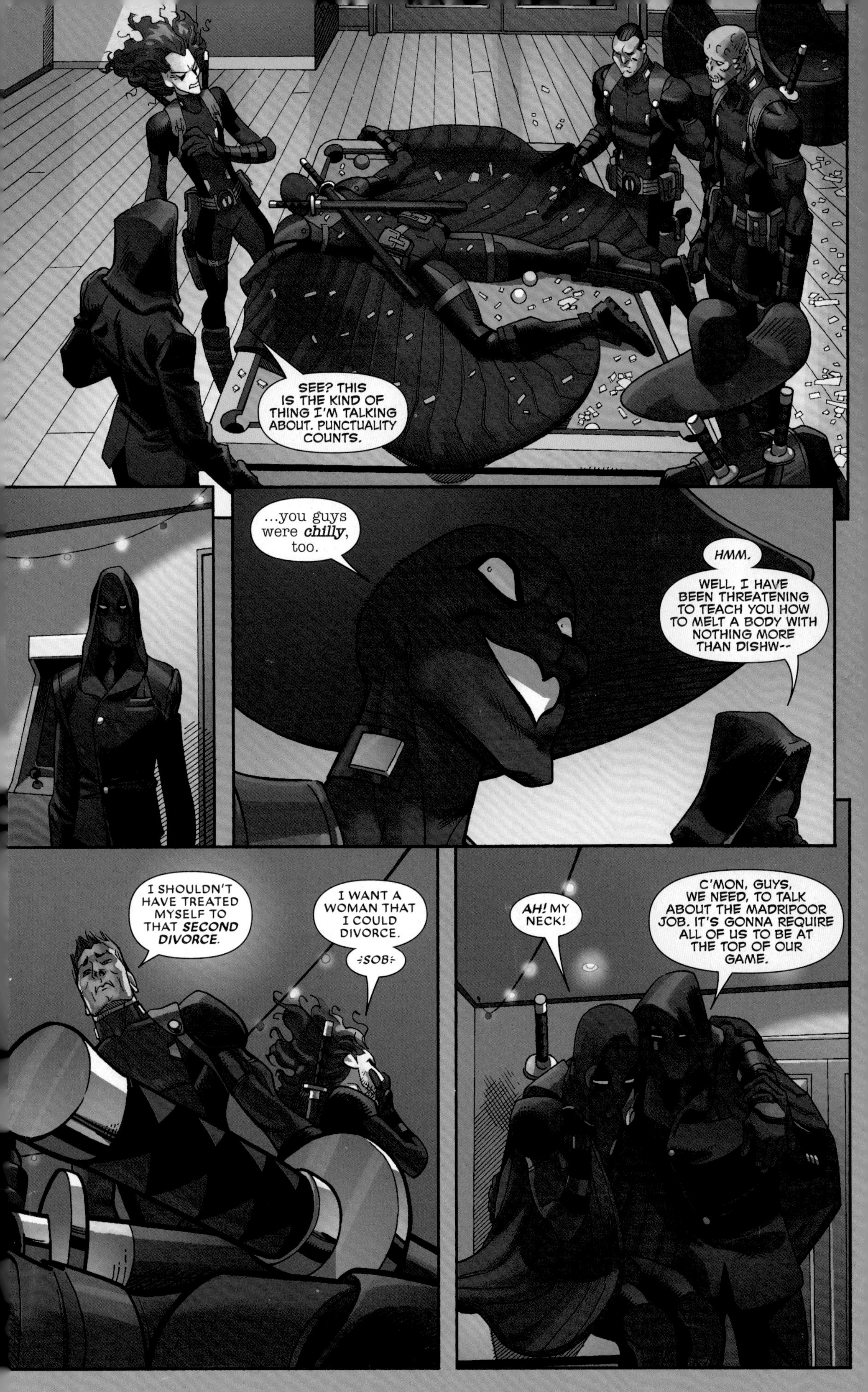
SEE? THIS IS THE KIND OF THING I'M TALKING ABOUT. PUNCTUALITY COUNTS.
...you guys were *chilly*, too.
HMM.
WELL, I HAVE BEEN THREATENING TO TEACH YOU HOW TO MELT A BODY WITH NOTHING MORE THAN DISHW--
I SHOULDN'T HAVE TREATED MYSELF TO THAT *SECOND DIVORCE*.
I WANT A WOMAN THAT I COULD DIVORCE.
SOB
AH! MY NECK!
C'MON, GUYS, WE NEED, TO TALK ABOUT THE MADRIPOOR JOB. IT'S GONNA REQUIRE ALL OF US TO BE AT THE TOP OF OUR GAME.

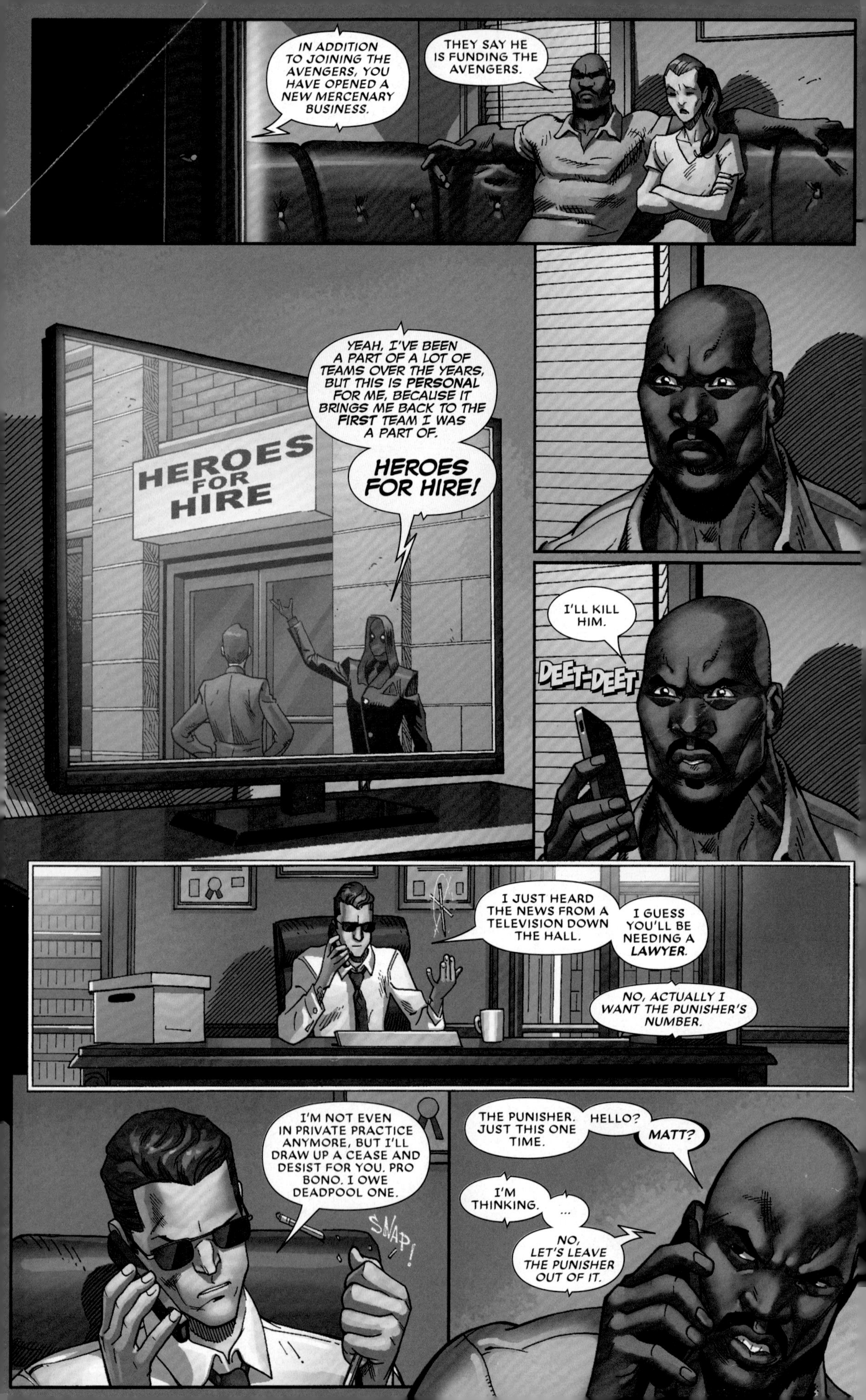
IN ADDITION TO JOINING THE AVENGERS, YOU HAVE OPENED A NEW MERCENARY BUSINESS.
THEY SAY HE IS FUNDING THE AVENGERS.
YEAH, I'VE BEEN A PART OF A LOT OF TEAMS OVER THE YEARS, BUT THIS IS PERSONAL FOR ME, BECAUSE IT BRINGS ME BACK TO THE FIRST TEAM I WAS A PART OF.
HEROES FOR HIRE!
HEROES FOR HIRE
I'LL KILL HIM.
DEET-DEET
I JUST HEARD THE NEWS FROM A TELEVISION DOWN THE HALL.
I GUESS YOU'LL BE NEEDING A LAWYER.
NO, ACTUALLY I WANT THE PUNISHER'S NUMBER.
I'M NOT EVEN IN PRIVATE PRACTICE ANYMORE, BUT I'LL DRAW UP A CEASE AND DESIST FOR YOU. PRO BONO. I OWE DEADPOOL ONE.
SNAP!
THE PUNISHER. JUST THIS ONE TIME.
HELLO?
MATT?
I'M THINKING.
...
NO, LET'S LEAVE THE PUNISHER OUT OF IT.

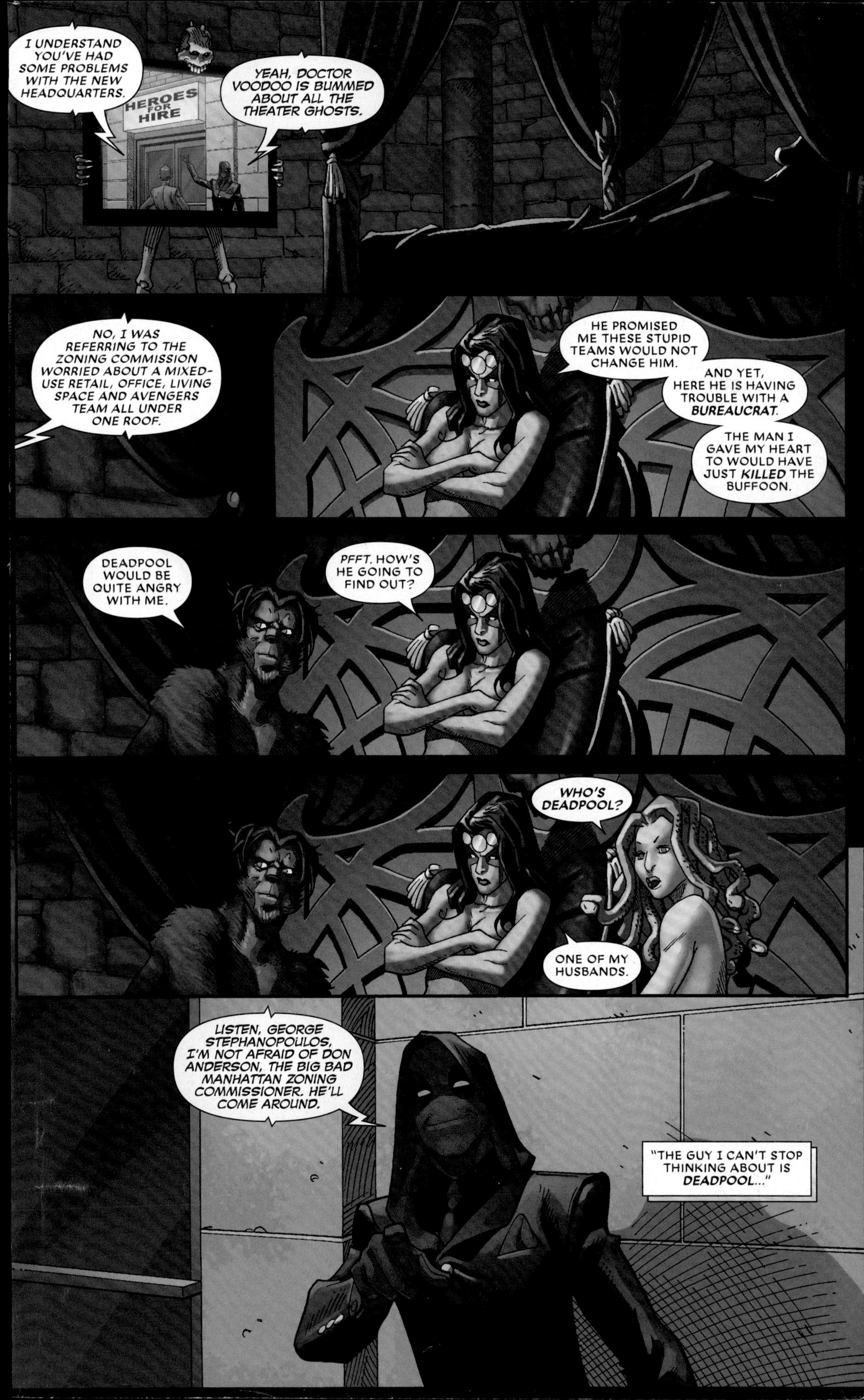
I UNDERSTAND YOU'VE HAD SOME PROBLEMS WITH THE NEW HEADQUARTERS.
HEROES FOR HIRE
YEAH, DOCTOR VOODOO IS BUMMED ABOUT ALL THE THEATER GHOSTS.
NO, I WAS REFERRING TO THE ZONING COMMISSION WORRIED ABOUT A MIXED-USE RETAIL, OFFICE, LIVING SPACE AND AVENGERS TEAM ALL UNDER ONE ROOF.
HE PROMISED ME THESE STUPID TEAMS WOULD NOT CHANGE HIM.
AND YET, HERE HE IS HAVING TROUBLE WITH A BUREAUCRAT.
THE MAN I GAVE MY HEART TO WOULD HAVE JUST KILLED THE BUFFOON.
DEADPOOL WOULD BE QUITE ANGRY WITH ME.
PFFT. HOW'S HE GOING TO FIND OUT?
WHO'S DEADPOOL?
ONE OF MY HUSBANDS.
LISTEN, GEORGE STEPHANOPOULOS, I'M NOT AFRAID OF DON ANDERSON, THE BIG BAD MANHATTAN ZONING COMMISSIONER. HE'LL COME AROUND.
"THE GUY I CAN'T STOP THINKING ABOUT IS DEADPOOL..."

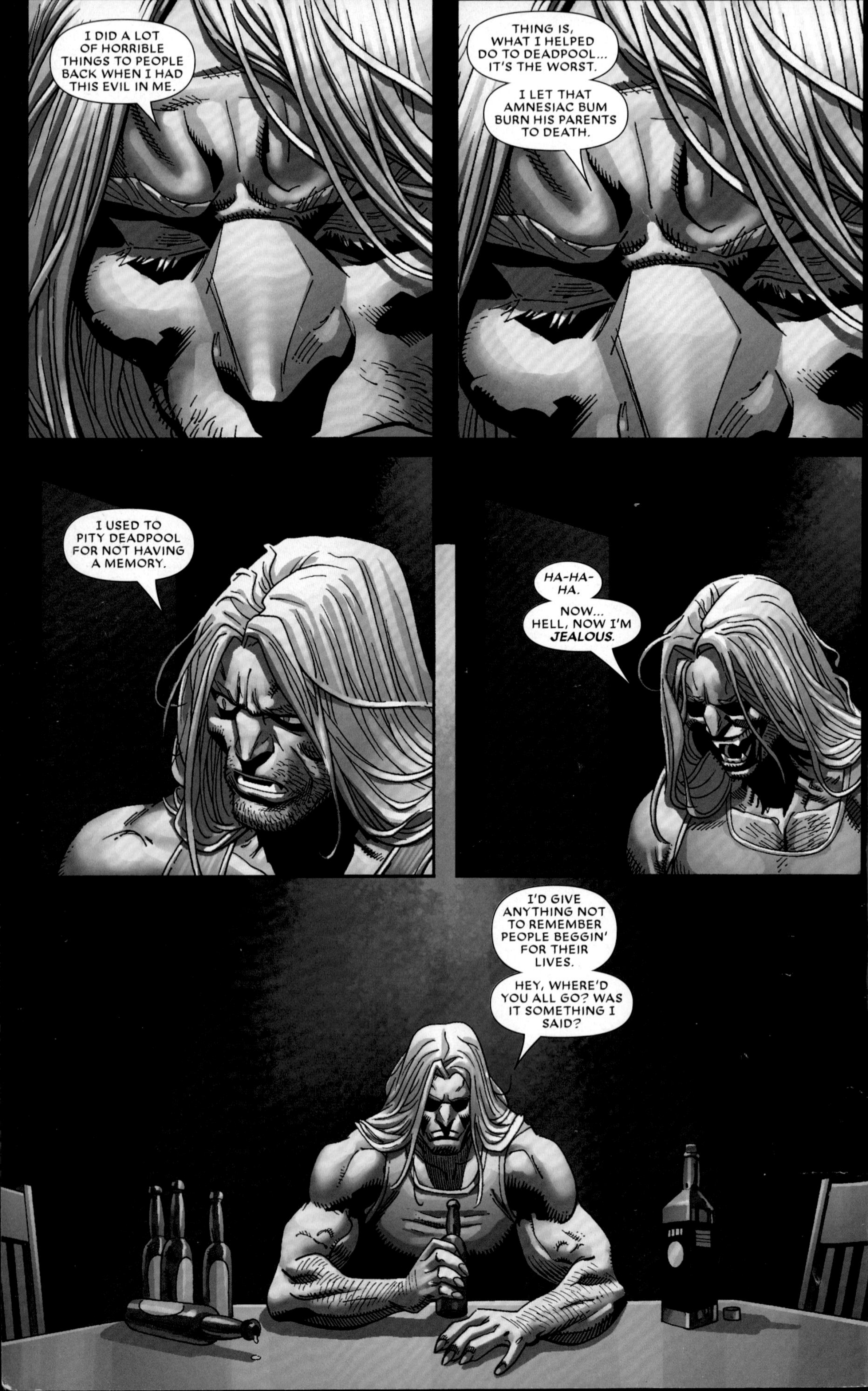
I DID A LOT OF HORRIBLE THINGS TO PEOPLE BACK WHEN I HAD THIS EVIL IN ME.
THING IS, WHAT I HELPED DO TO DEADPOOL... IT'S THE WORST.
I LET THAT AMNESIAC BUM BURN HIS PARENTS TO DEATH.
I USED TO PITY DEADPOOL FOR NOT HAVING A MEMORY.
HA-HA-HA.
NOW... HELL, NOW I'M ***JEALOUS***.
I'D GIVE ANYTHING NOT TO REMEMBER PEOPLE BEGGIN' FOR THEIR LIVES.
HEY, WHERE'D YOU ALL GO? WAS IT SOMETHING I SAID?

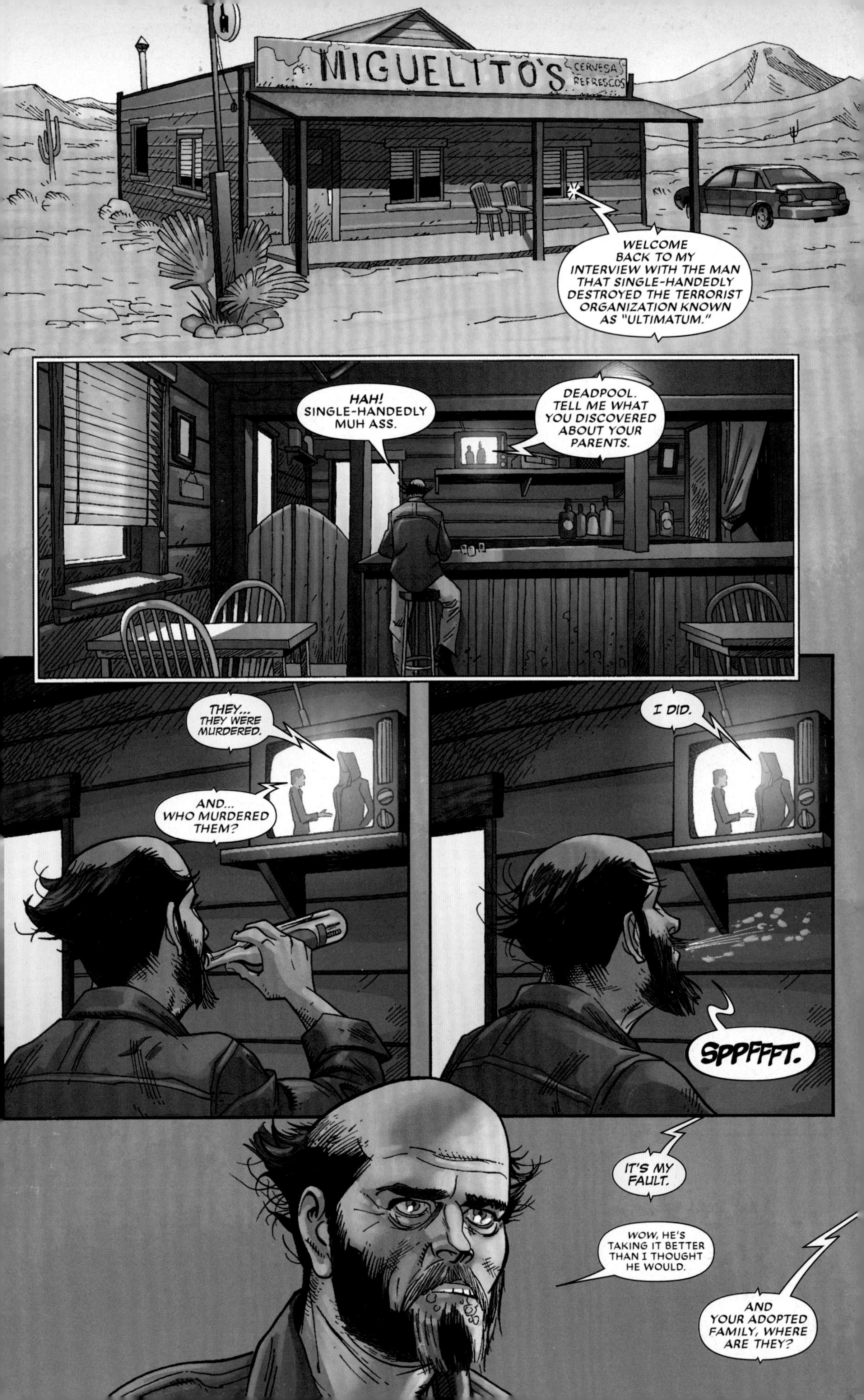
MIGUELITO'S
CERVESA
REFRESCOS
WELCOME BACK TO MY INTERVIEW WITH THE MAN THAT SINGLE-HANDEDLY DESTROYED THE TERRORIST ORGANIZATION KNOWN AS "ULTIMATUM."
HAH! SINGLE-HANDEDLY MUH ASS.
DEADPOOL. TELL ME WHAT YOU DISCOVERED ABOUT YOUR PARENTS.
THEY... THEY WERE MURDERED.
AND... WHO MURDERED THEM?
I DID.
SPPFFFT.
IT'S MY FAULT.
WOW, HE'S TAKING IT BETTER THAN I THOUGHT HE WOULD.
AND YOUR ADOPTED FAMILY, WHERE ARE THEY?

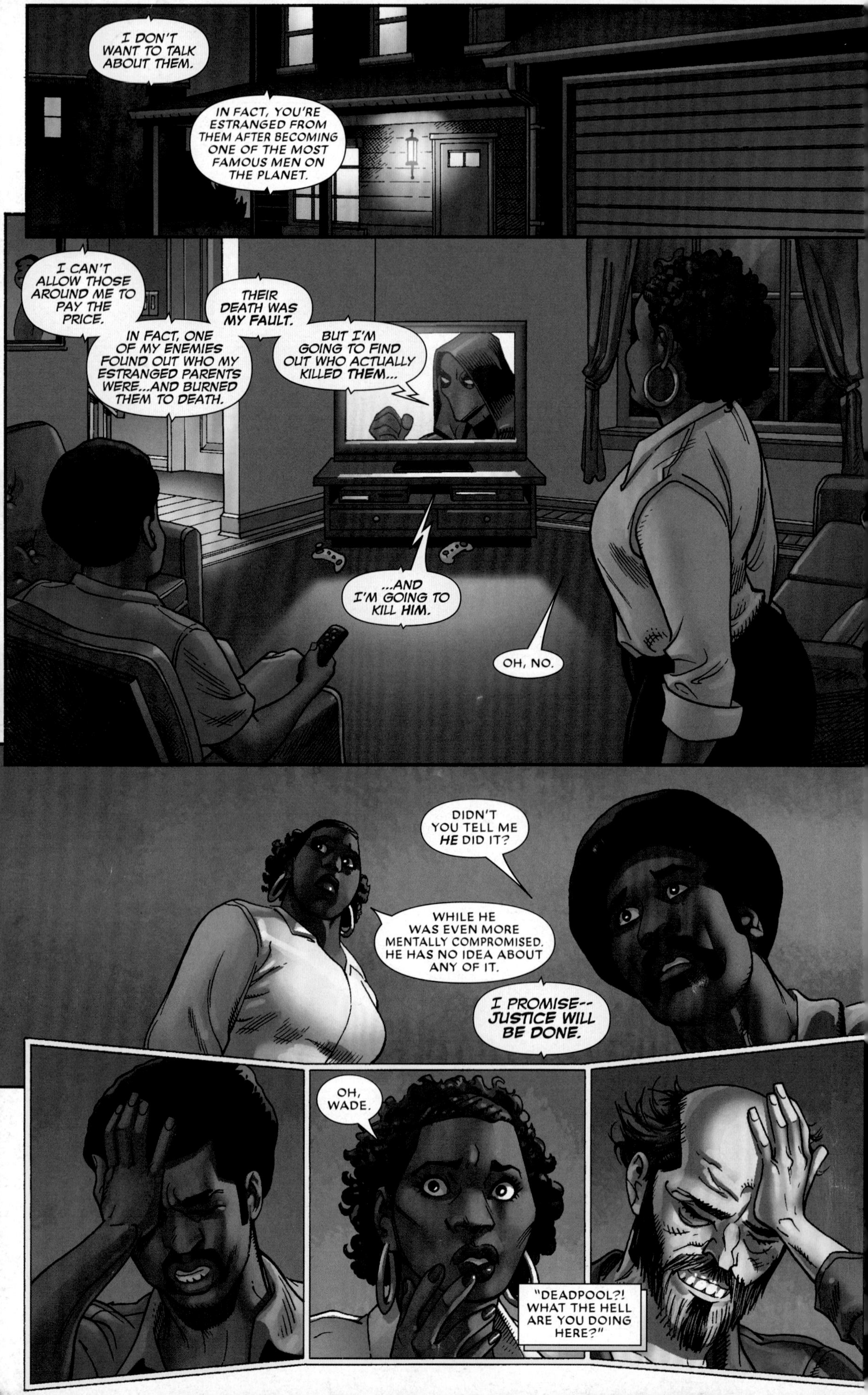
I DON'T WANT TO TALK ABOUT THEM.
IN FACT, YOU'RE ESTRANGED FROM THEM AFTER BECOMING ONE OF THE MOST FAMOUS MEN ON THE PLANET.
I CAN'T ALLOW THOSE AROUND ME TO PAY THE PRICE.
IN FACT, ONE OF MY ENEMIES FOUND OUT WHO MY ESTRANGED PARENTS WERE...AND BURNED THEM TO DEATH.
THEIR DEATH WAS MY FAULT.
BUT I'M GOING TO FIND OUT WHO ACTUALLY KILLED THEM...
...AND I'M GOING TO KILL HIM.
OH, NO.
DIDN'T YOU TELL ME HE DID IT?
WHILE HE WAS EVEN MORE MENTALLY COMPROMISED. HE HAS NO IDEA ABOUT ANY OF IT.
I PROMISE-- JUSTICE WILL BE DONE.
OH, WADE.
"DEADPOOL?! WHAT THE HELL ARE YOU DOING HERE?"

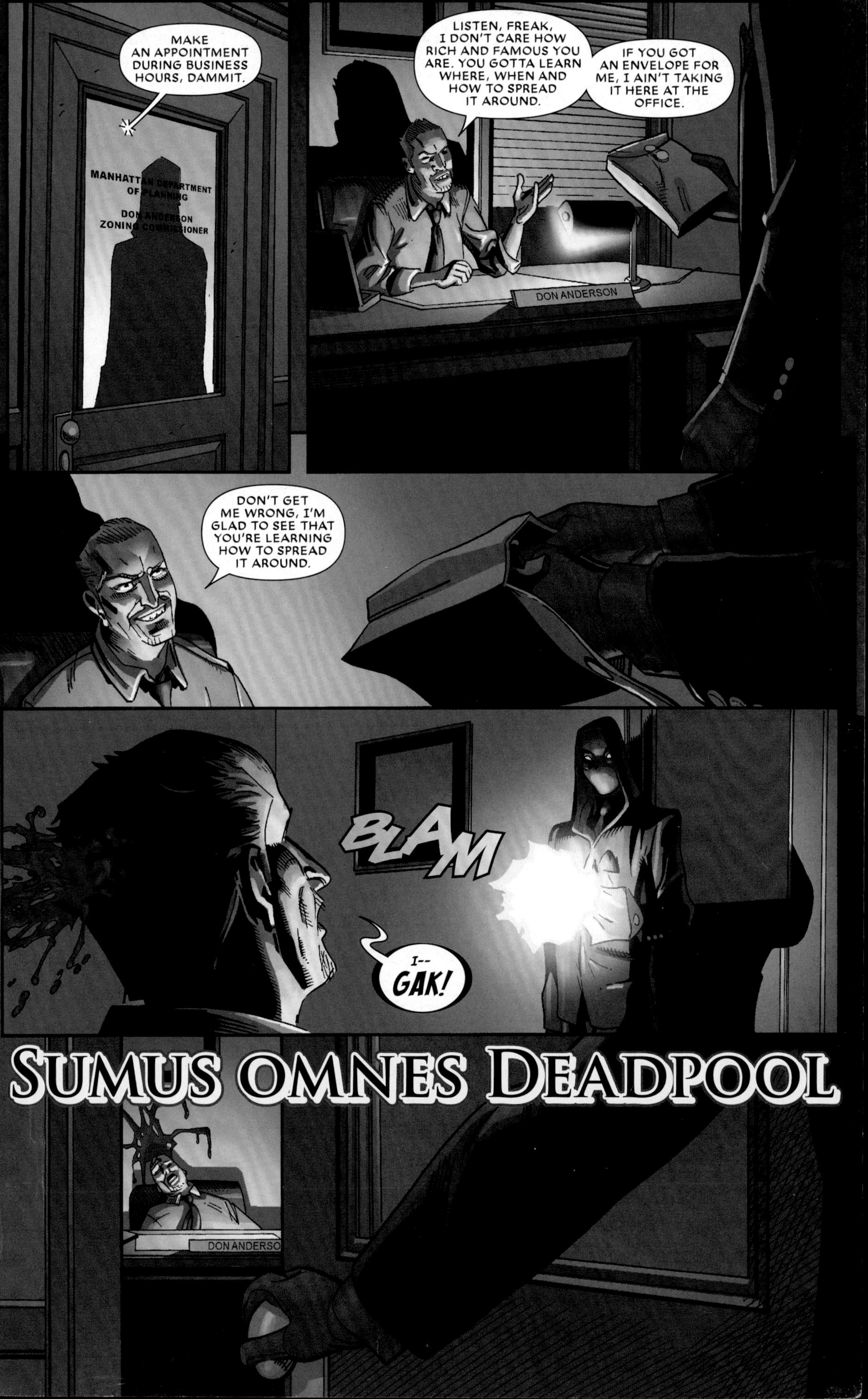
MAKE AN APPOINTMENT DURING BUSINESS HOURS, DAMMIT.
MANHATTAN DEPARTMENT OF PLANNING
DON ANDERSON ZONING COMMISSIONER
LISTEN, FREAK, I DON'T CARE HOW RICH AND FAMOUS YOU ARE. YOU GOTTA LEARN WHERE, WHEN AND HOW TO SPREAD IT AROUND.
IF YOU GOT AN ENVELOPE FOR ME, I AIN'T TAKING IT HERE AT THE OFFICE.
DON ANDERSON
DON'T GET ME WRONG, I'M GLAD TO SEE THAT YOU'RE LEARNING HOW TO SPREAD IT AROUND.
BLAM
I-- GAK!
SUMUS OMNES DEADPOOL
DON ANDERSO

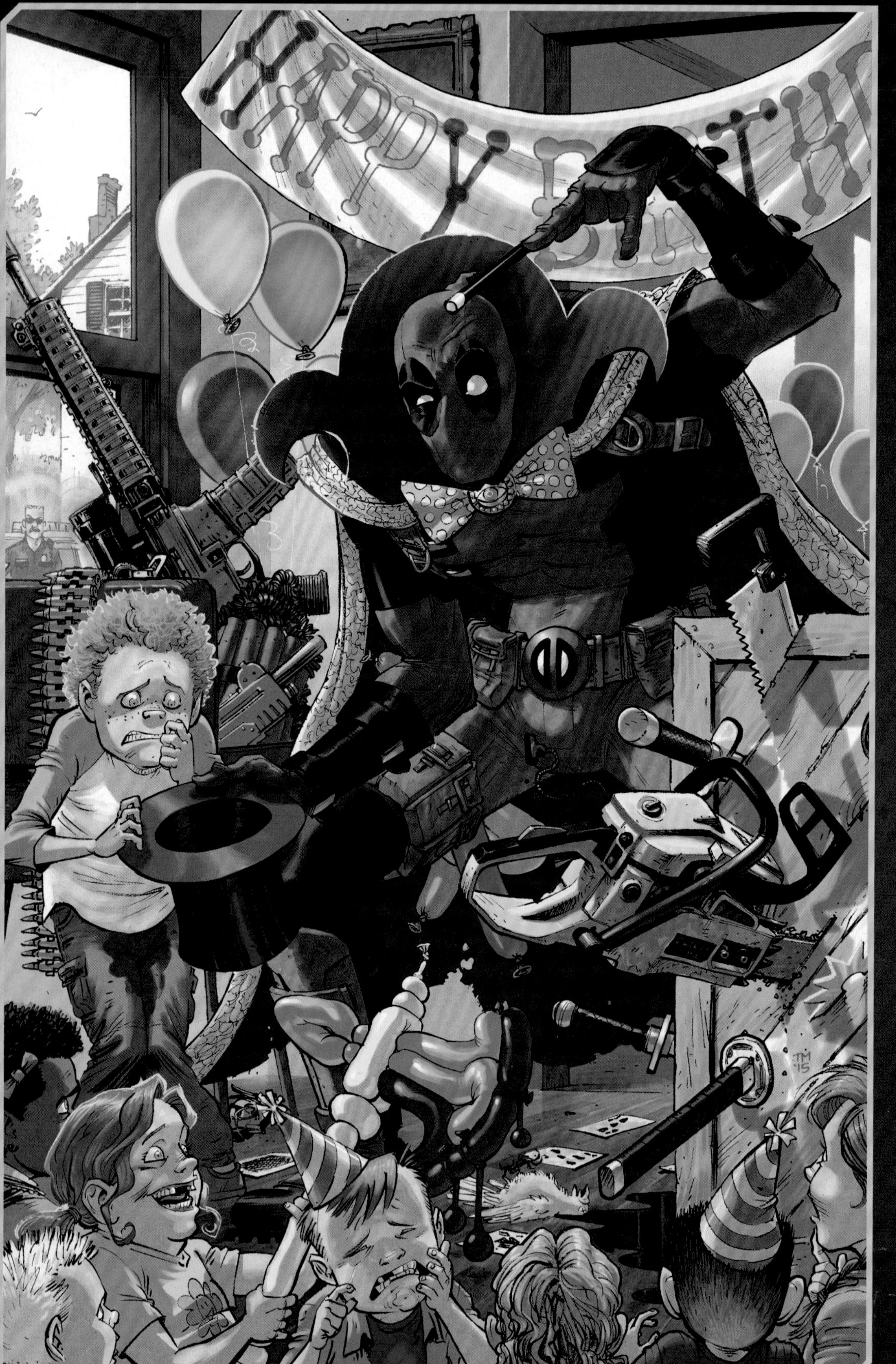

Z | THE MORE WE GIVE, THE MORE WE HAVE

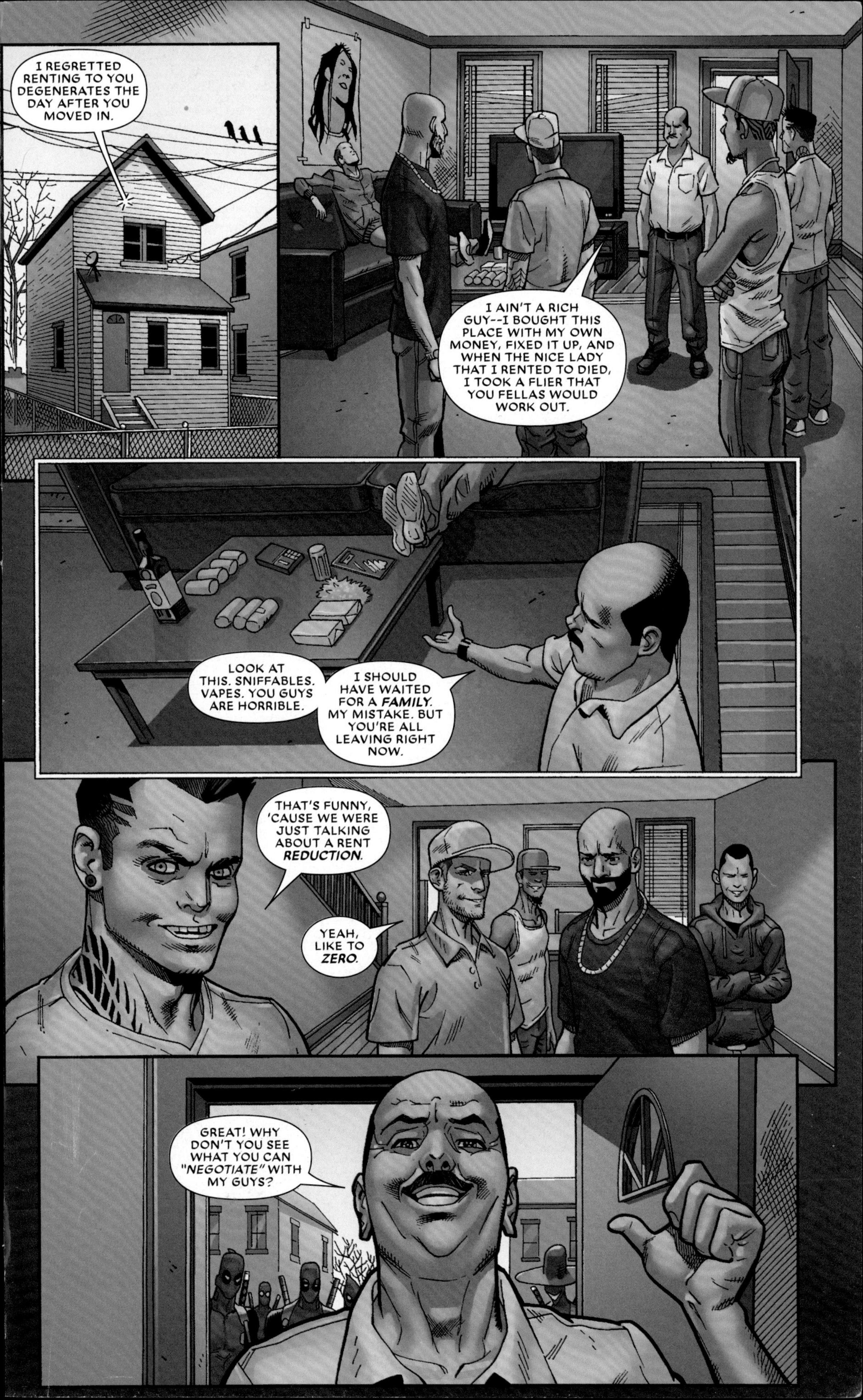
I REGRETTED RENTING TO YOU DEGENERATES THE DAY AFTER YOU MOVED IN.
I AIN'T A RICH GUY--I BOUGHT THIS PLACE WITH MY OWN MONEY, FIXED IT UP, AND WHEN THE NICE LADY THAT I RENTED TO DIED, I TOOK A FLIER THAT YOU FELLAS WOULD WORK OUT.
LOOK AT THIS. SNIFFABLES. VAPES. YOU GUYS ARE HORRIBLE.
I SHOULD HAVE WAITED FOR A *FAMILY*. MY MISTAKE. BUT YOU'RE ALL LEAVING RIGHT NOW.
THAT'S FUNNY, 'CAUSE WE WERE JUST TALKING ABOUT A RENT ***REDUCTION***.
YEAH, LIKE TO ***ZERO***.
GREAT! WHY DON'T YOU SEE WHAT YOU CAN "*NEGOTIATE*" WITH MY GUYS?

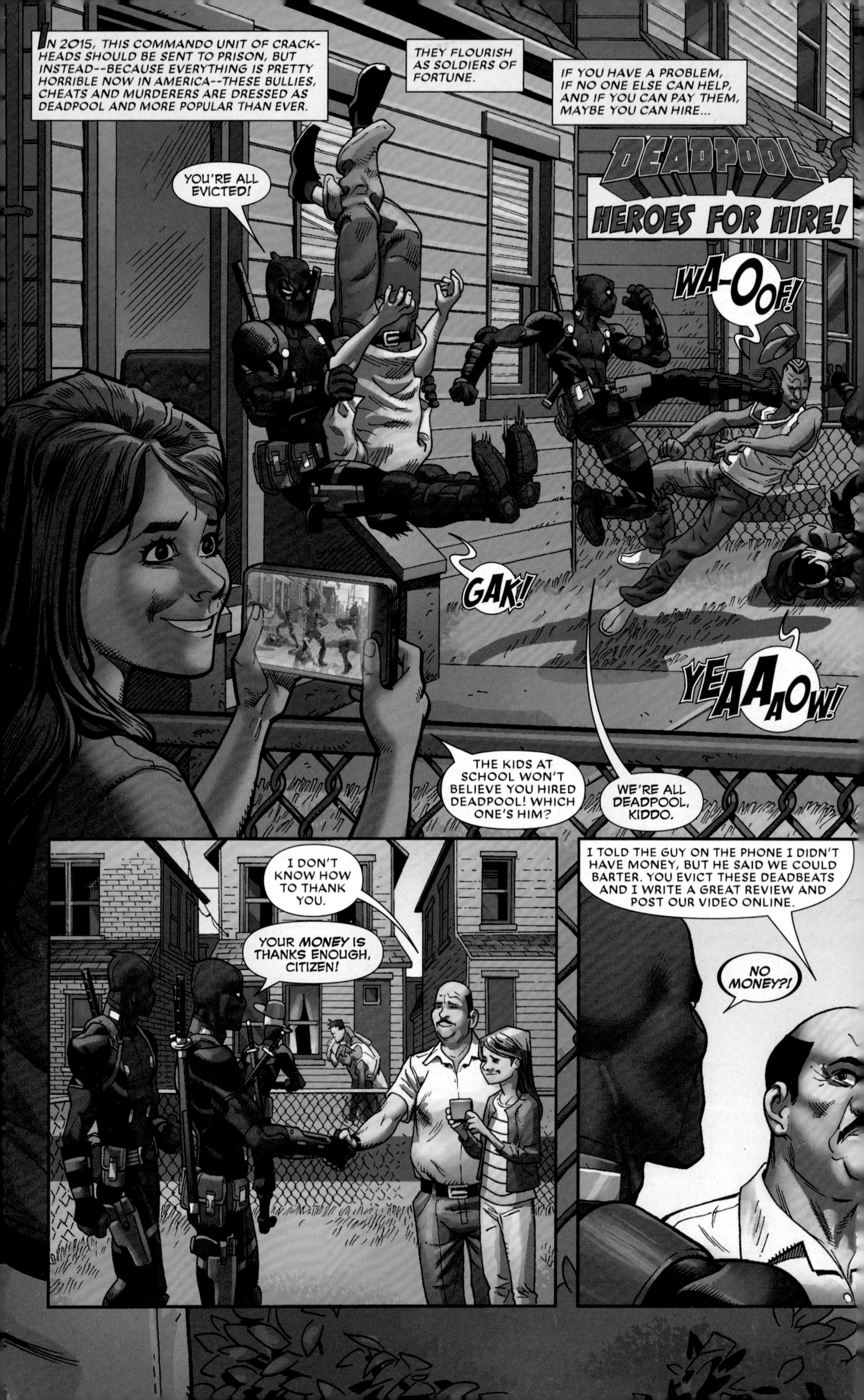
IN 2015, THIS COMMANDO UNIT OF CRACK-HEADS SHOULD BE SENT TO PRISON, BUT INSTEAD--BECAUSE EVERYTHING IS PRETTY HORRIBLE NOW IN AMERICA--THESE BULLIES, CHEATS AND MURDERERS ARE DRESSED AS DEADPOOL AND MORE POPULAR THAN EVER.
THEY FLOURISH AS SOLDIERS OF FORTUNE.
IF YOU HAVE A PROBLEM, IF NO ONE ELSE CAN HELP, AND IF YOU CAN PAY THEM, MAYBE YOU CAN HIRE...
DEADPOOL'S
HEROES FOR HIRE!
YOU'RE ALL EVICTED!
WA-OOF!
GAK!
YEAAAAOW!
THE KIDS AT SCHOOL WON'T BELIEVE YOU HIRED DEADPOOL! WHICH ONE'S HIM?
WE'RE ALL DEADPOOL, KIDDO.
I DON'T KNOW HOW TO THANK YOU.
YOUR MONEY IS THANKS ENOUGH, CITIZEN!
I TOLD THE GUY ON THE PHONE I DIDN'T HAVE MONEY, BUT HE SAID WE COULD BARTER. YOU EVICT THESE DEADBEATS AND I WRITE A GREAT REVIEW AND POST OUR VIDEO ONLINE.
NO MONEY?!

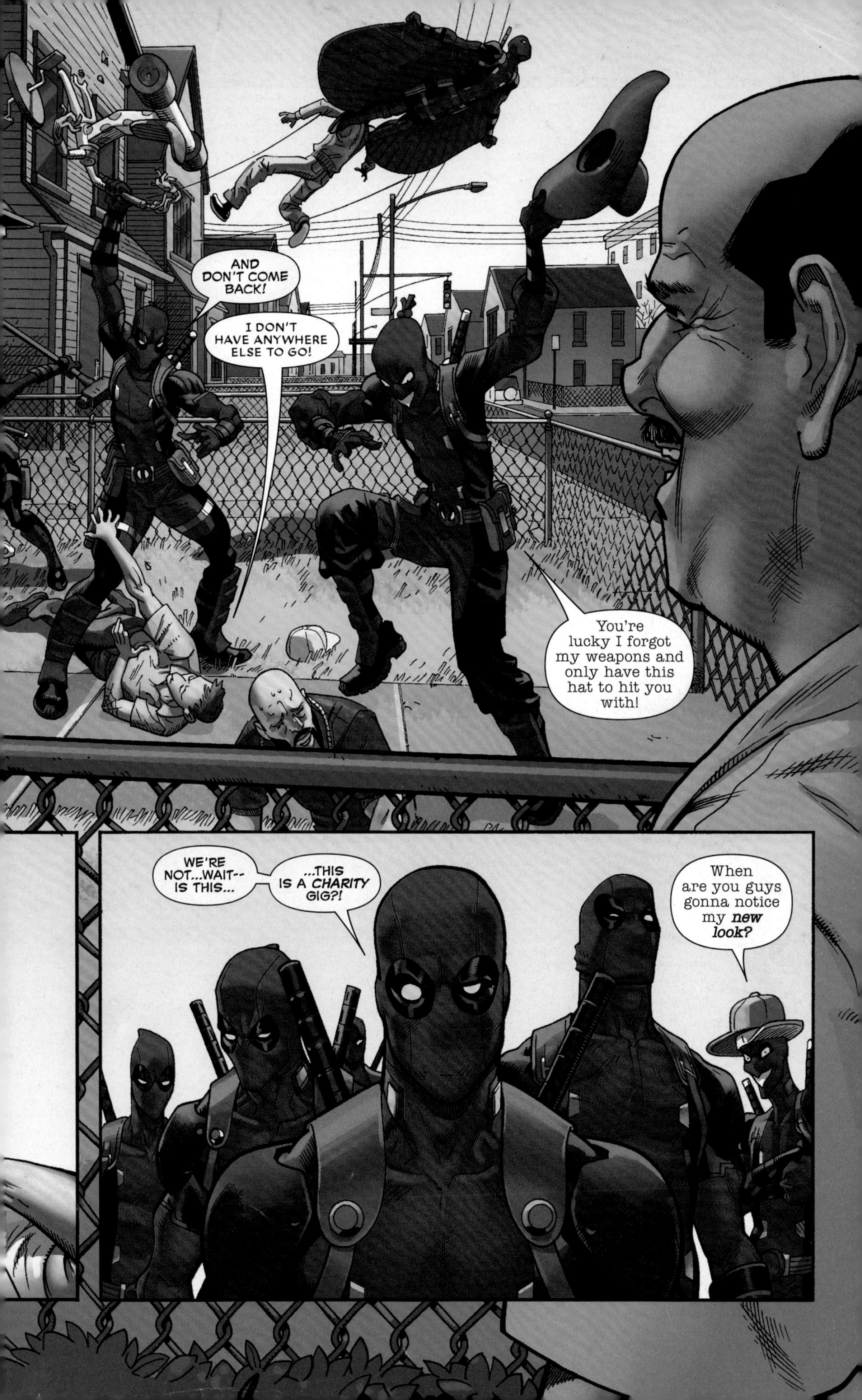
AND DON'T COME BACK!
I DON'T HAVE ANYWHERE ELSE TO GO!
You're lucky I forgot my weapons and only have this hat to hit you with!
WE'RE NOT...WAIT-- IS THIS...
...THIS IS A *CHARITY* GIG?!
When are you guys gonna notice my ***new look?***

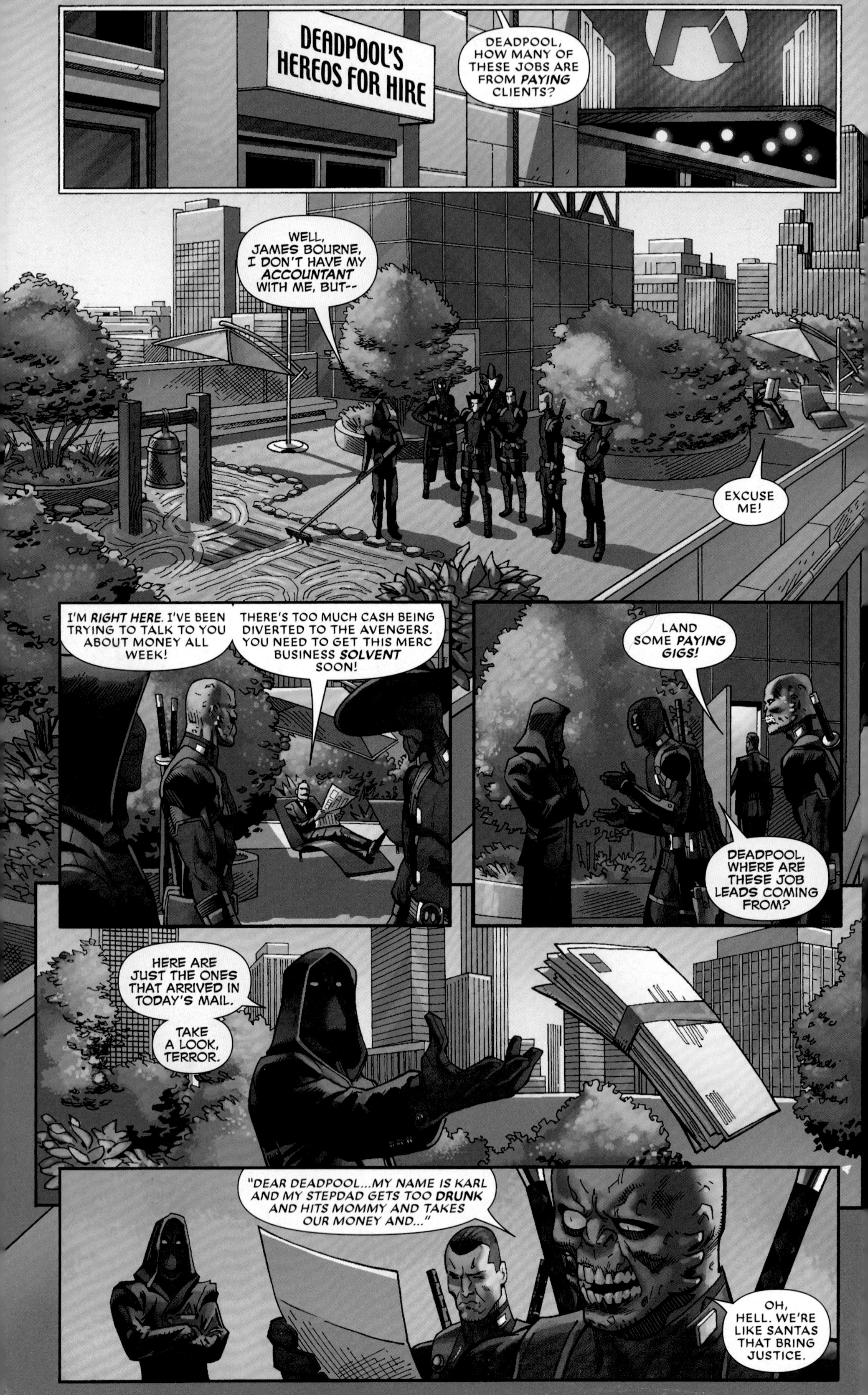
DEADPOOL'S HEREOS FOR HIRE
DEADPOOL, HOW MANY OF THESE JOBS ARE FROM PAYING CLIENTS?
WELL, JAMES BOURNE, I DON'T HAVE MY ACCOUNTANT WITH ME, BUT--
EXCUSE ME!
I'M RIGHT HERE. I'VE BEEN TRYING TO TALK TO YOU ABOUT MONEY ALL WEEK!
THERE'S TOO MUCH CASH BEING DIVERTED TO THE AVENGERS. YOU NEED TO GET THIS MERC BUSINESS SOLVENT SOON!
LAND SOME PAYING GIGS!
DEADPOOL, WHERE ARE THESE JOB LEADS COMING FROM?
HERE ARE JUST THE ONES THAT ARRIVED IN TODAY'S MAIL.
TAKE A LOOK, TERROR.
"DEAR DEADPOOL...MY NAME IS KARL AND MY STEPDAD GETS TOO DRUNK AND HITS MOMMY AND TAKES OUR MONEY AND..."
OH, HELL. WE'RE LIKE SANTAS THAT BRING JUSTICE.

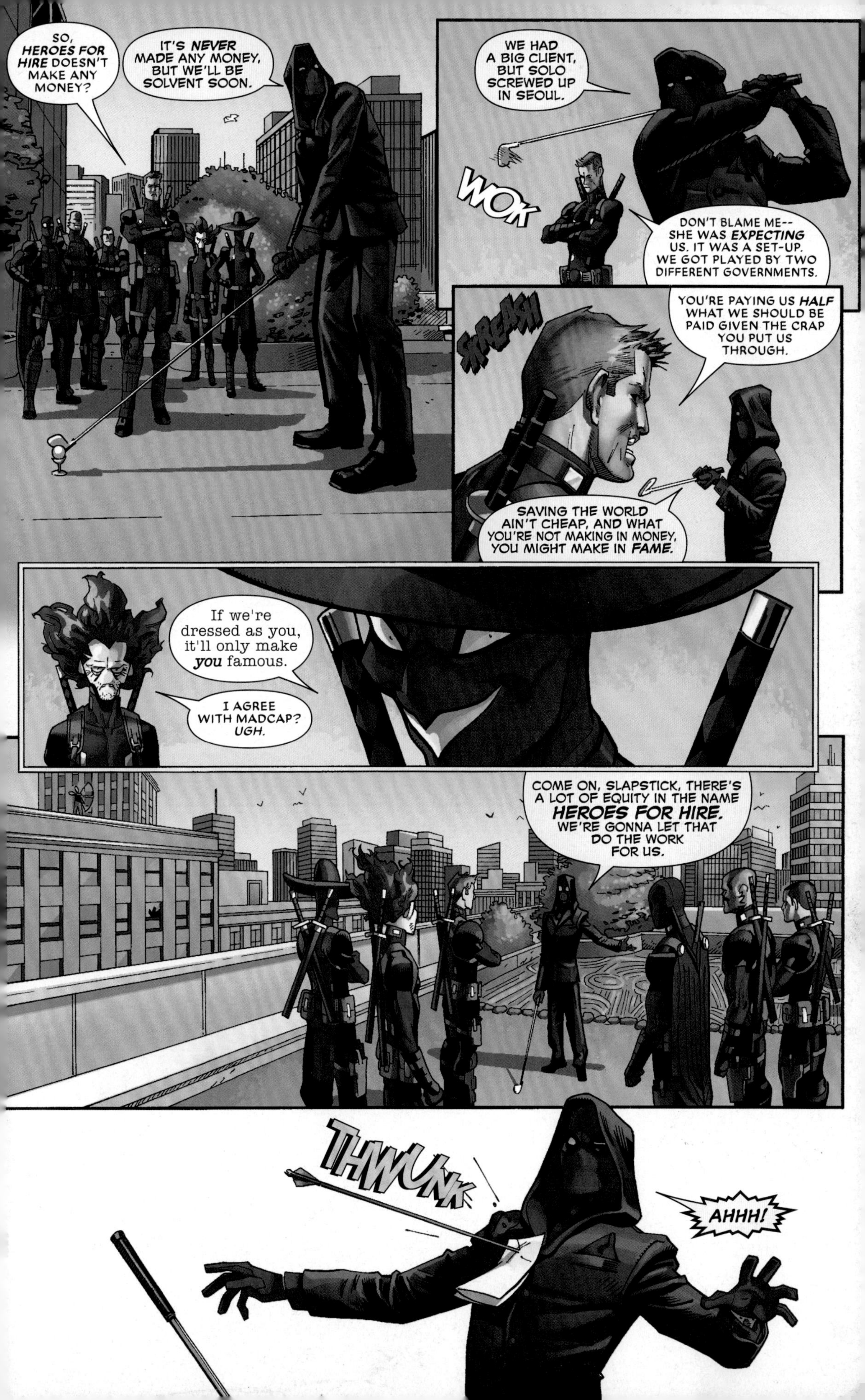
SO, HEROES FOR HIRE DOESN'T MAKE ANY MONEY?
IT'S NEVER MADE ANY MONEY, BUT WE'LL BE SOLVENT SOON.
WE HAD A BIG CLIENT, BUT SOLO SCREWED UP IN SEOUL.
WOK
DON'T BLAME ME-- SHE WAS EXPECTING US. IT WAS A SET-UP. WE GOT PLAYED BY TWO DIFFERENT GOVERNMENTS.
SKREASH
YOU'RE PAYING US HALF WHAT WE SHOULD BE PAID GIVEN THE CRAP YOU PUT US THROUGH.
SAVING THE WORLD AIN'T CHEAP, AND WHAT YOU'RE NOT MAKING IN MONEY, YOU MIGHT MAKE IN FAME.
If we're dressed as you, it'll only make you famous.
I AGREE WITH MADCAP? UGH.
COME ON, SLAPSTICK, THERE'S A LOT OF EQUITY IN THE NAME HEROES FOR HIRE. WE'RE GONNA LET THAT DO THE WORK FOR US.
THWUNK
AHHH!

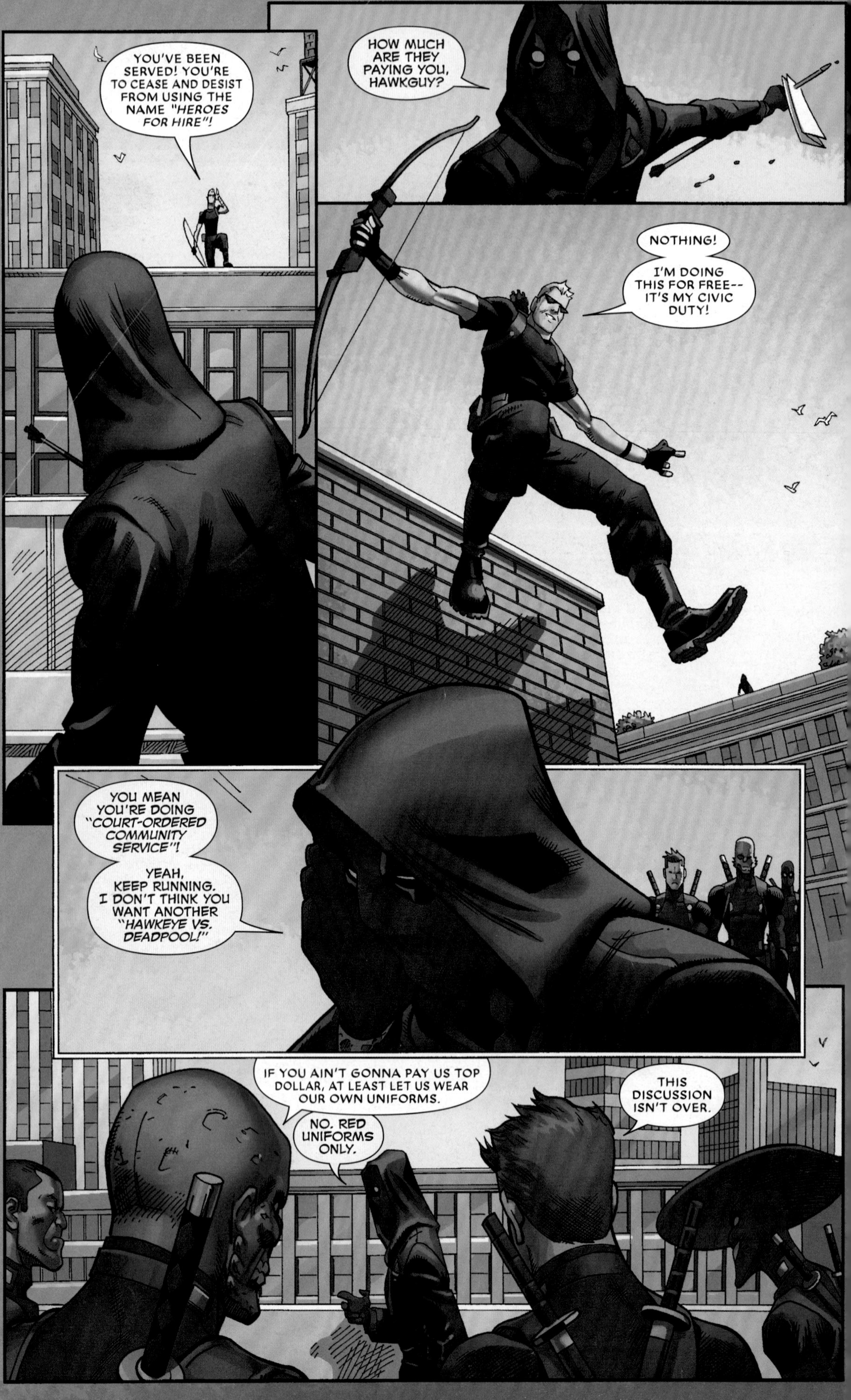

YOU'VE BEEN SERVED! YOU'RE TO CEASE AND DESIST FROM USING THE NAME "HEROES FOR HIRE"!
HOW MUCH ARE THEY PAYING YOU, HAWKGUY?
NOTHING!
I'M DOING THIS FOR FREE-- IT'S MY CIVIC DUTY!
YOU MEAN YOU'RE DOING "COURT-ORDERED COMMUNITY SERVICE"!
YEAH, KEEP RUNNING. I DON'T THINK YOU WANT ANOTHER "HAWKEYE VS. DEADPOOL!"
IF YOU AIN'T GONNA PAY US TOP DOLLAR, AT LEAST LET US WEAR OUR OWN UNIFORMS.
NO. RED UNIFORMS ONLY.
THIS DISCUSSION ISN'T OVER.

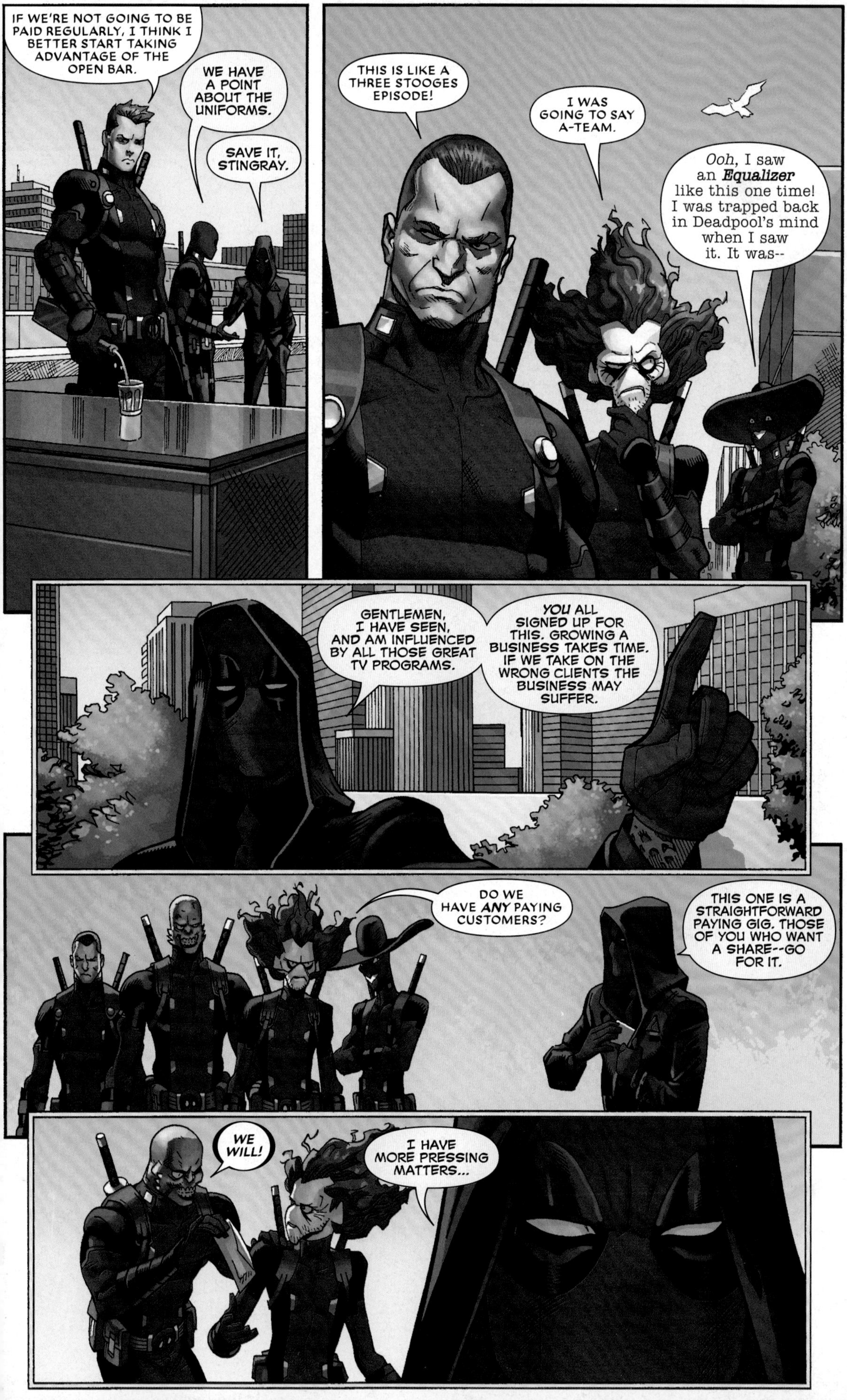

IF WE'RE NOT GOING TO BE PAID REGULARLY, I THINK I BETTER START TAKING ADVANTAGE OF THE OPEN BAR.
WE HAVE A POINT ABOUT THE UNIFORMS.
SAVE IT, STINGRAY.
THIS IS LIKE A THREE STOOGES EPISODE!
I WAS GOING TO SAY A-TEAM.
Ooh, I saw an Equalizer like this one time! I was trapped back in Deadpool's mind when I saw it. It was--
GENTLEMEN, I HAVE SEEN, AND AM INFLUENCED BY ALL THOSE GREAT TV PROGRAMS.
YOU ALL SIGNED UP FOR THIS. GROWING A BUSINESS TAKES TIME. IF WE TAKE ON THE WRONG CLIENTS THE BUSINESS MAY SUFFER.
DO WE HAVE ANY PAYING CUSTOMERS?
THIS ONE IS A STRAIGHTFORWARD PAYING GIG. THOSE OF YOU WHO WANT A SHARE--GO FOR IT.
WE WILL!
I HAVE MORE PRESSING MATTERS...

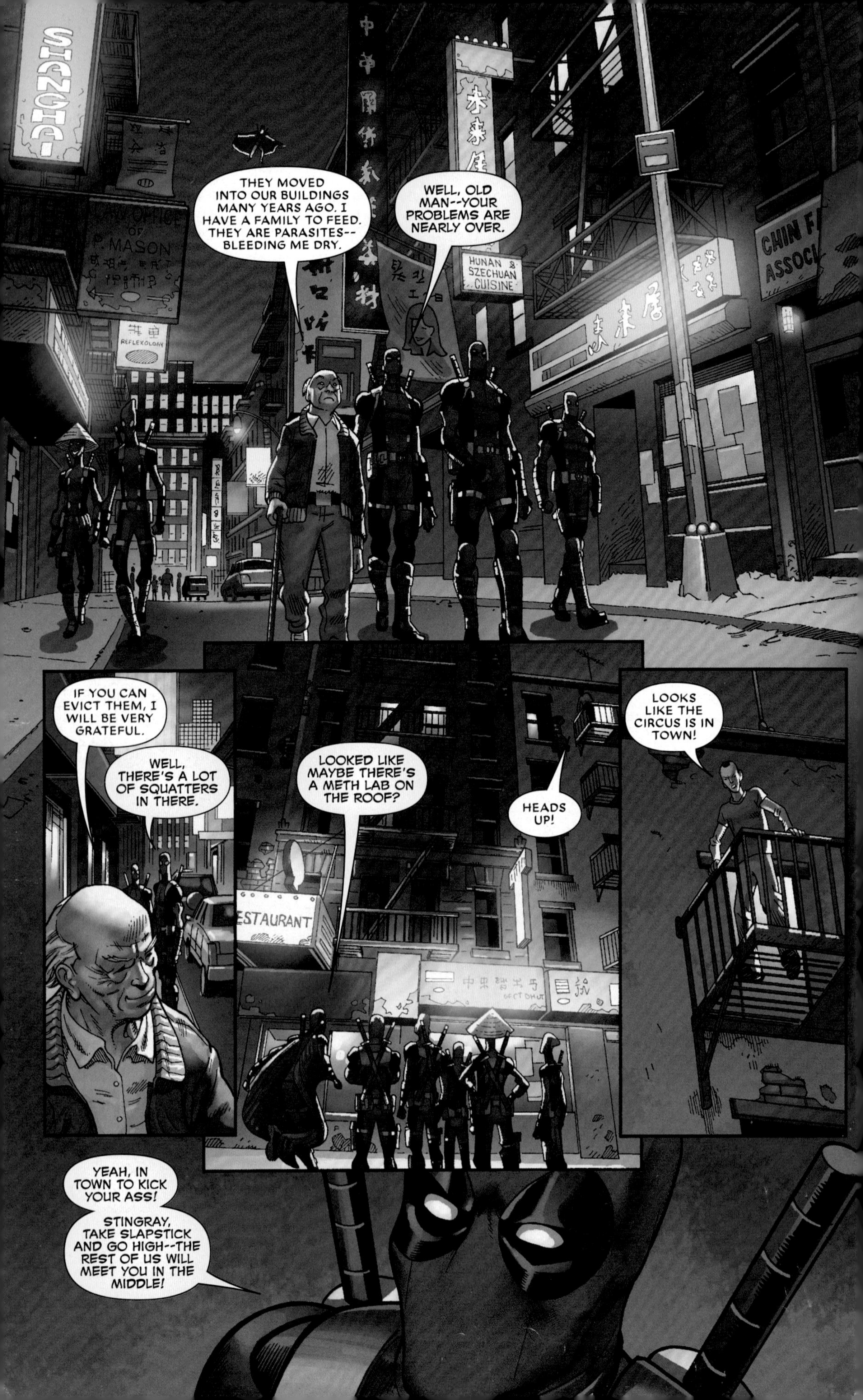
SHANGHAI
LAW OFFICE OF P. MASON
REFLEXOLOGY
THEY MOVED INTO OUR BUILDINGS MANY YEARS AGO. I HAVE A FAMILY TO FEED. THEY ARE PARASITES--BLEEDING ME DRY.
WELL, OLD MAN--YOUR PROBLEMS ARE NEARLY OVER.
HUNAN & SZECHUAN CUISINE
IF YOU CAN EVICT THEM, I WILL BE VERY GRATEFUL.
WELL, THERE'S A LOT OF SQUATTERS IN THERE.
LOOKED LIKE MAYBE THERE'S A METH LAB ON THE ROOF?
ESTAURANT
HEADS UP!
LOOKS LIKE THE CIRCUS IS IN TOWN!
YEAH, IN TOWN TO KICK YOUR ASS!
STINGRAY, TAKE SLAPSTICK AND GO HIGH--THE REST OF US WILL MEET YOU IN THE MIDDLE!

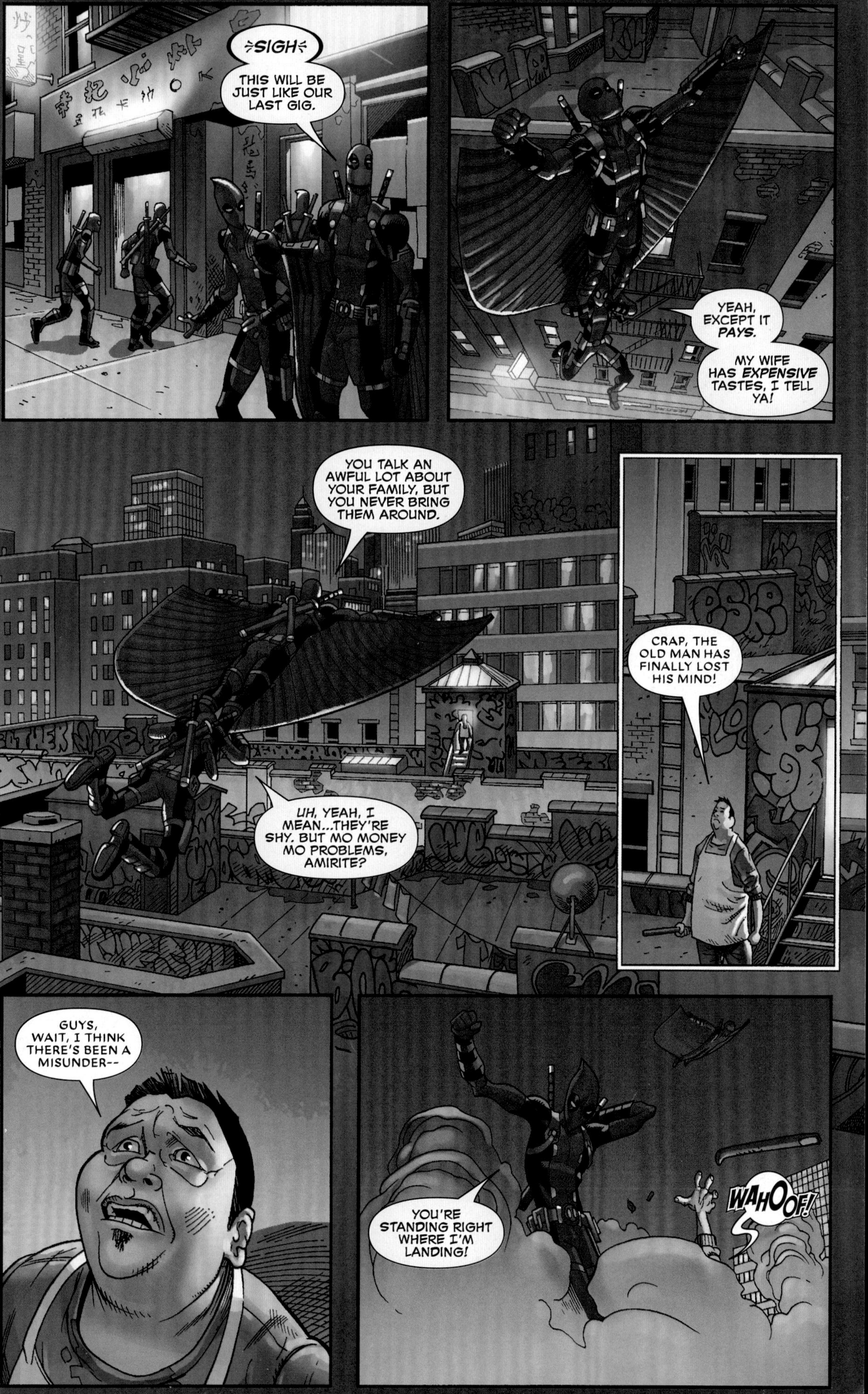

SIGH
THIS WILL BE JUST LIKE OUR LAST GIG.
YEAH, EXCEPT IT PAYS.
MY WIFE HAS EXPENSIVE TASTES, I TELL YA!
YOU TALK AN AWFUL LOT ABOUT YOUR FAMILY, BUT YOU NEVER BRING THEM AROUND.
UH, YEAH, I MEAN...THEY'RE SHY. BUT MO MONEY MO PROBLEMS, AMIRITE?
CRAP, THE OLD MAN HAS FINALLY LOST HIS MIND!
GUYS, WAIT, I THINK THERE'S BEEN A MISUNDER--
YOU'RE STANDING RIGHT WHERE I'M LANDING!
WAHOOF!

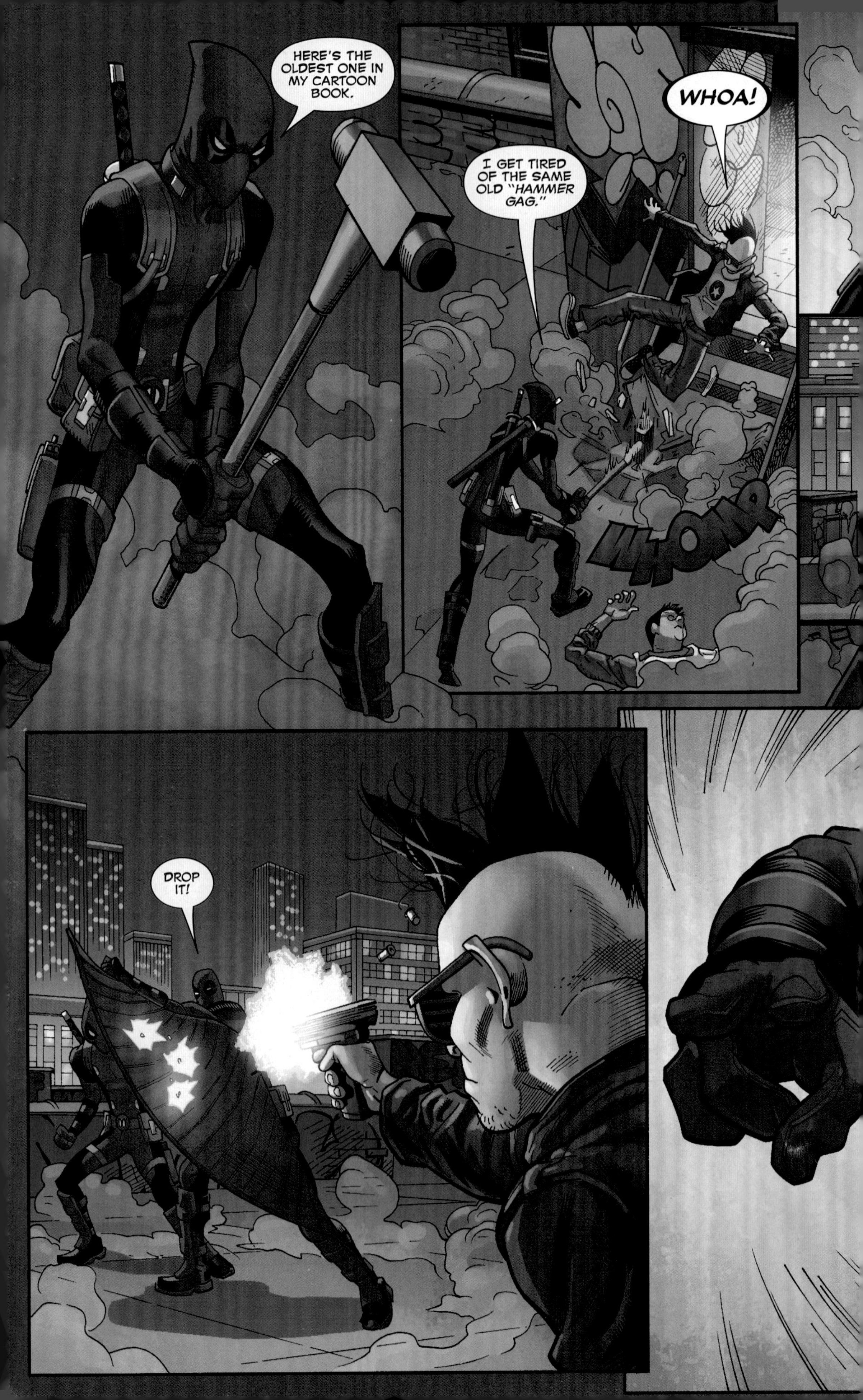
HERE'S THE OLDEST ONE IN MY CARTOON BOOK.
I GET TIRED OF THE SAME OLD "HAMMER GAG."
WHOA!
WHOMP
DROP IT!

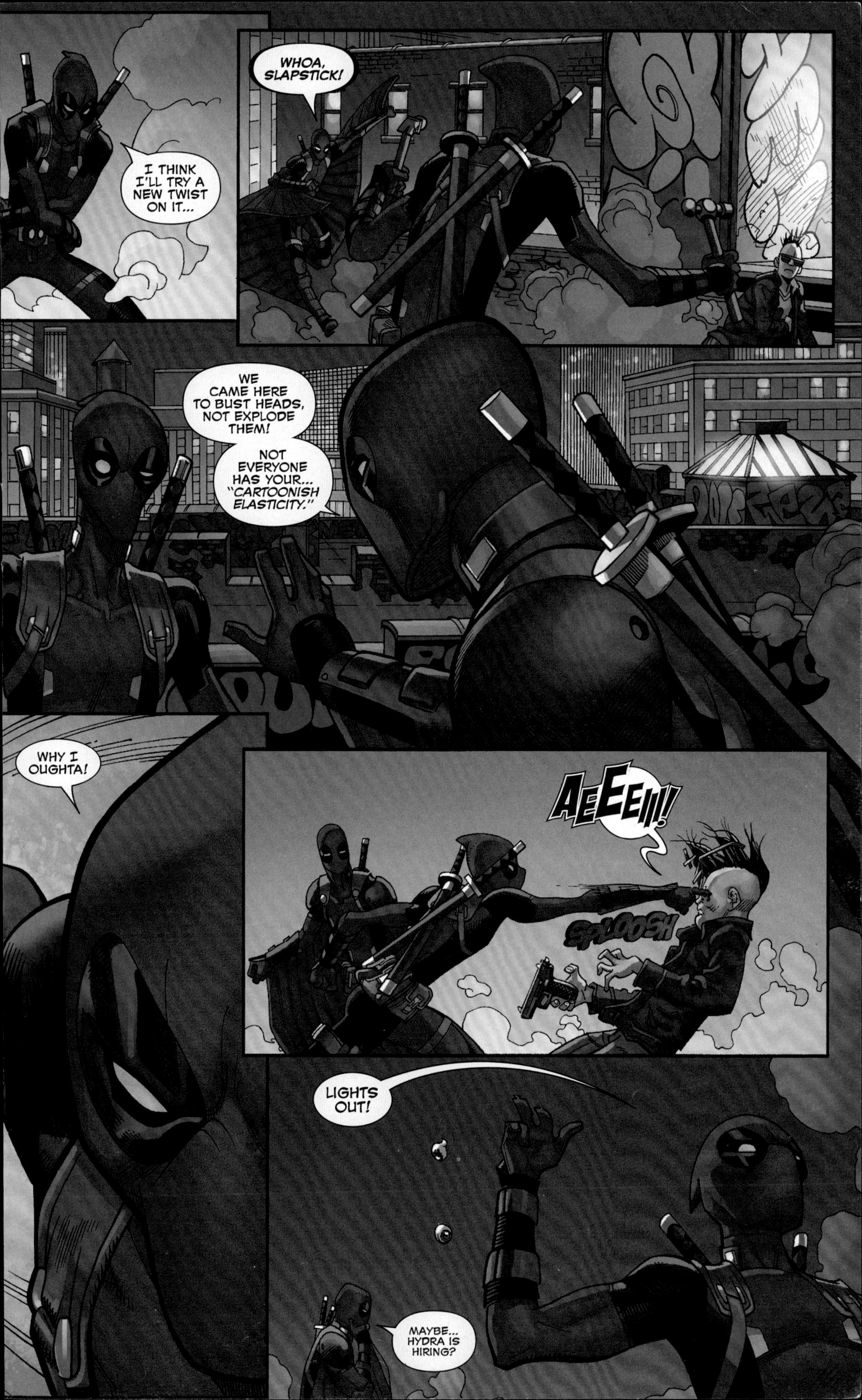
I THINK I'LL TRY A NEW TWIST ON IT...
WHOA, SLAPSTICK!
WE CAME HERE TO BUST HEADS, NOT EXPLODE THEM!
NOT EVERYONE HAS YOUR... "CARTOONISH ELASTICITY."
WHY I OUGHTA!
AEEEIII!
SPLOOSH
LIGHTS OUT!
MAYBE... HYDRA IS HIRING?

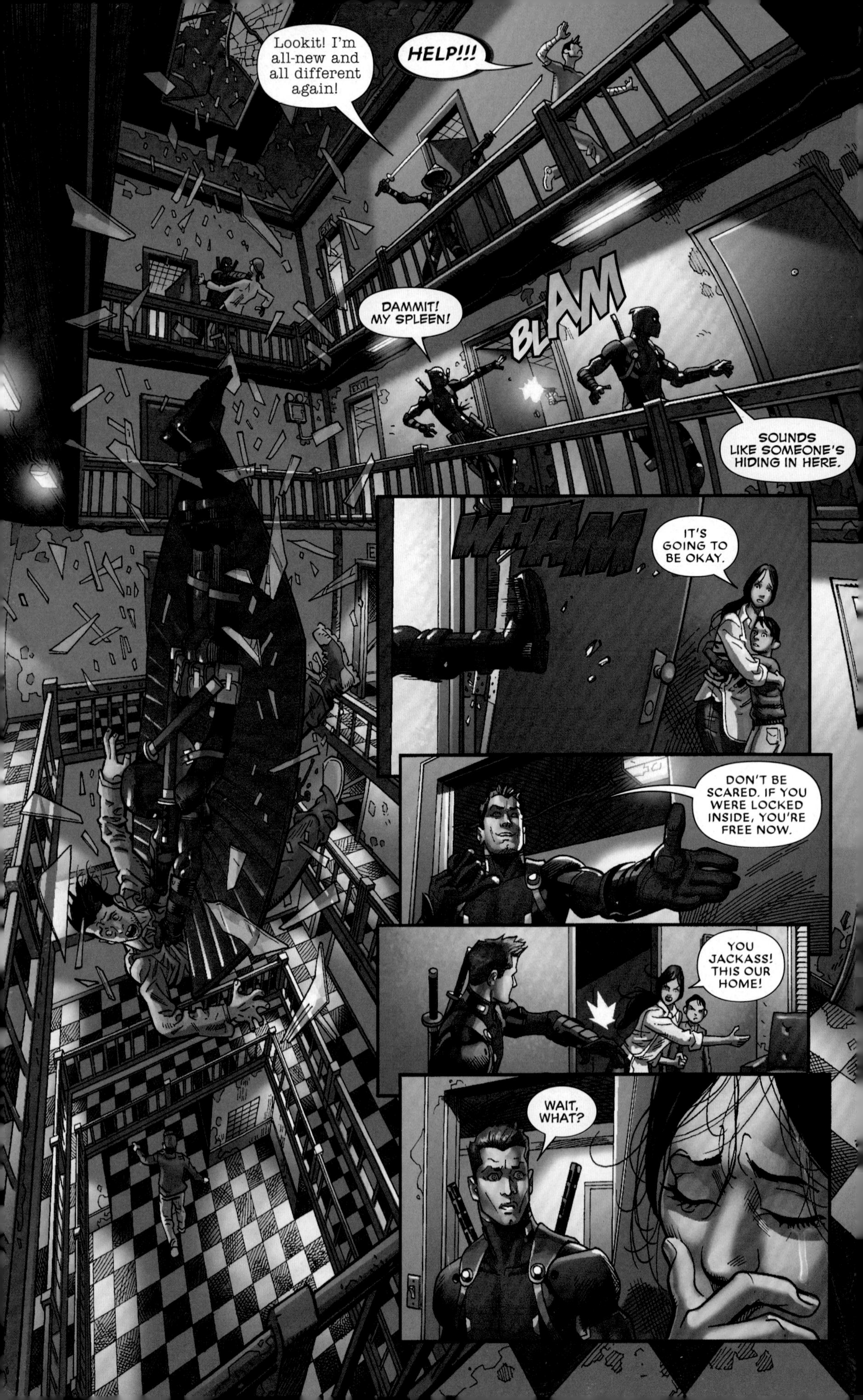
Lookit! I'm all-new and all different again!
HELP!!!
BLAM
DAMMIT! MY SPLEEN!
SOUNDS LIKE SOMEONE'S HIDING IN HERE.
WHAM
IT'S GOING TO BE OKAY.
DON'T BE SCARED. IF YOU WERE LOCKED INSIDE, YOU'RE FREE NOW.
YOU JACKASS! THIS OUR HOME!
WAIT, WHAT?

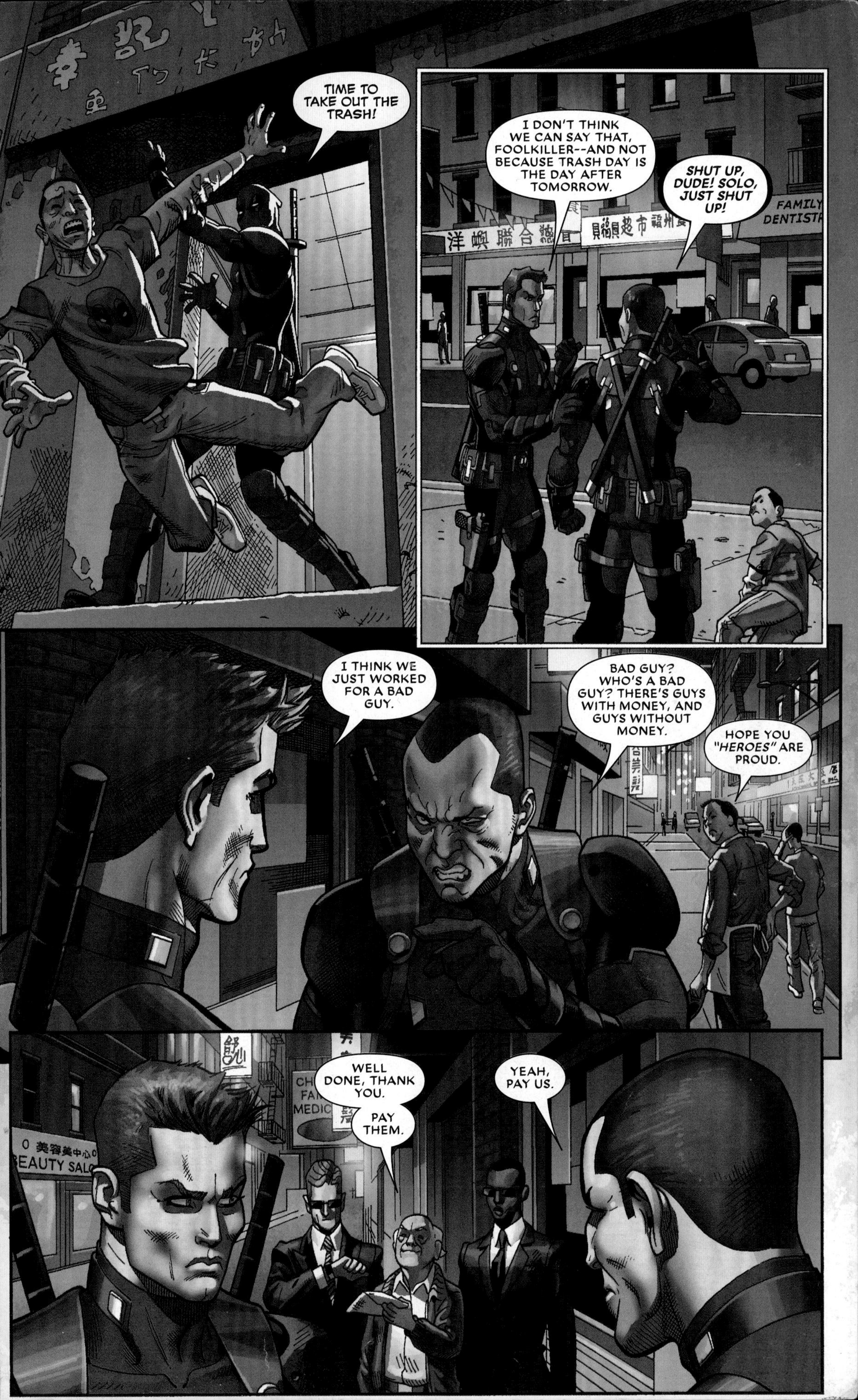
TIME TO TAKE OUT THE TRASH!
I DON'T THINK WE CAN SAY THAT, FOOLKILLER--AND NOT BECAUSE TRASH DAY IS THE DAY AFTER TOMORROW.
SHUT UP, DUDE! SOLO, JUST SHUT UP!
FAMILY DENTISTR
I THINK WE JUST WORKED FOR A BAD GUY.
BAD GUY? WHO'S A BAD GUY? THERE'S GUYS WITH MONEY, AND GUYS WITHOUT MONEY.
HOPE YOU "HEROES" ARE PROUD.
WELL DONE, THANK YOU.
PAY THEM.
YEAH, PAY US.
BEAUTY SALO

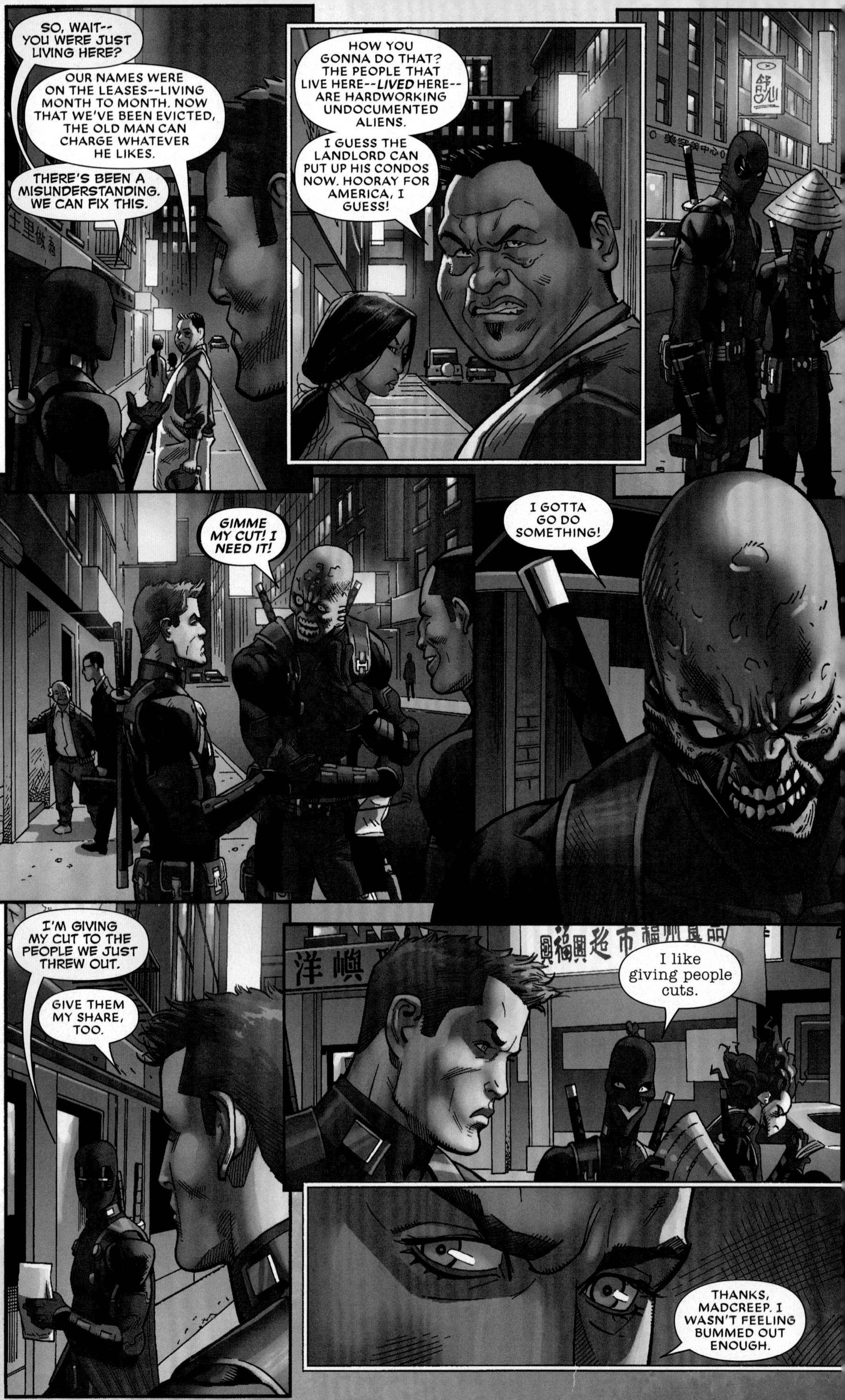
SO, WAIT-- YOU WERE JUST LIVING HERE?
OUR NAMES WERE ON THE LEASES--LIVING MONTH TO MONTH. NOW THAT WE'VE BEEN EVICTED, THE OLD MAN CAN CHARGE WHATEVER HE LIKES.
THERE'S BEEN A MISUNDERSTANDING. WE CAN FIX THIS.
HOW YOU GONNA DO THAT? THE PEOPLE THAT LIVE HERE--*LIVED* HERE--ARE HARDWORKING UNDOCUMENTED ALIENS.
I GUESS THE LANDLORD CAN PUT UP HIS CONDOS NOW. HOORAY FOR AMERICA, I GUESS!
GIMME MY CUT! I NEED IT!
I GOTTA GO DO SOMETHING!
I'M GIVING MY CUT TO THE PEOPLE WE JUST THREW OUT.
GIVE THEM MY SHARE, TOO.
I like giving people cuts.
THANKS, MADCREEP. I WASN'T FEELING BUMMED OUT ENOUGH.

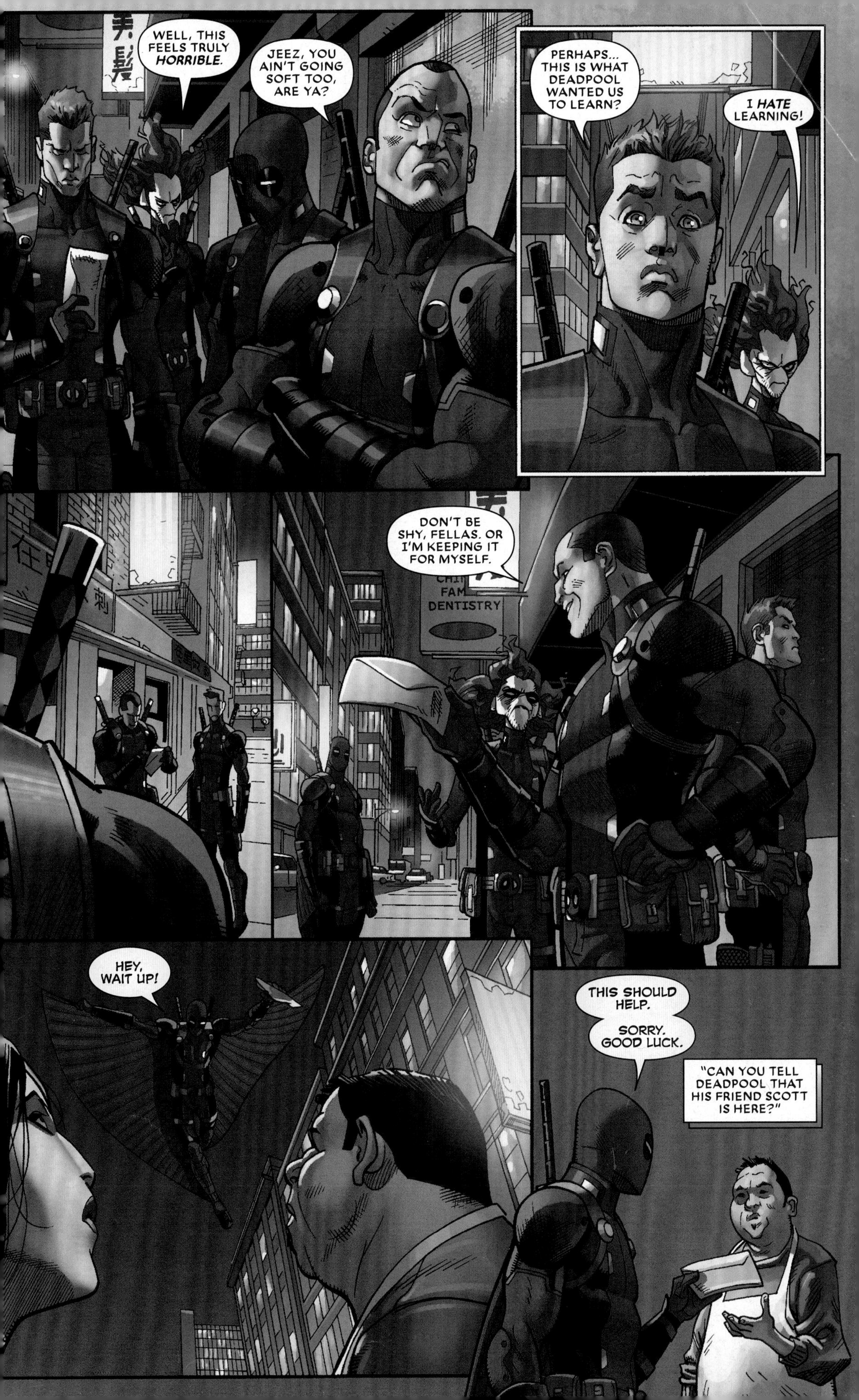
WELL, THIS FEELS TRULY *HORRIBLE*.
JEEZ, YOU AIN'T GOING SOFT TOO, ARE YA?
PERHAPS... THIS IS WHAT DEADPOOL WANTED US TO LEARN?
I *HATE* LEARNING!
DON'T BE SHY, FELLAS. OR I'M KEEPING IT FOR MYSELF.
DENTISTRY
HEY, WAIT UP!
THIS SHOULD HELP.
SORRY. GOOD LUCK.
"CAN YOU TELL DEADPOOL THAT HIS FRIEND SCOTT IS HERE?"

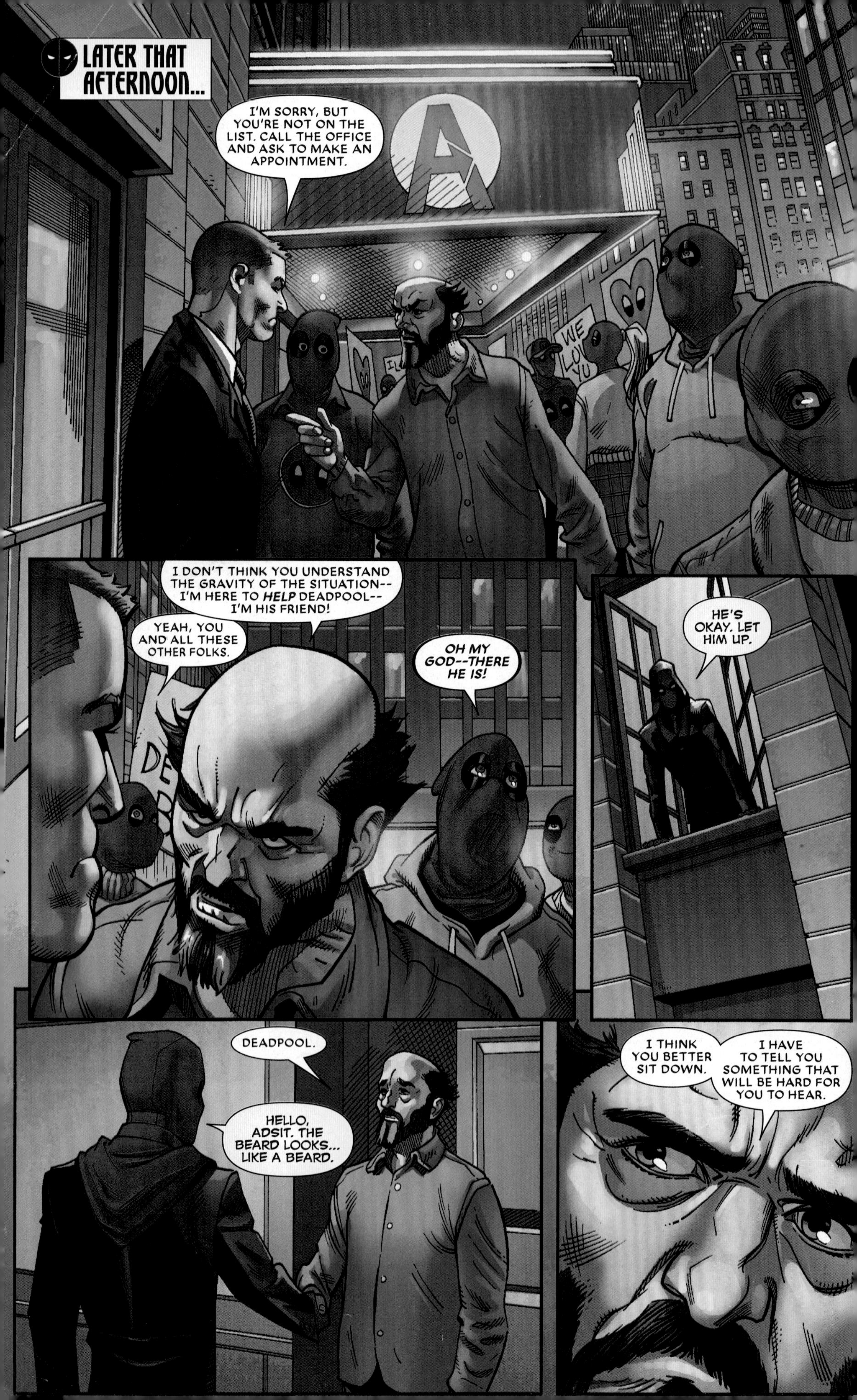
LATER THAT AFTERNOON...
I'M SORRY, BUT YOU'RE NOT ON THE LIST. CALL THE OFFICE AND ASK TO MAKE AN APPOINTMENT.
I DON'T THINK YOU UNDERSTAND THE GRAVITY OF THE SITUATION-- I'M HERE TO HELP DEADPOOL-- I'M HIS FRIEND!
YEAH, YOU AND ALL THESE OTHER FOLKS.
OH MY GOD--THERE HE IS!
HE'S OKAY. LET HIM UP.
DEADPOOL.
HELLO, ADSIT. THE BEARD LOOKS... LIKE A BEARD.
I THINK YOU BETTER SIT DOWN.
I HAVE TO TELL YOU SOMETHING THAT WILL BE HARD FOR YOU TO HEAR.

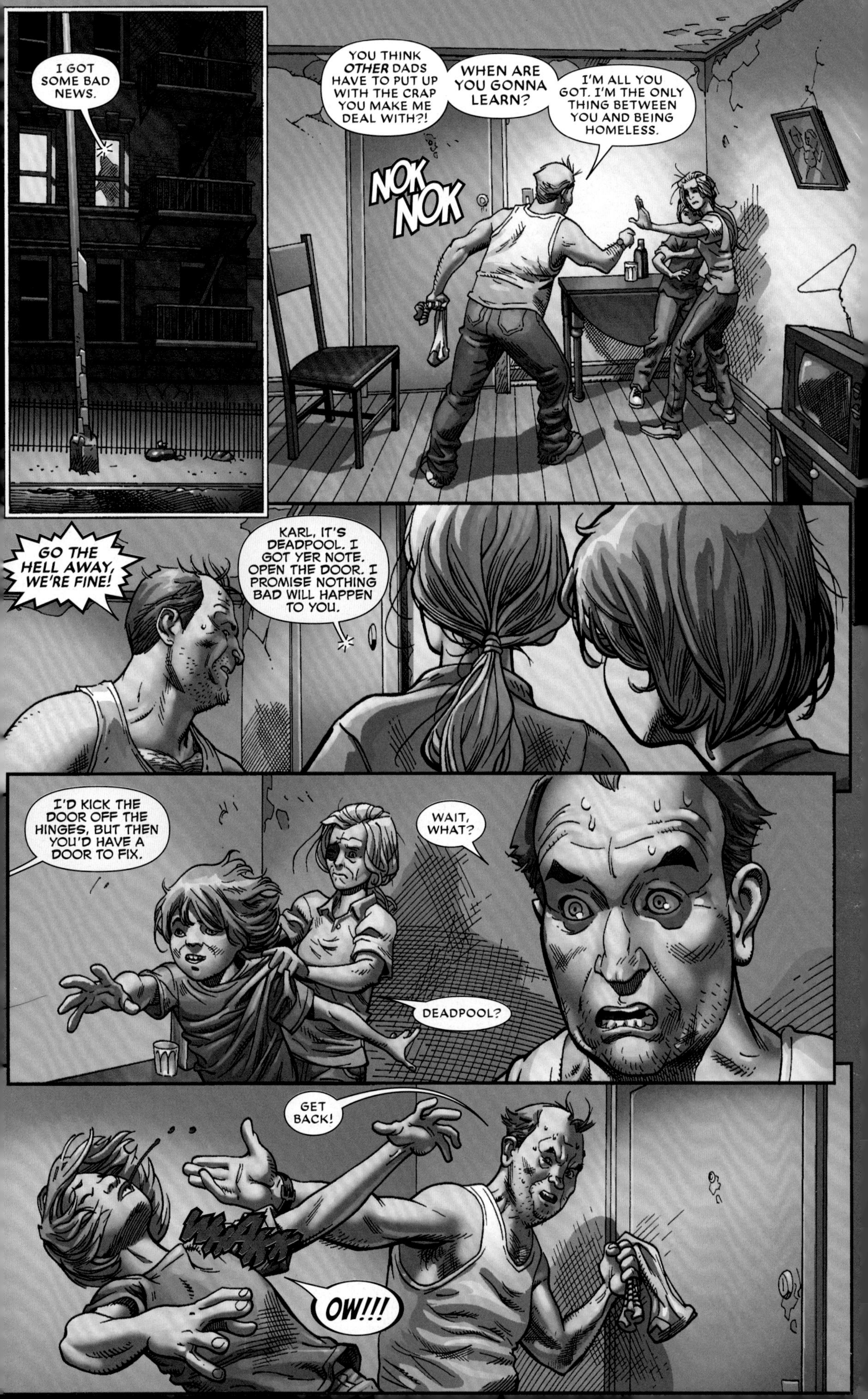
I GOT SOME BAD NEWS.
YOU THINK OTHER DADS HAVE TO PUT UP WITH THE CRAP YOU MAKE ME DEAL WITH?!
WHEN ARE YOU GONNA LEARN?
I'M ALL YOU GOT. I'M THE ONLY THING BETWEEN YOU AND BEING HOMELESS.
NOK NOK
GO THE HELL AWAY, WE'RE FINE!
KARL, IT'S DEADPOOL. I GOT YER NOTE. OPEN THE DOOR. I PROMISE NOTHING BAD WILL HAPPEN TO YOU.
I'D KICK THE DOOR OFF THE HINGES, BUT THEN YOU'D HAVE A DOOR TO FIX.
WAIT, WHAT?
DEADPOOL?
GET BACK!
OW!!!

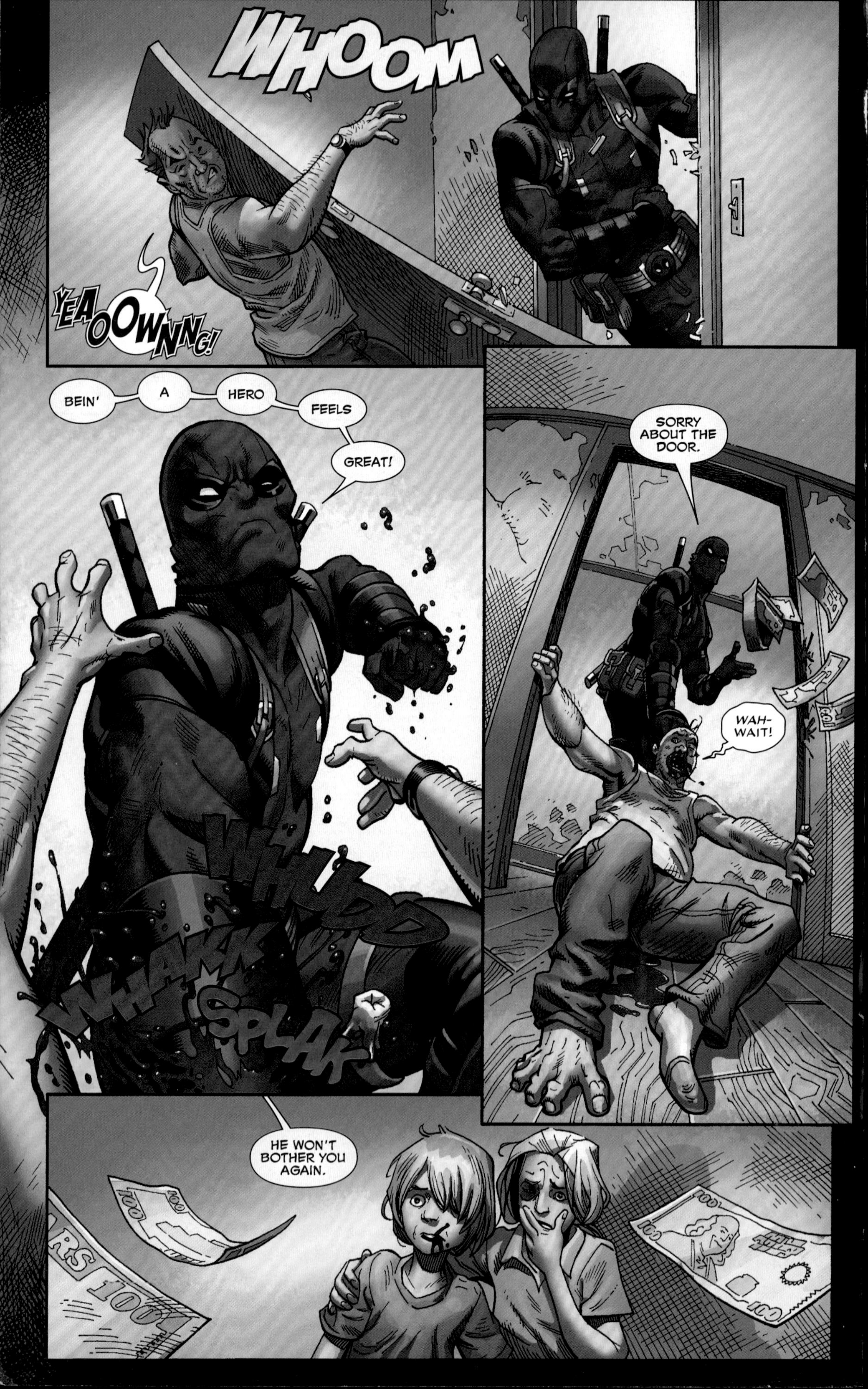
WHOOM
YEAOOWNNG!
BEIN' A HERO FEELS GREAT!
WHUDD
WHAKK
SPLAK
SORRY ABOUT THE DOOR.
WAH-WAIT!
HE WON'T BOTHER YOU AGAIN.

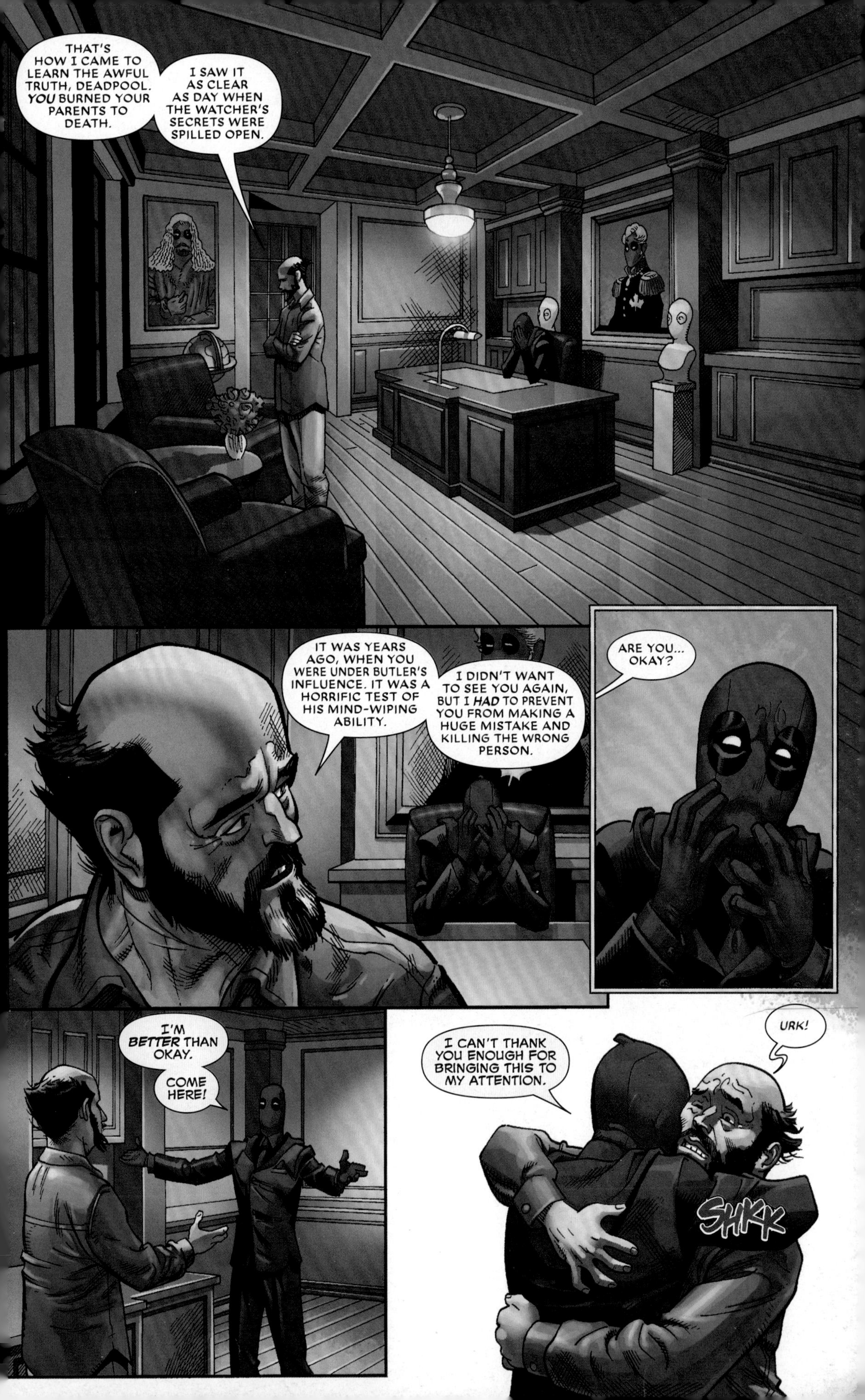
THAT'S HOW I CAME TO LEARN THE AWFUL TRUTH, DEADPOOL. *YOU* BURNED YOUR PARENTS TO DEATH.
I SAW IT AS CLEAR AS DAY WHEN THE WATCHER'S SECRETS WERE SPILLED OPEN.
IT WAS YEARS AGO, WHEN YOU WERE UNDER BUTLER'S INFLUENCE. IT WAS A HORRIFIC TEST OF HIS MIND-WIPING ABILITY.
I DIDN'T WANT TO SEE YOU AGAIN, BUT I *HAD* TO PREVENT YOU FROM MAKING A HUGE MISTAKE AND KILLING THE WRONG PERSON.
ARE YOU... OKAY?
I'M *BETTER* THAN OKAY.
COME HERE!
I CAN'T THANK YOU ENOUGH FOR BRINGING THIS TO MY ATTENTION.
URK!
SHKK

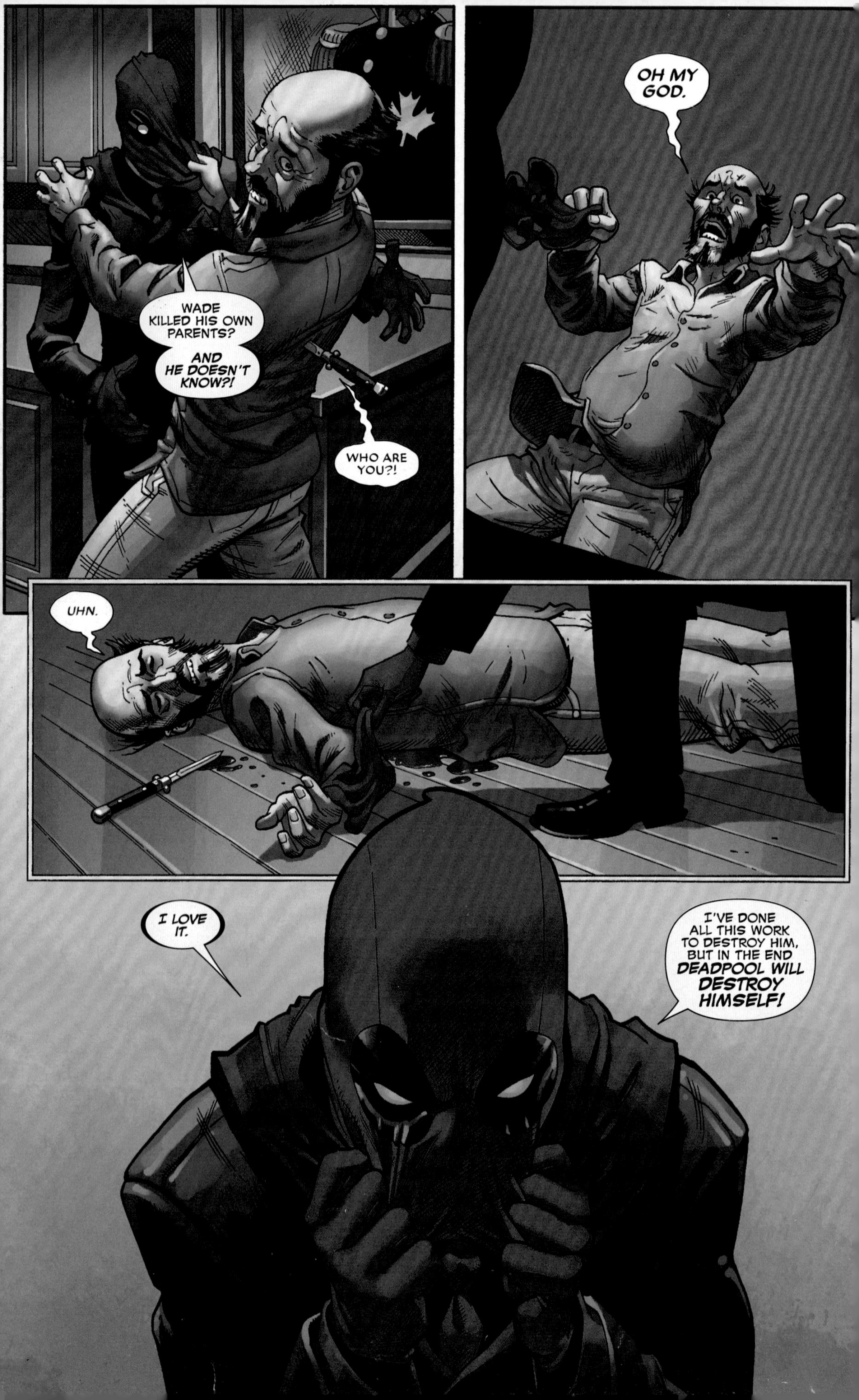
WADE KILLED HIS OWN PARENTS?
AND HE DOESN'T KNOW?!
WHO ARE YOU?!
OH MY GOD.
UHN.
I LOVE IT.
I'VE DONE ALL THIS WORK TO DESTROY HIM, BUT IN THE END DEADPOOL WILL DESTROY HIMSELF!

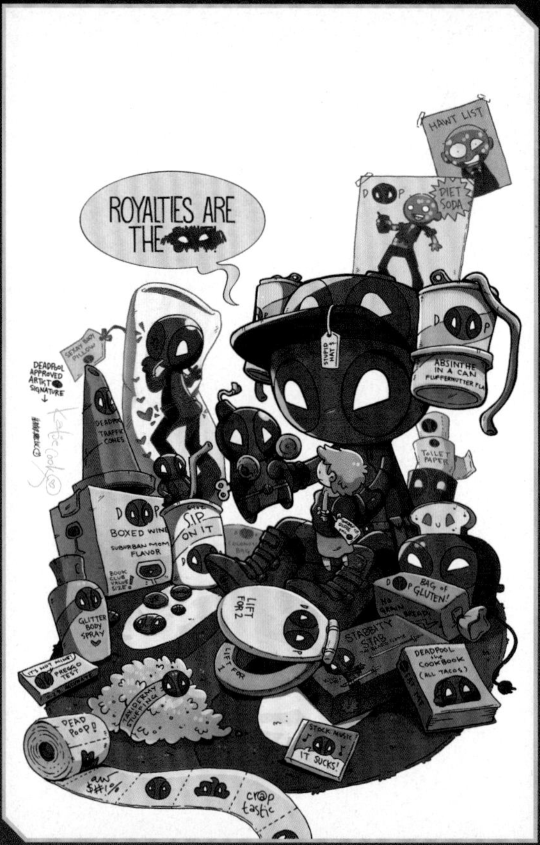
ROYALTIES ARE THE
HAWT LIST
DIET SODA
SEXAY BODY PILLOW
STUPID HAT
ABSINTHE IN A CAN
FLUFFERNUTTER FLA
DEADPOOL APPROVED ARTIST SIGNATURE
DEADPOOL TRAFFIC CONES
TOILET PAPER
BOXED WINE
SUBURBAN MOM FLAVOR
BOOK CLUB VALUE SIZE!
SIP ON IT
BAG of GLUTEN!
NO GRAIN BREAD
GLITTER BODY SPRAY
LIFT FOR 2
LIFT FOR 1
STABBITY STAB
DEADPOOL the COOKBOOK (ALL TACOS)
IT'S NOT MINE! PREGGO TEST
TAXIDERMY STUFFING
DEAD POOP!
STOCK MUSIC IT SUCKS!
aw $#!%
cr@p tastic

#1 variant by
KATIE COOK & HEATHER BRECKEL

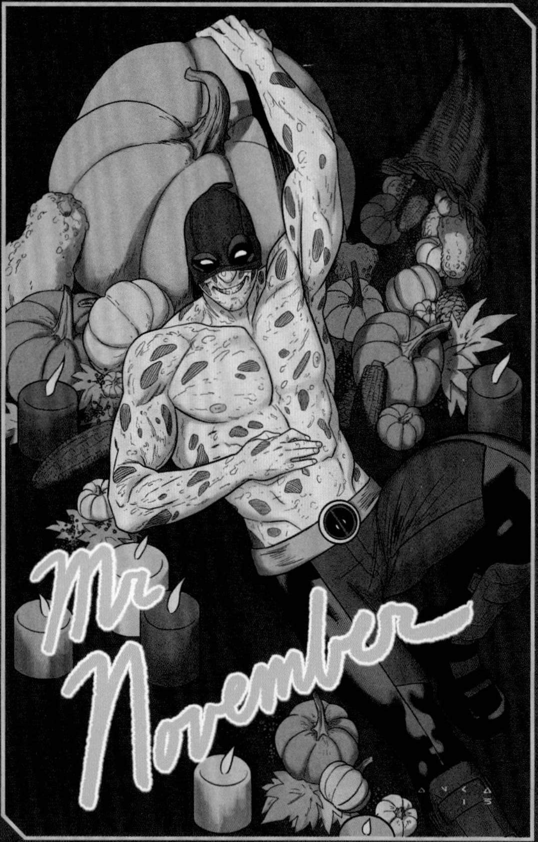
Mr November

#1 variant by
KRIS ANKA

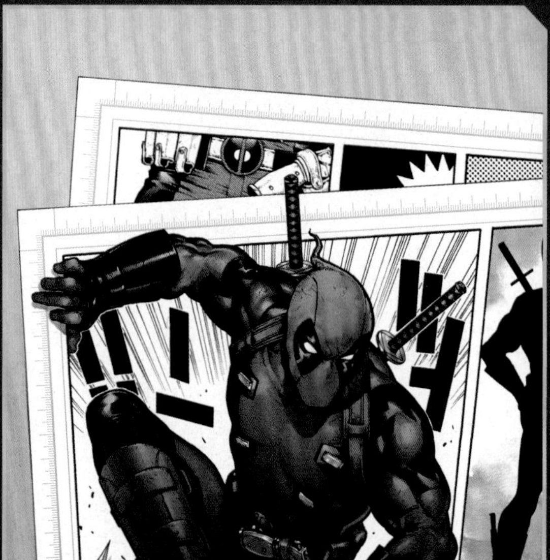

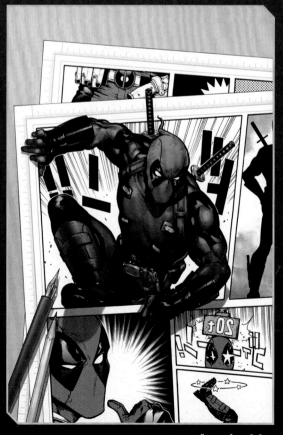

#1 variant by
KAMOME SHIRAHAMA

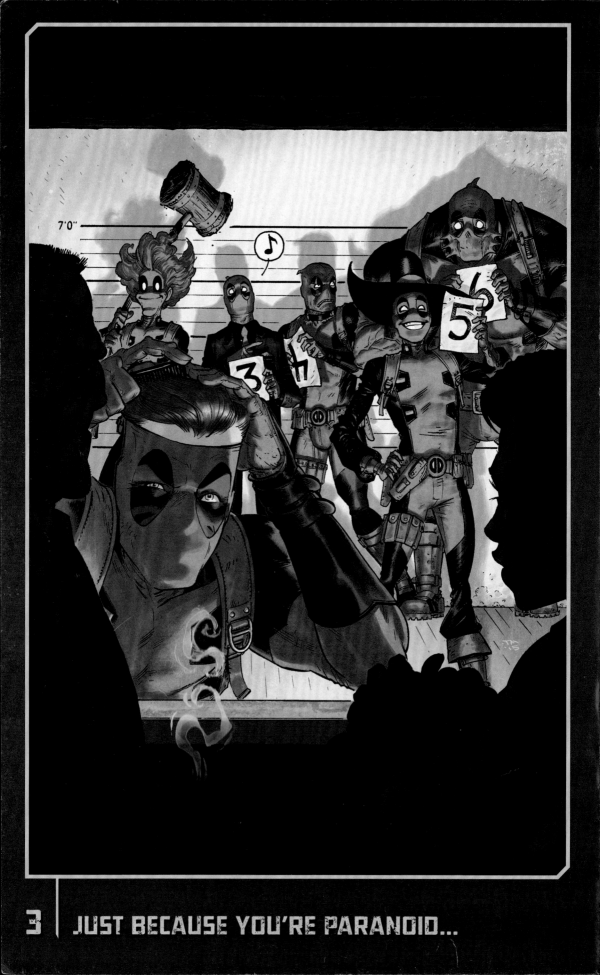

| JUST BECAUSE YOU'RE PARANOID...

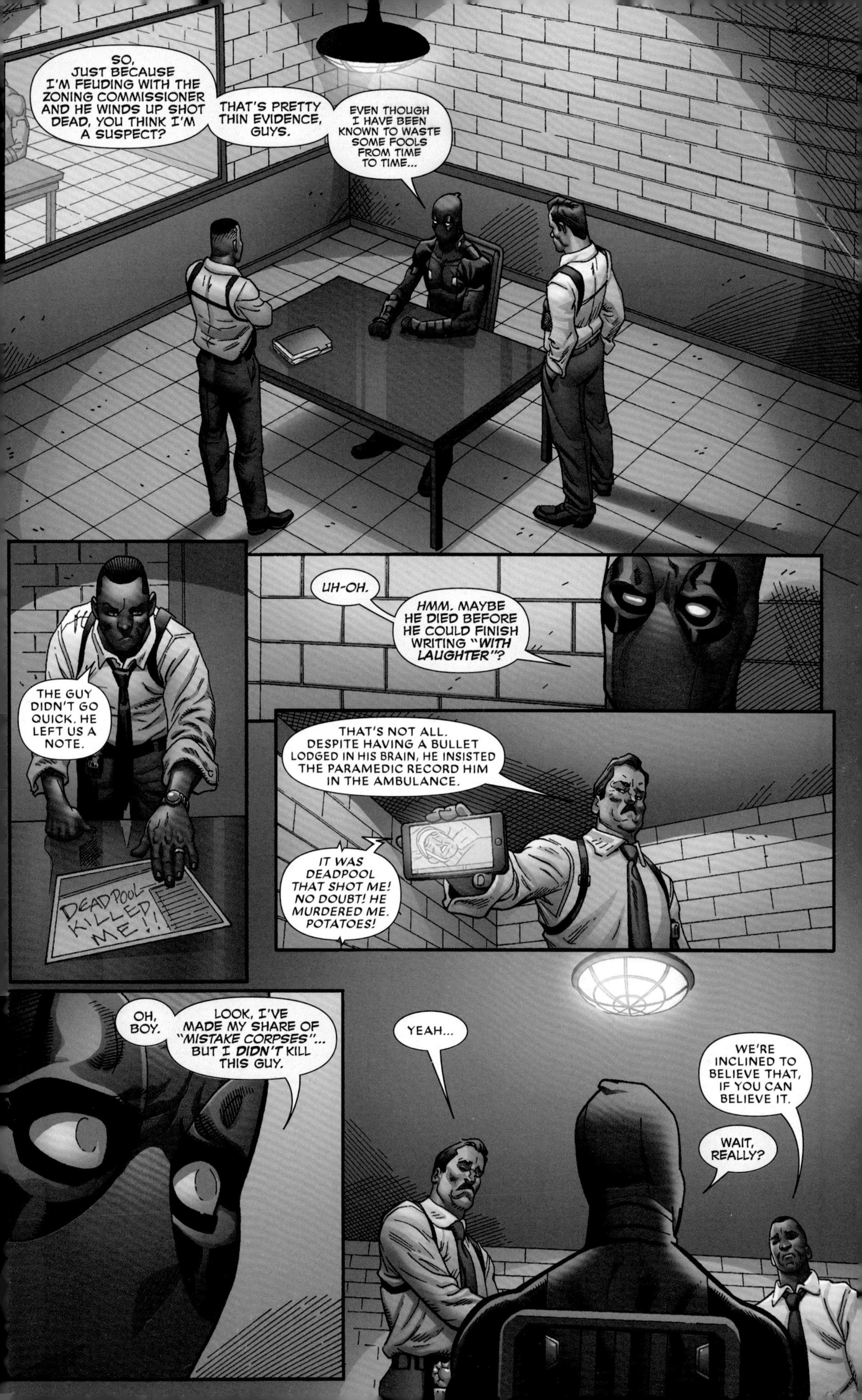
SO, JUST BECAUSE I'M FEUDING WITH THE ZONING COMMISSIONER AND HE WINDS UP SHOT DEAD, YOU THINK I'M A SUSPECT?
THAT'S PRETTY THIN EVIDENCE, GUYS.
EVEN THOUGH I HAVE BEEN KNOWN TO WASTE SOME FOOLS FROM TIME TO TIME...
THE GUY DIDN'T GO QUICK. HE LEFT US A NOTE.
DEADPOOL KILLED ME!!
UH-OH.
HMM. MAYBE HE DIED BEFORE HE COULD FINISH WRITING "WITH LAUGHTER"?
THAT'S NOT ALL. DESPITE HAVING A BULLET LODGED IN HIS BRAIN, HE INSISTED THE PARAMEDIC RECORD HIM IN THE AMBULANCE.
IT WAS DEADPOOL THAT SHOT ME! NO DOUBT! HE MURDERED ME. POTATOES!
OH, BOY.
LOOK, I'VE MADE MY SHARE OF "MISTAKE CORPSES"... BUT I DIDN'T KILL THIS GUY.
YEAH...
WE'RE INCLINED TO BELIEVE THAT, IF YOU CAN BELIEVE IT.
WAIT, REALLY?

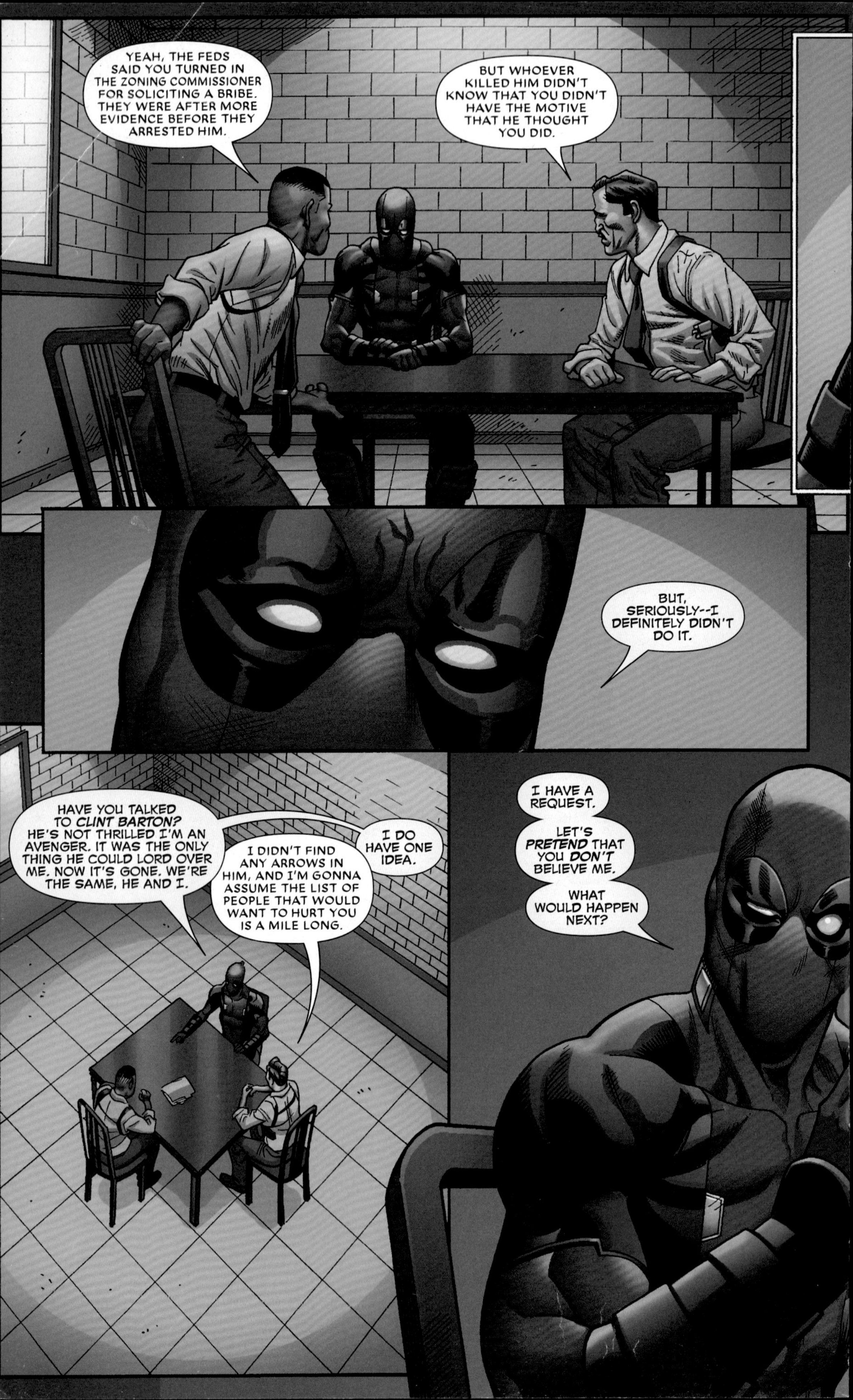
YEAH, THE FEDS SAID YOU TURNED IN THE ZONING COMMISSIONER FOR SOLICITING A BRIBE. THEY WERE AFTER MORE EVIDENCE BEFORE THEY ARRESTED HIM.
BUT WHOEVER KILLED HIM DIDN'T KNOW THAT YOU DIDN'T HAVE THE MOTIVE THAT HE THOUGHT YOU DID.
BUT, SERIOUSLY--I DEFINITELY DIDN'T DO IT.
HAVE YOU TALKED TO *CLINT BARTON?* HE'S NOT THRILLED I'M AN AVENGER. IT WAS THE ONLY THING HE COULD LORD OVER ME. NOW IT'S GONE. WE'RE THE SAME, HE AND I.
I DIDN'T FIND ANY ARROWS IN HIM, AND I'M GONNA ASSUME THE LIST OF PEOPLE THAT WOULD WANT TO HURT YOU IS A MILE LONG.
I DO HAVE ONE IDEA.
I HAVE A REQUEST.
LET'S ***PRETEND*** THAT YOU ***DON'T*** BELIEVE ME.
WHAT WOULD HAPPEN NEXT?

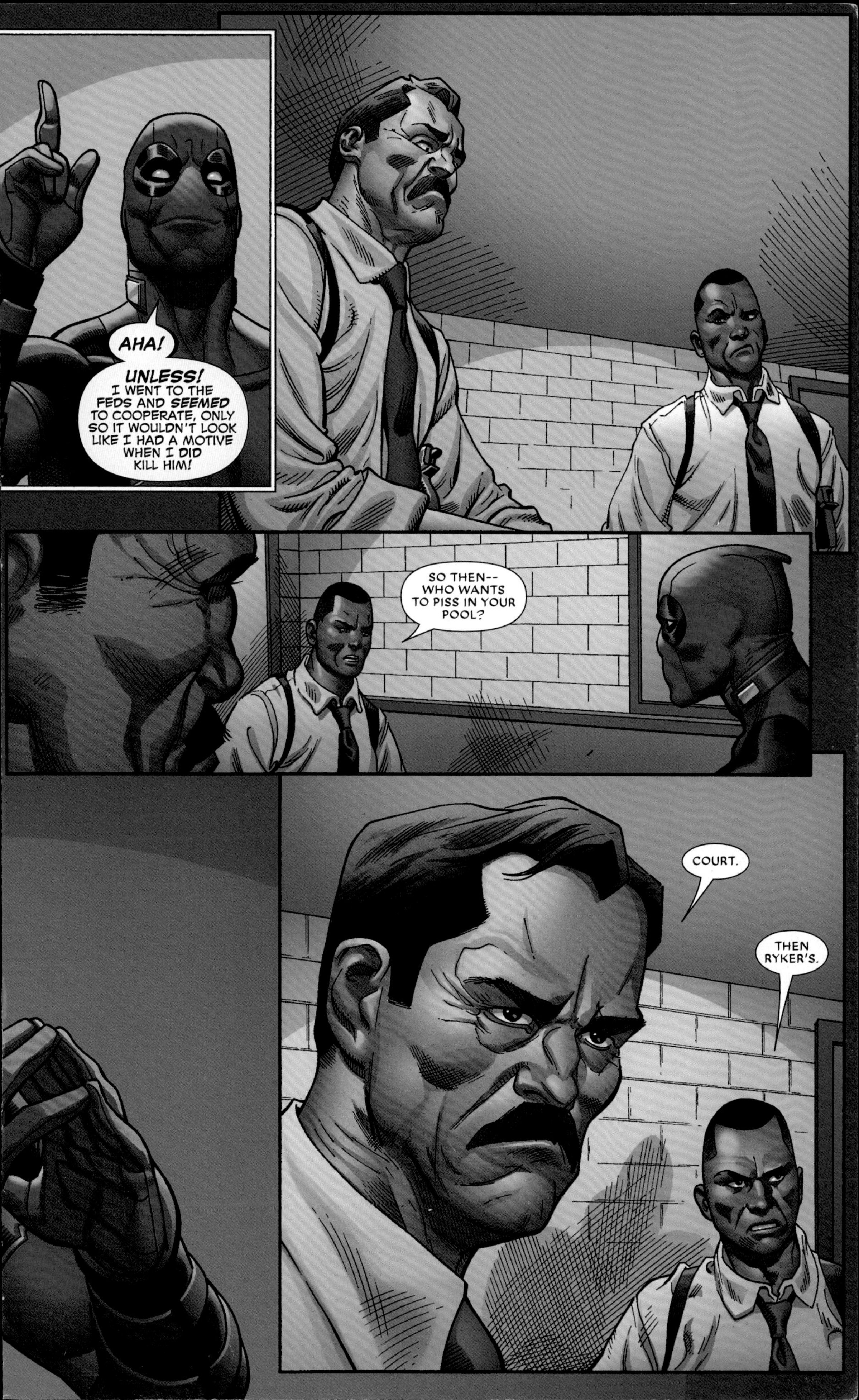
AHA!
UNLESS! I WENT TO THE FEDS AND SEEMED TO COOPERATE, ONLY SO IT WOULDN'T LOOK LIKE I HAD A MOTIVE WHEN I DID KILL HIM!
SO THEN-- WHO WANTS TO PISS IN YOUR POOL?
COURT.
THEN RYKER'S.

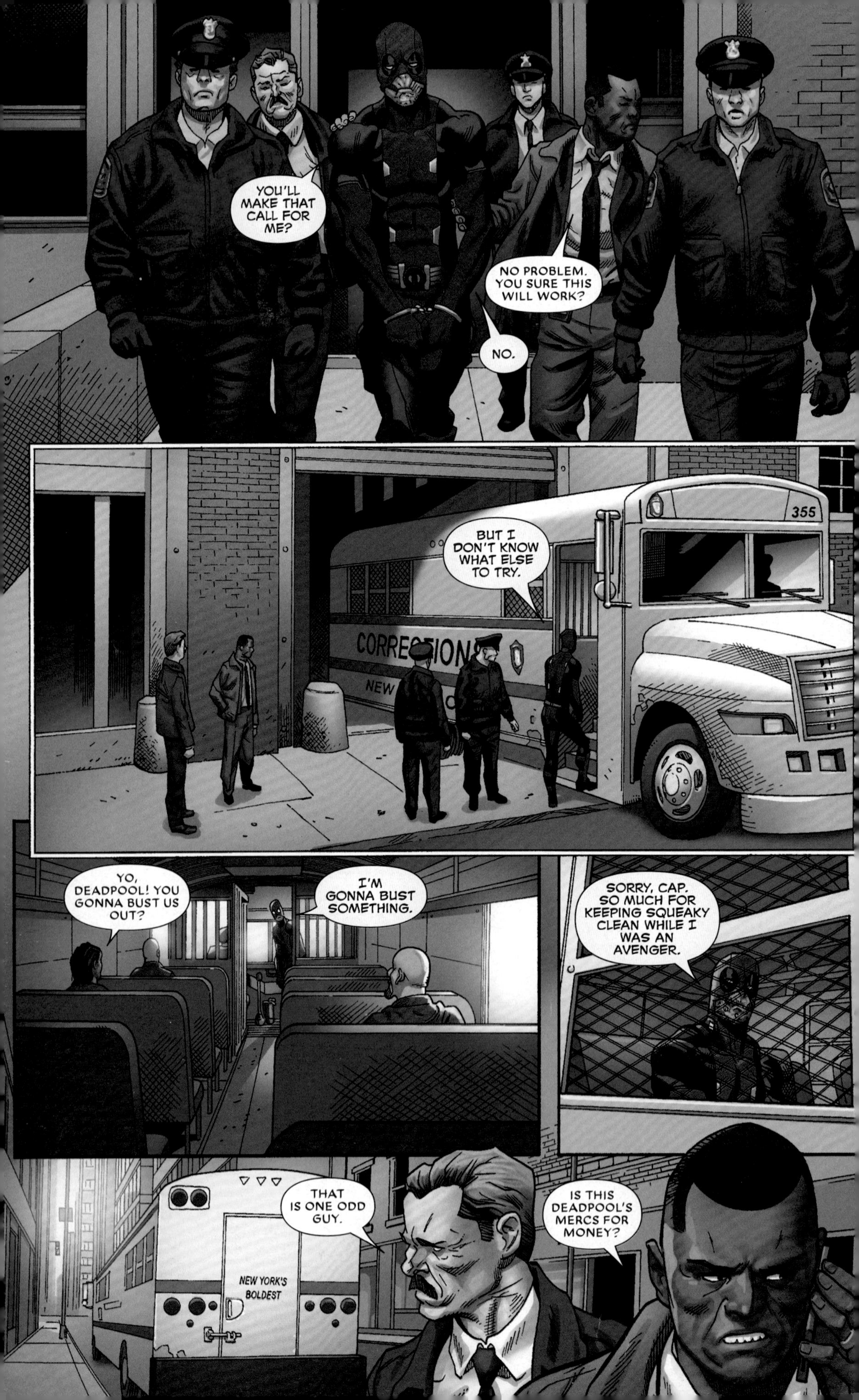
YOU'LL MAKE THAT CALL FOR ME?
NO PROBLEM. YOU SURE THIS WILL WORK?
NO.
BUT I DON'T KNOW WHAT ELSE TO TRY.
355
CORRECTIONS
NEW
YO, DEADPOOL! YOU GONNA BUST US OUT?
I'M GONNA BUST SOMETHING.
SORRY, CAP. SO MUCH FOR KEEPING SQUEAKY CLEAN WHILE I WAS AN AVENGER.
NEW YORK'S BOLDEST
THAT IS ONE ODD GUY.
IS THIS DEADPOOL'S MERCS FOR MONEY?

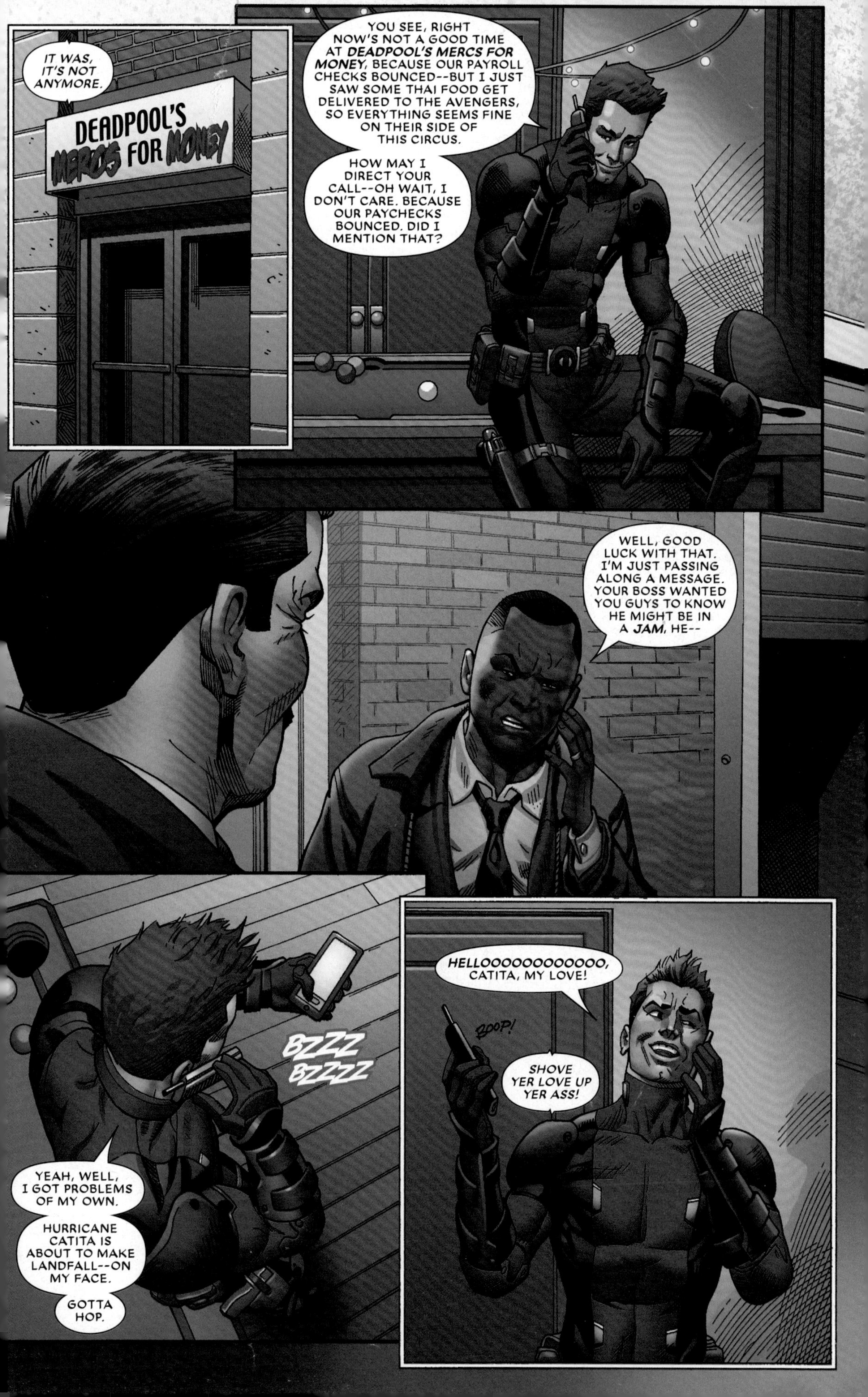

IT WAS, IT'S NOT ANYMORE.
DEADPOOL'S MERCS FOR MONEY
YOU SEE, RIGHT NOW'S NOT A GOOD TIME AT DEADPOOL'S MERCS FOR MONEY, BECAUSE OUR PAYROLL CHECKS BOUNCED--BUT I JUST SAW SOME THAI FOOD GET DELIVERED TO THE AVENGERS, SO EVERYTHING SEEMS FINE ON THEIR SIDE OF THIS CIRCUS.
HOW MAY I DIRECT YOUR CALL--OH WAIT, I DON'T CARE. BECAUSE OUR PAYCHECKS BOUNCED. DID I MENTION THAT?
WELL, GOOD LUCK WITH THAT. I'M JUST PASSING ALONG A MESSAGE. YOUR BOSS WANTED YOU GUYS TO KNOW HE MIGHT BE IN A JAM, HE--
BZZZ BZZZZ
YEAH, WELL, I GOT PROBLEMS OF MY OWN.
HURRICANE CATITA IS ABOUT TO MAKE LANDFALL--ON MY FACE.
GOTTA HOP.
HELLOOOOOOOOOOOO, CATITA, MY LOVE!
BOOP!
SHOVE YER LOVE UP YER ASS!

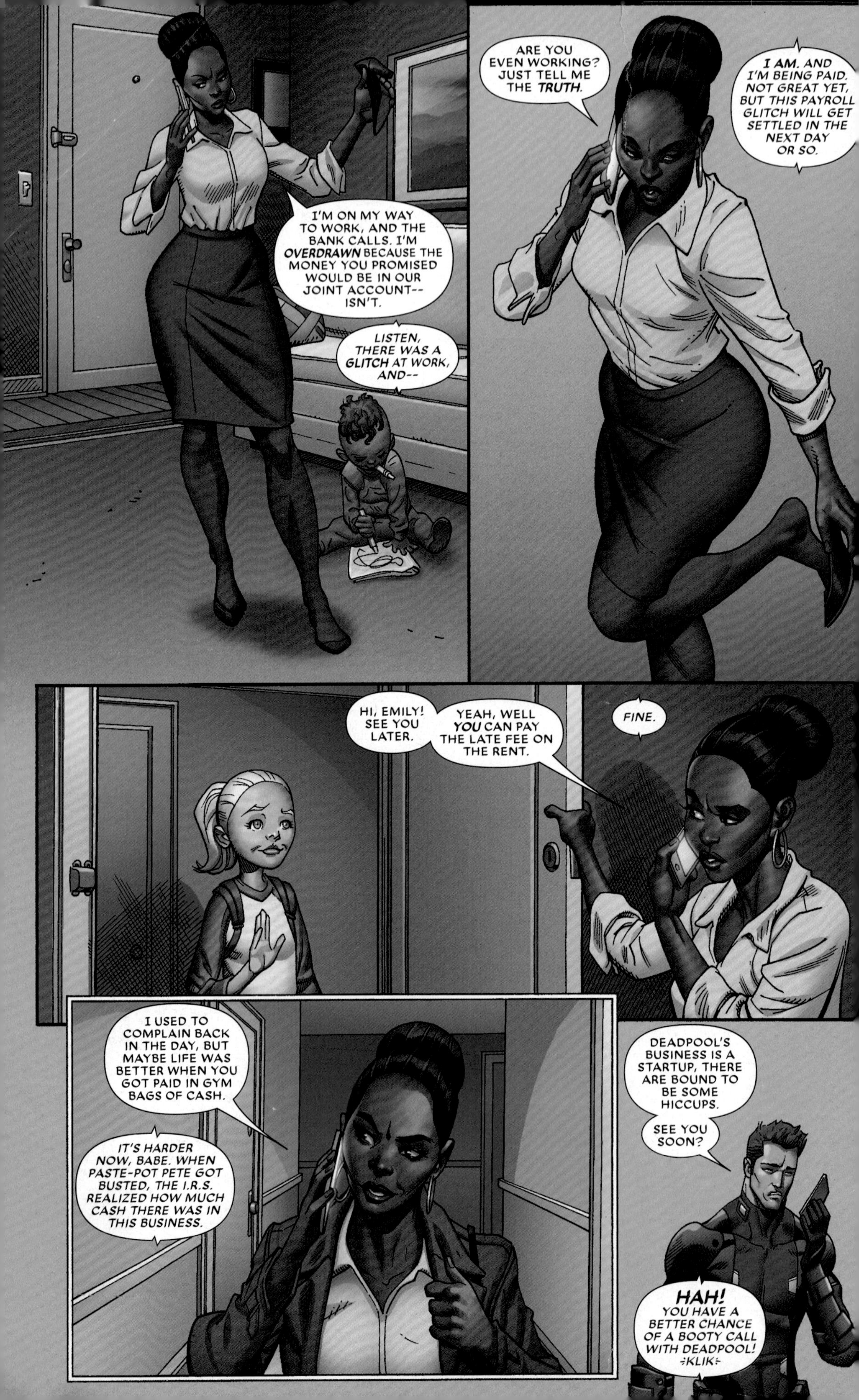
I'M ON MY WAY TO WORK, AND THE BANK CALLS. I'M OVERDRAWN BECAUSE THE MONEY YOU PROMISED WOULD BE IN OUR JOINT ACCOUNT-- ISN'T.
LISTEN, THERE WAS A GLITCH AT WORK, AND--
ARE YOU EVEN WORKING? JUST TELL ME THE TRUTH.
I AM. AND I'M BEING PAID. NOT GREAT YET, BUT THIS PAYROLL GLITCH WILL GET SETTLED IN THE NEXT DAY OR SO.
HI, EMILY! SEE YOU LATER.
YEAH, WELL YOU CAN PAY THE LATE FEE ON THE RENT.
FINE.
I USED TO COMPLAIN BACK IN THE DAY, BUT MAYBE LIFE WAS BETTER WHEN YOU GOT PAID IN GYM BAGS OF CASH.
IT'S HARDER NOW, BABE. WHEN PASTE-POT PETE GOT BUSTED, THE I.R.S. REALIZED HOW MUCH CASH THERE WAS IN THIS BUSINESS.
DEADPOOL'S BUSINESS IS A STARTUP, THERE ARE BOUND TO BE SOME HICCUPS.
SEE YOU SOON?
HAH! YOU HAVE A BETTER CHANCE OF A BOOTY CALL WITH DEADPOOL!
KLIK

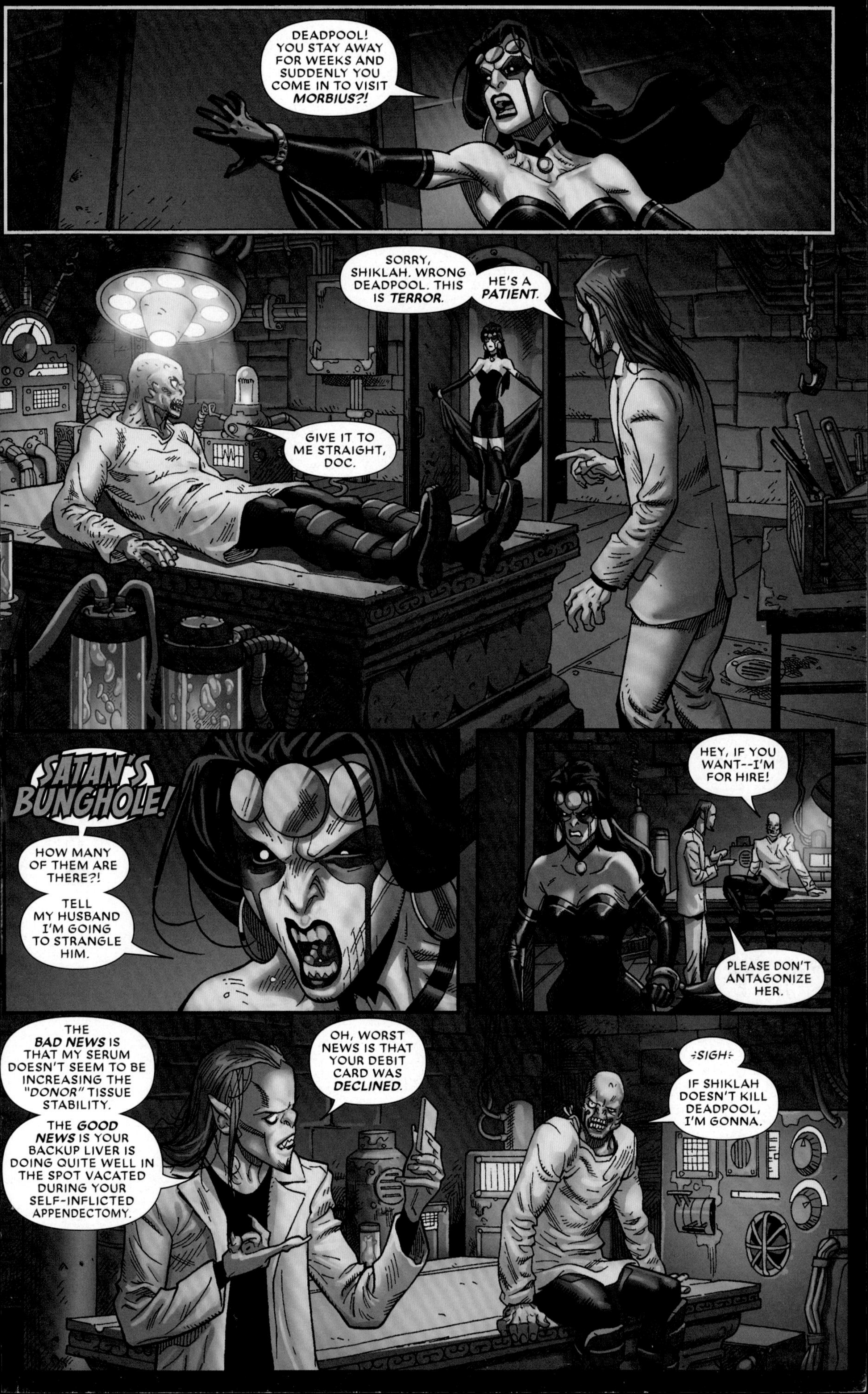
DEADPOOL! YOU STAY AWAY FOR WEEKS AND SUDDENLY YOU COME IN TO VISIT *MORBIUS?!*
SORRY, SHIKLAH. WRONG DEADPOOL. THIS IS *TERROR*.
HE'S A *PATIENT*.
GIVE IT TO ME STRAIGHT, DOC.
SATAN'S BUNGHOLE!
HOW MANY OF THEM ARE THERE?!
TELL MY HUSBAND I'M GOING TO STRANGLE HIM.
HEY, IF YOU WANT--I'M FOR HIRE!
PLEASE DON'T ANTAGONIZE HER.
THE *BAD NEWS* IS THAT MY SERUM DOESN'T SEEM TO BE INCREASING THE *"DONOR"* TISSUE STABILITY.
THE *GOOD NEWS* IS YOUR BACKUP LIVER IS DOING QUITE WELL IN THE SPOT VACATED DURING YOUR SELF-INFLICTED APPENDECTOMY.
OH, WORST NEWS IS THAT YOUR DEBIT CARD WAS *DECLINED*.
SIGH
IF SHIKLAH DOESN'T KILL DEADPOOL, I'M GONNA.

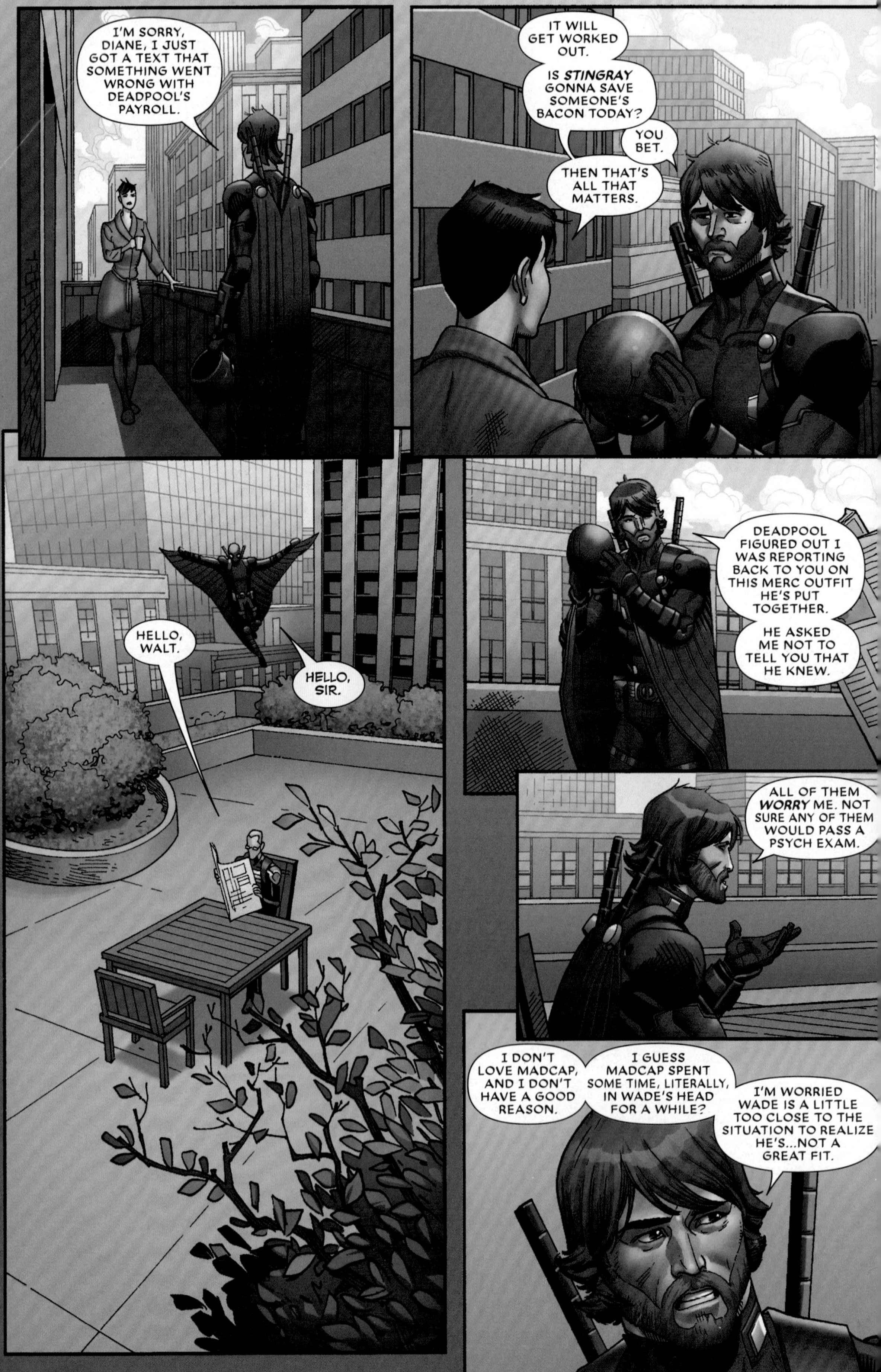
I'M SORRY, DIANE, I JUST GOT A TEXT THAT SOMETHING WENT WRONG WITH DEADPOOL'S PAYROLL.
IT WILL GET WORKED OUT.
IS STINGRAY GONNA SAVE SOMEONE'S BACON TODAY?
YOU BET.
THEN THAT'S ALL THAT MATTERS.
HELLO, WALT.
HELLO, SIR.
DEADPOOL FIGURED OUT I WAS REPORTING BACK TO YOU ON THIS MERC OUTFIT HE'S PUT TOGETHER.
HE ASKED ME NOT TO TELL YOU THAT HE KNEW.
ALL OF THEM WORRY ME. NOT SURE ANY OF THEM WOULD PASS A PSYCH EXAM.
I DON'T LOVE MADCAP, AND I DON'T HAVE A GOOD REASON.
I GUESS MADCAP SPENT SOME TIME, LITERALLY, IN WADE'S HEAD FOR A WHILE?
I'M WORRIED WADE IS A LITTLE TOO CLOSE TO THE SITUATION TO REALIZE HE'S...NOT A GREAT FIT.

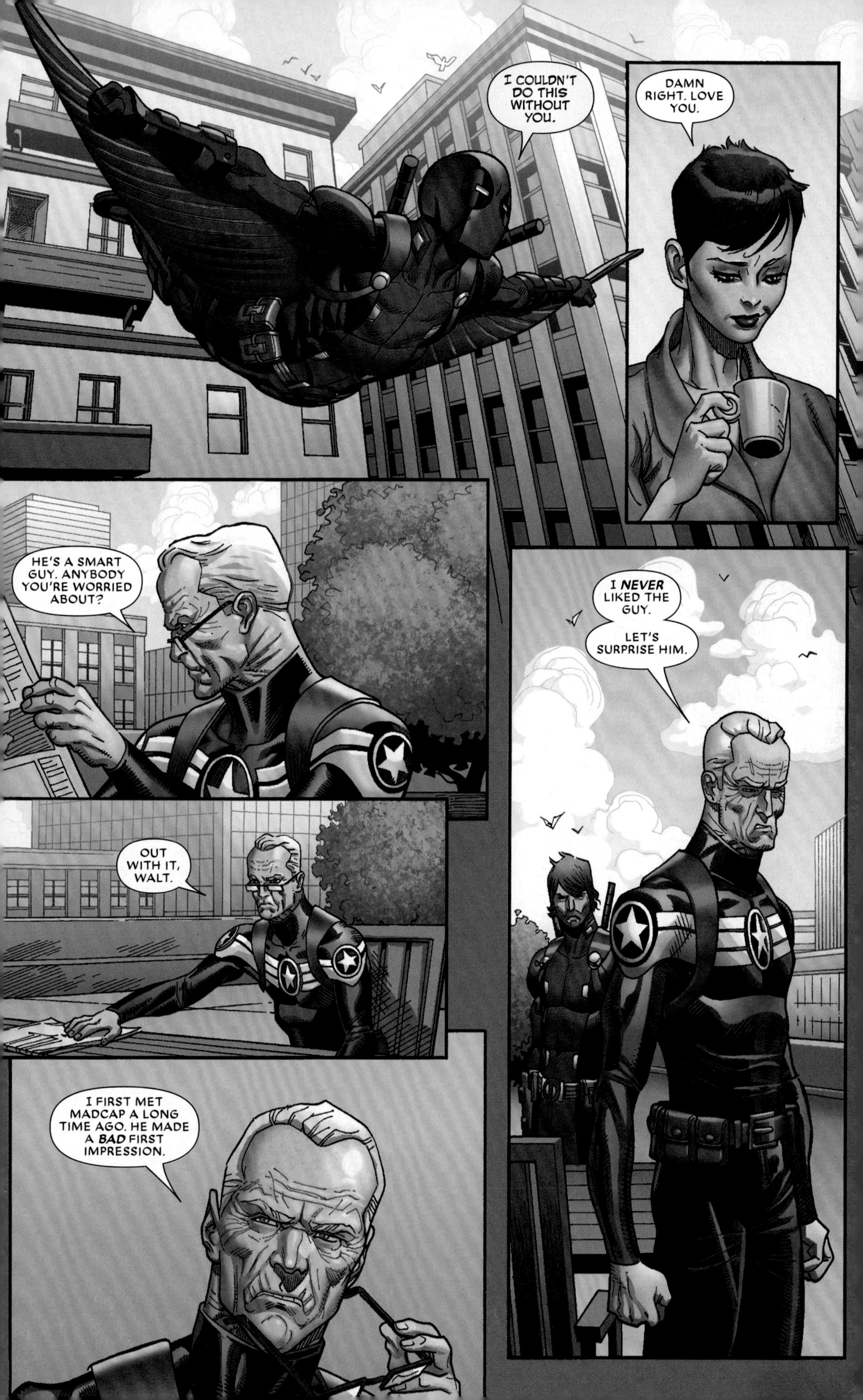
I COULDN'T DO THIS WITHOUT YOU.
DAMN RIGHT. LOVE YOU.
HE'S A SMART GUY. ANYBODY YOU'RE WORRIED ABOUT?
OUT WITH IT, WALT.
I FIRST MET MADCAP A LONG TIME AGO. HE MADE A *BAD* FIRST IMPRESSION.
I *NEVER* LIKED THE GUY.
LET'S SURPRISE HIM.

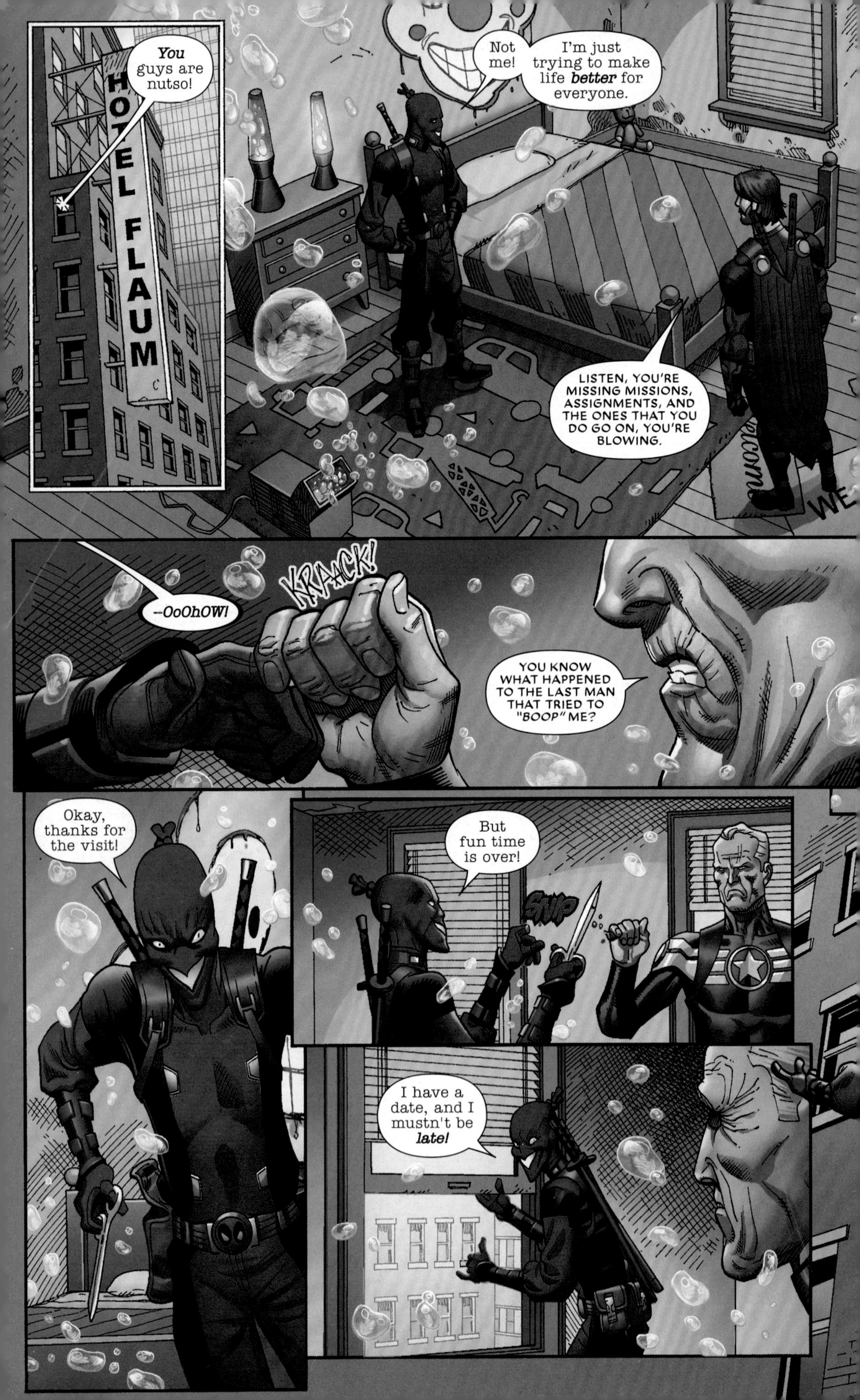

HOTEL FLAUM
You guys are nutso!
Not me!
I'm just trying to make life ***better*** for everyone.
LISTEN, YOU'RE MISSING MISSIONS, ASSIGNMENTS, AND THE ONES THAT YOU DO GO ON, YOU'RE BLOWING.
WE
--OoOhOW!
KRAACK!
YOU KNOW WHAT HAPPENED TO THE LAST MAN THAT TRIED TO "*BOOP*" ME?
Okay, thanks for the visit!
But fun time is over!
SNIP
I have a date, and I mustn't be ***late!***

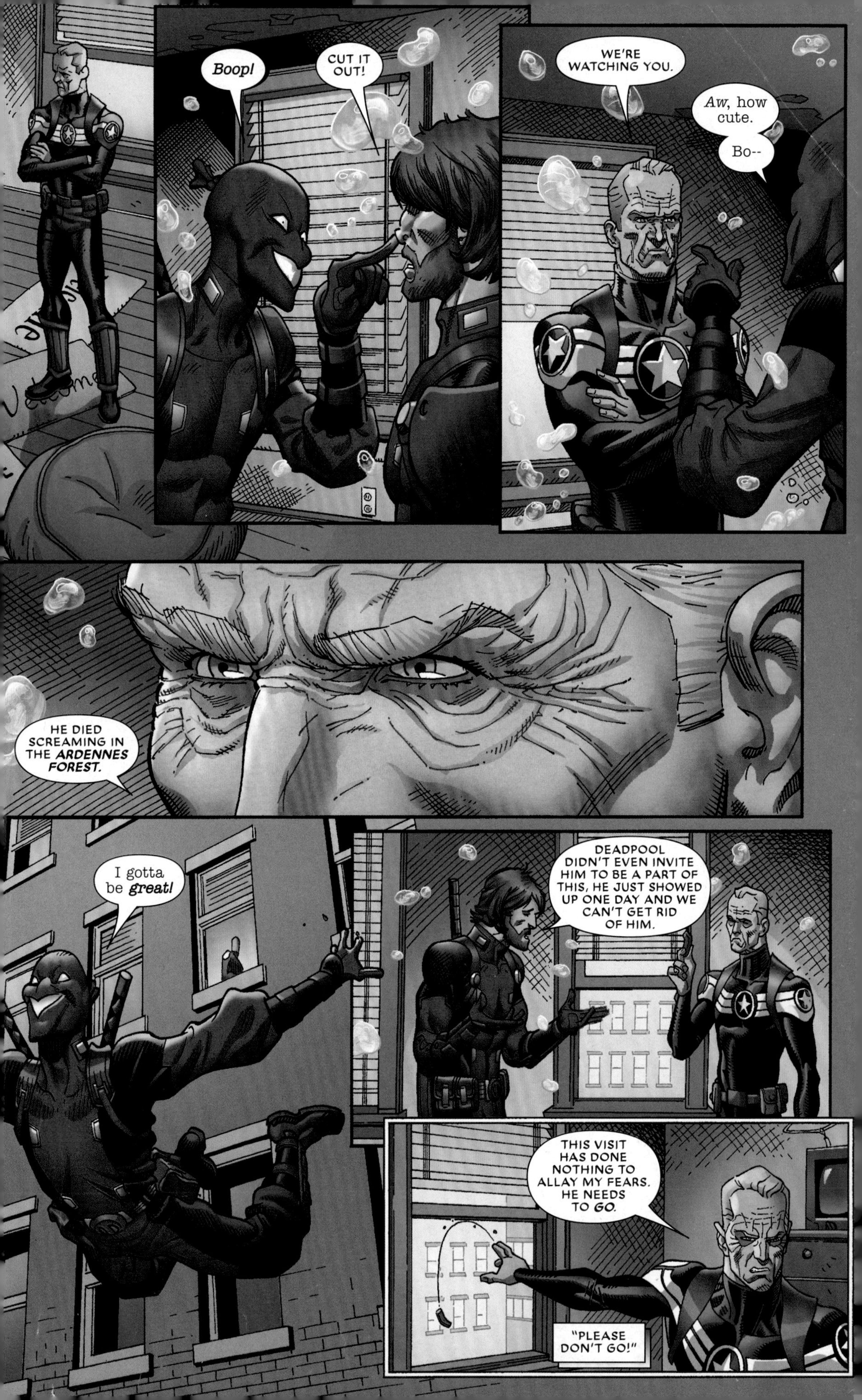
Boop!
CUT IT OUT!
WE'RE WATCHING YOU.
Aw, how cute.
Bo--
HE DIED SCREAMING IN THE ARDENNES FOREST.
I gotta be great!
DEADPOOL DIDN'T EVEN INVITE HIM TO BE A PART OF THIS, HE JUST SHOWED UP ONE DAY AND WE CAN'T GET RID OF HIM.
THIS VISIT HAS DONE NOTHING TO ALLAY MY FEARS. HE NEEDS TO GO.
"PLEASE DON'T GO!"

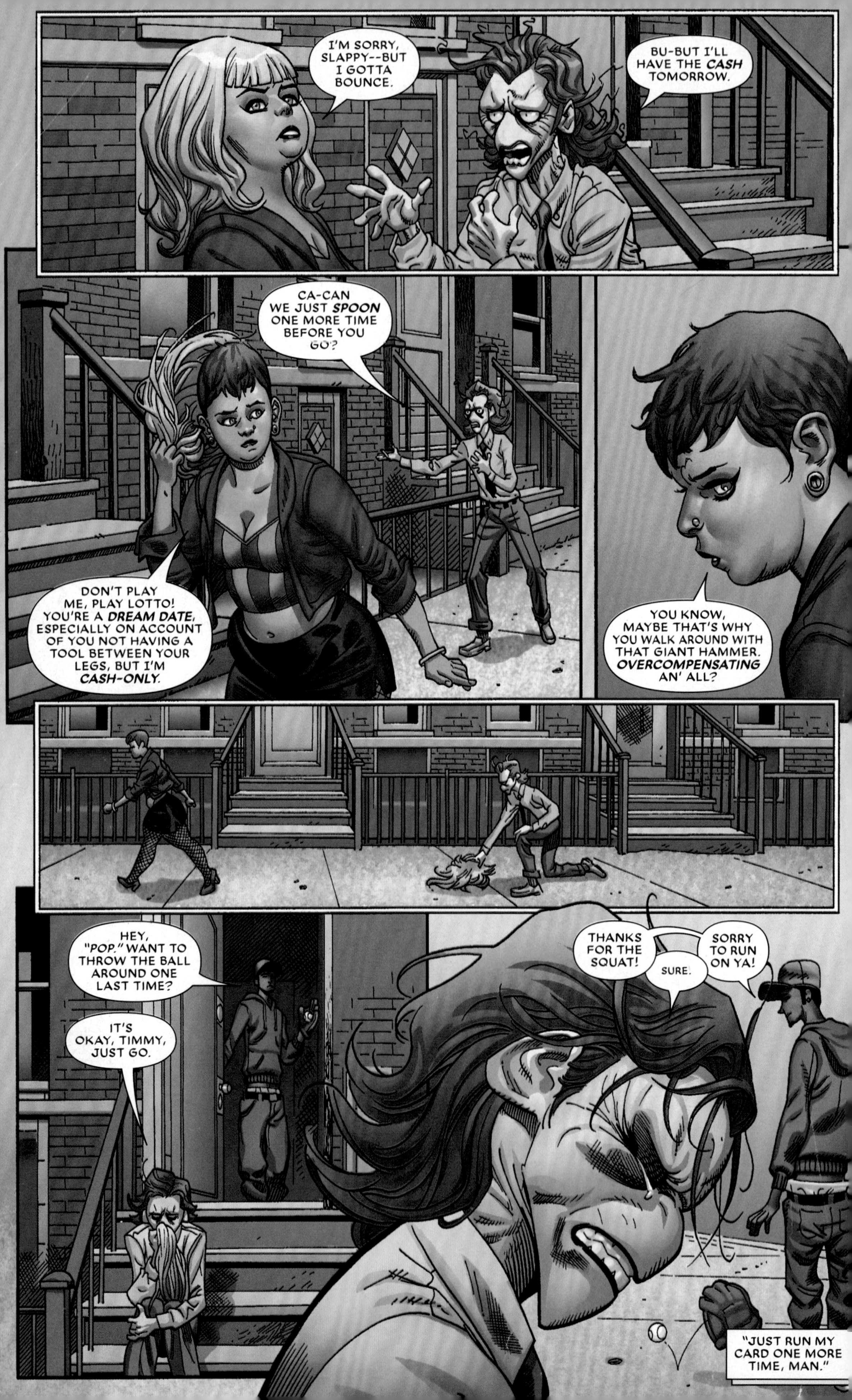
I'M SORRY, SLAPPY--BUT I GOTTA BOUNCE.
BU-BUT I'LL HAVE THE *CASH* TOMORROW.
CA-CAN WE JUST *SPOON* ONE MORE TIME BEFORE YOU GO?
DON'T PLAY ME, PLAY LOTTO! YOU'RE A *DREAM DATE*, ESPECIALLY ON ACCOUNT OF YOU NOT HAVING A TOOL BETWEEN YOUR LEGS, BUT I'M *CASH-ONLY*.
YOU KNOW, MAYBE THAT'S WHY YOU WALK AROUND WITH THAT GIANT HAMMER. *OVERCOMPENSATING* AN' ALL?
HEY, "*POP*." WANT TO THROW THE BALL AROUND ONE LAST TIME?
IT'S OKAY, TIMMY, JUST GO.
THANKS FOR THE SQUAT!
SORRY TO RUN ON YA!
SURE.
"JUST RUN MY CARD ONE MORE TIME, MAN."

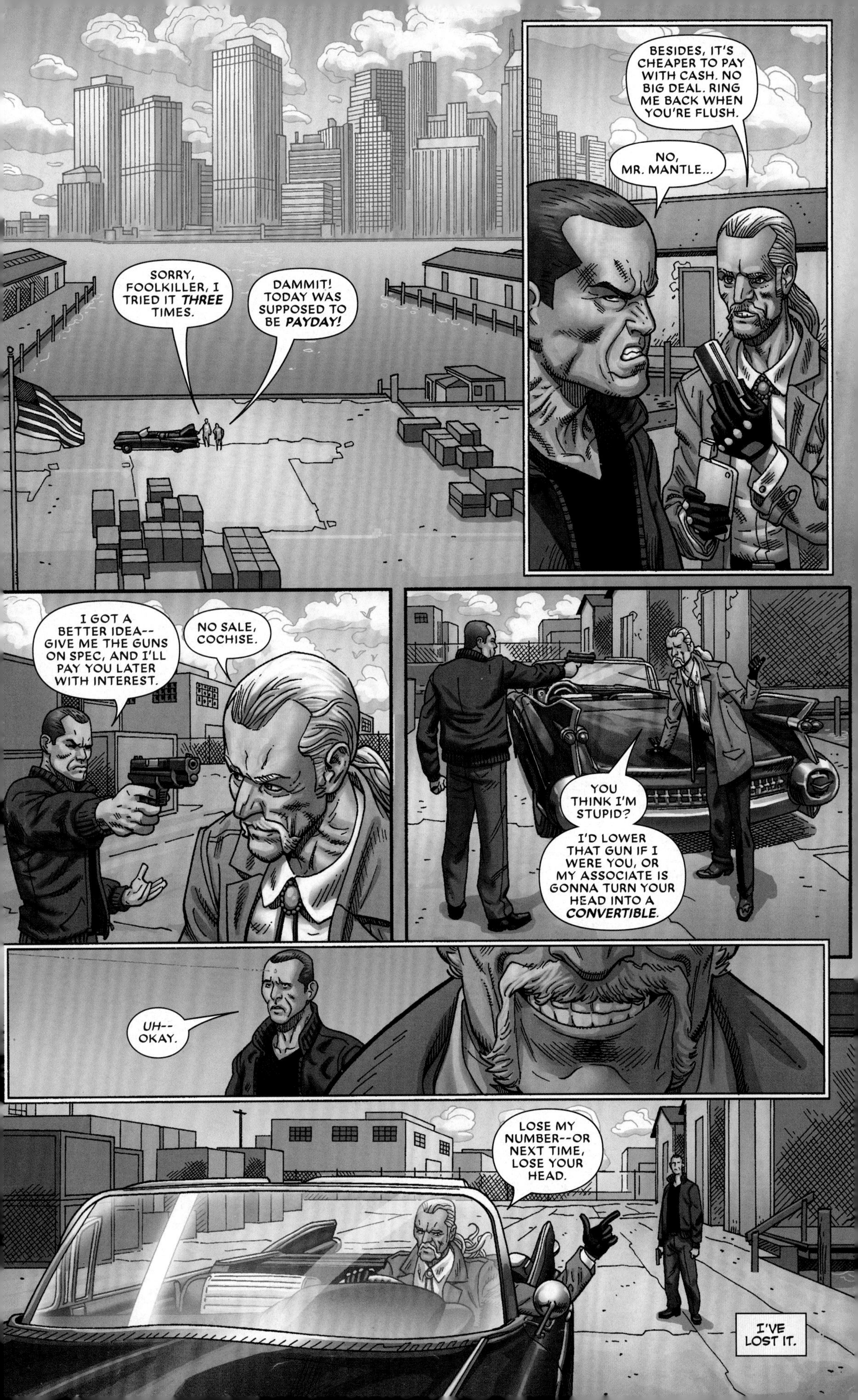

SORRY, FOOLKILLER, I TRIED IT *THREE* TIMES.
DAMMIT! TODAY WAS SUPPOSED TO BE *PAYDAY!*
BESIDES, IT'S CHEAPER TO PAY WITH CASH. NO BIG DEAL. RING ME BACK WHEN YOU'RE FLUSH.
NO, MR. MANTLE...
I GOT A BETTER IDEA-- GIVE ME THE GUNS ON SPEC, AND I'LL PAY YOU LATER WITH INTEREST.
NO SALE, COCHISE.
YOU THINK I'M STUPID?
I'D LOWER THAT GUN IF I WERE YOU, OR MY ASSOCIATE IS GONNA TURN YOUR HEAD INTO A *CONVERTIBLE*.
UH-- OKAY.
LOSE MY NUMBER--OR NEXT TIME, LOSE YOUR HEAD.
I'VE LOST IT.

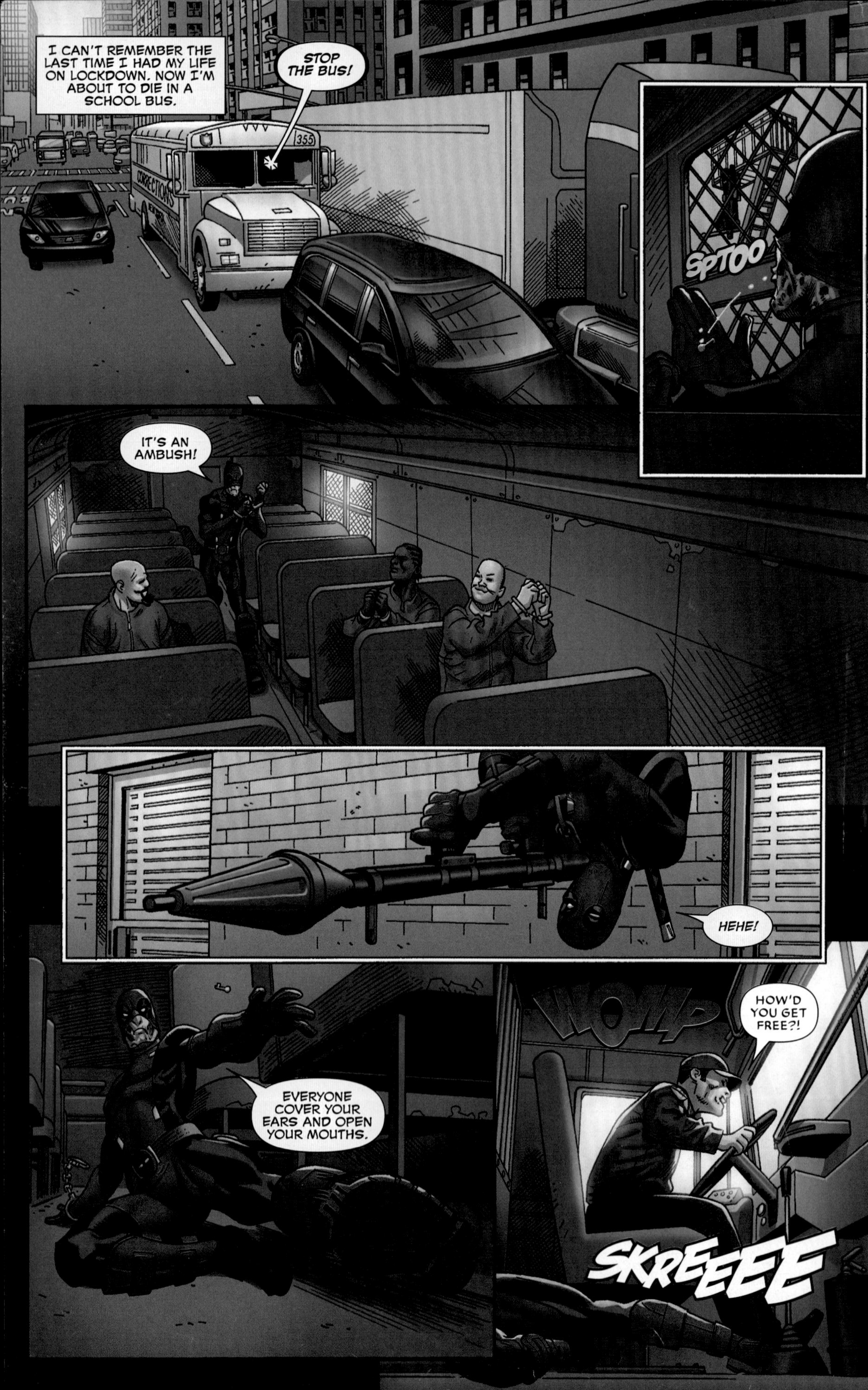
I CAN'T REMEMBER THE LAST TIME I HAD MY LIFE ON LOCKDOWN. NOW I'M ABOUT TO DIE IN A SCHOOL BUS.
STOP THE BUS!
355
CORRECTIONS
SPTOO
IT'S AN AMBUSH!
HEHE!
EVERYONE COVER YOUR EARS AND OPEN YOUR MOUTHS.
WOMP
HOW'D YOU GET FREE?!
SKREEEEE

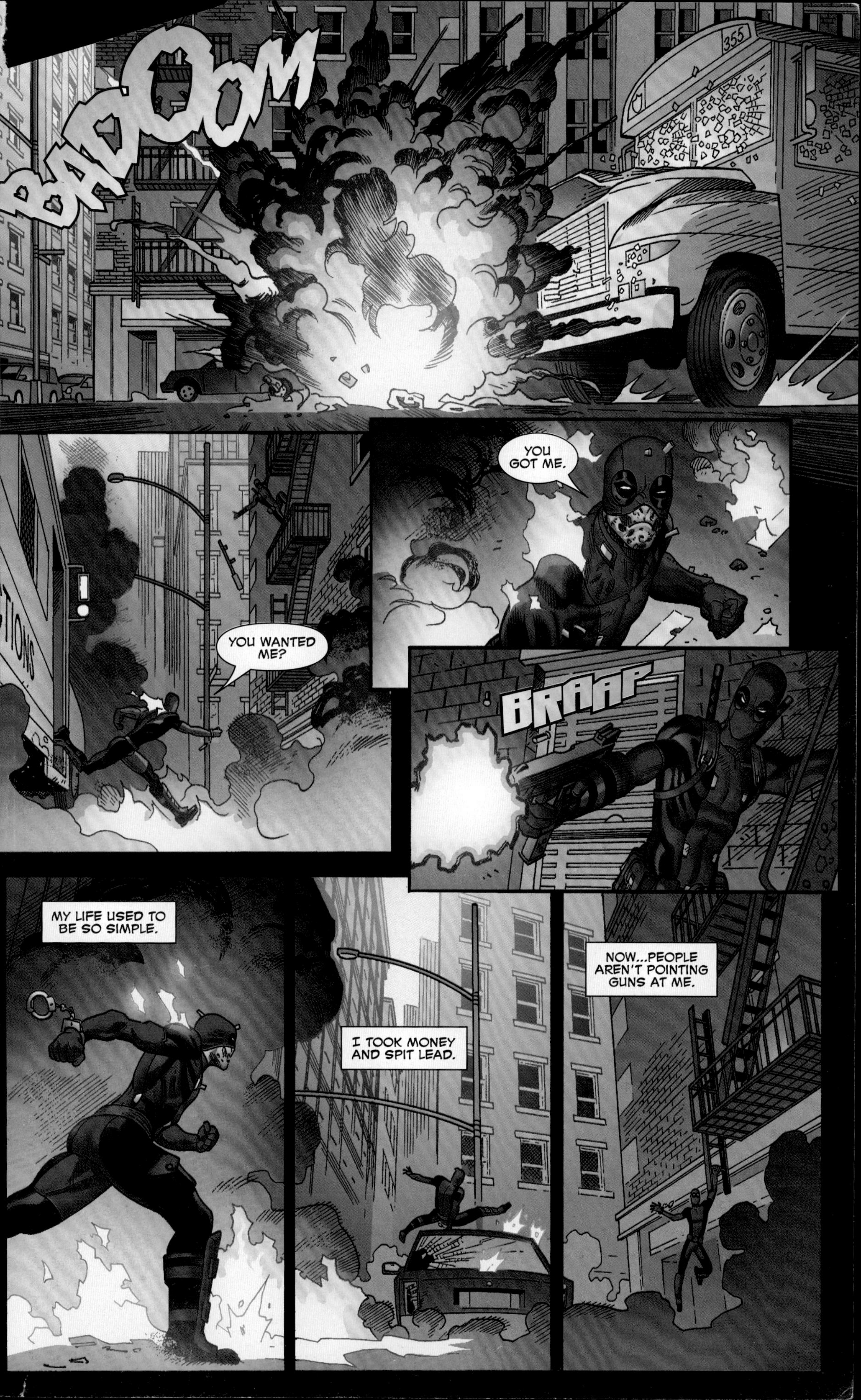
BADOOM
355
YOU WANTED ME?
YOU GOT ME.
BRAAP
MY LIFE USED TO BE SO SIMPLE.
I TOOK MONEY AND SPIT LEAD.
NOW...PEOPLE AREN'T POINTING GUNS AT ME.

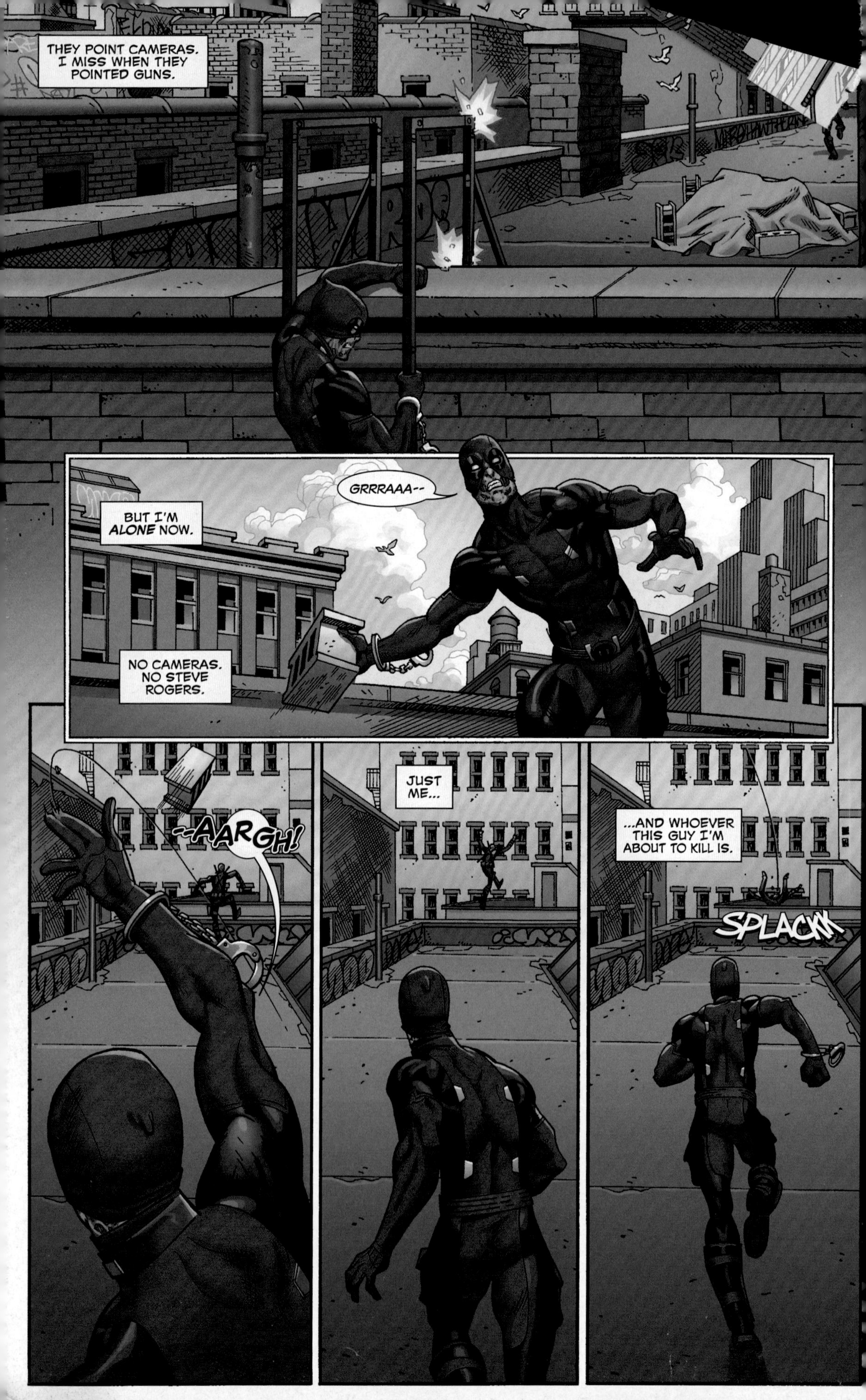
THEY POINT CAMERAS. I MISS WHEN THEY POINTED GUNS.
BUT I'M *ALONE* NOW.
GRRRAAA--
NO CAMERAS. NO STEVE ROGERS.
--AARGH!
JUST ME...
...AND WHOEVER THIS GUY I'M ABOUT TO KILL IS.
SPLACK!!

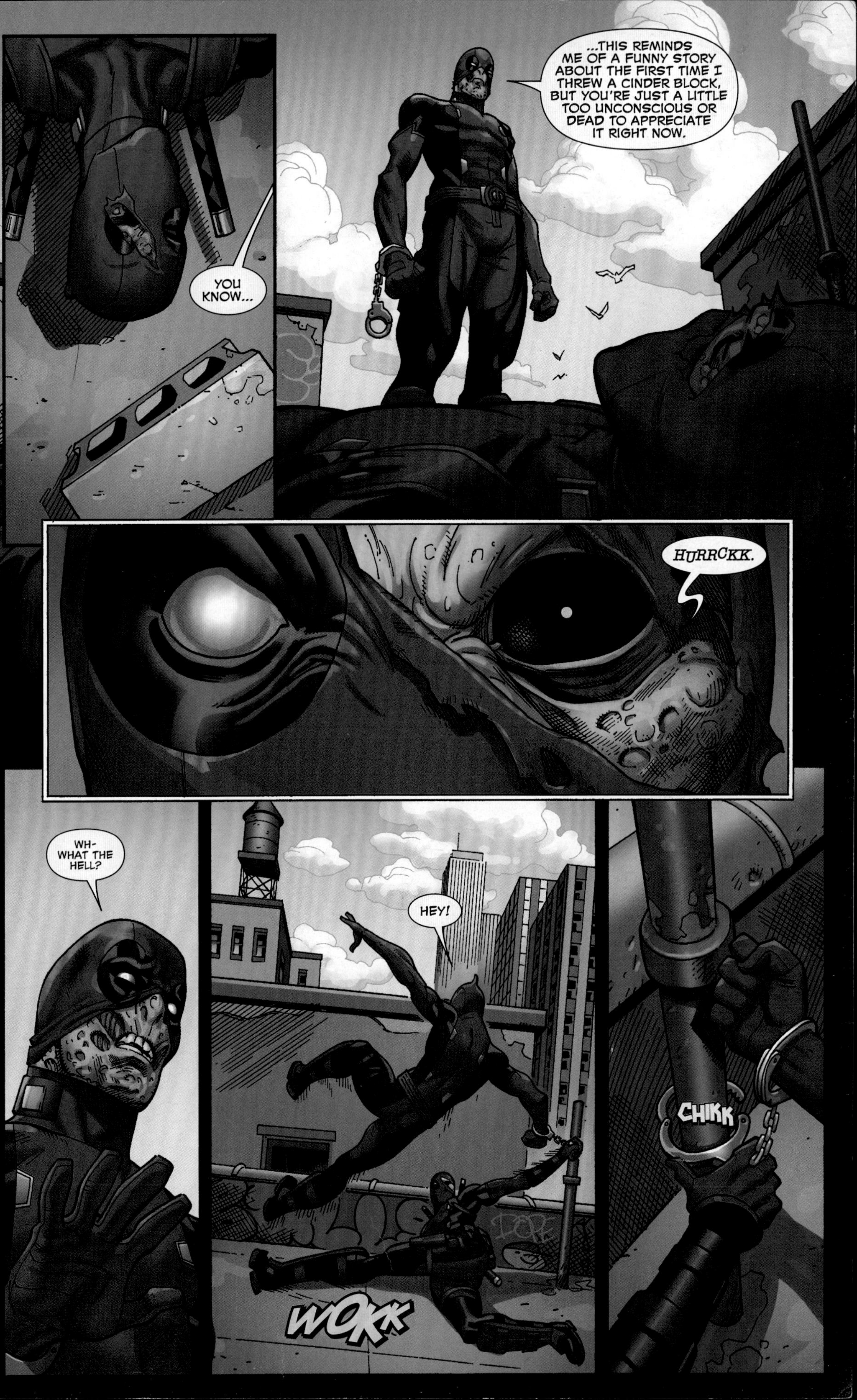
YOU KNOW...
...THIS REMINDS ME OF A FUNNY STORY ABOUT THE FIRST TIME I THREW A CINDER BLOCK, BUT YOU'RE JUST A LITTLE TOO UNCONSCIOUS OR DEAD TO APPRECIATE IT RIGHT NOW.
HURRCKK.
WH- WHAT THE HELL?
HEY!
WOKK
CHIKK

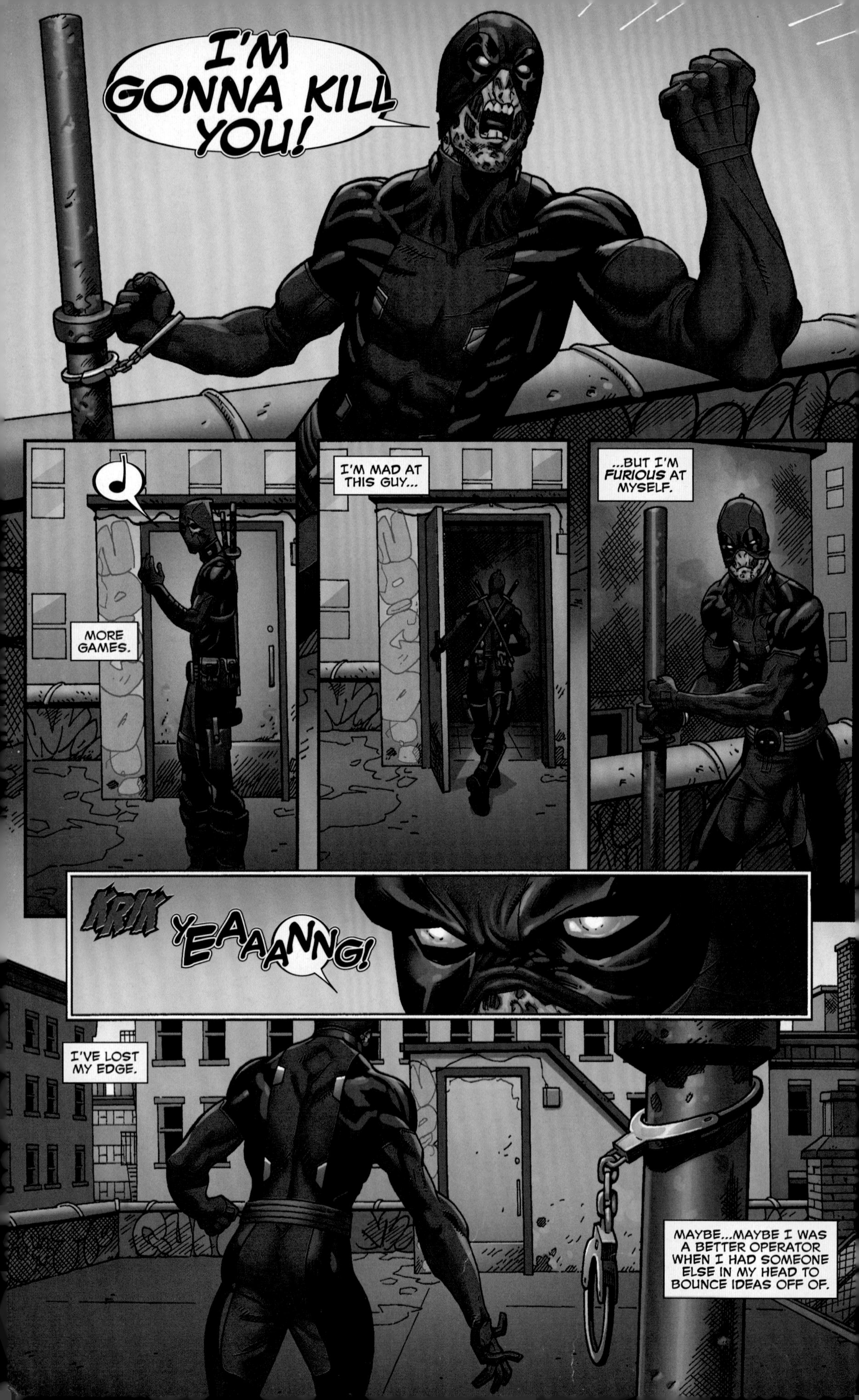

I'M GONNA KILL YOU!
MORE GAMES.
I'M MAD AT THIS GUY...
...BUT I'M *FURIOUS* AT MYSELF.
KRIK
YEAAANNG!
I'VE LOST MY EDGE.
MAYBE...MAYBE I WAS A BETTER OPERATOR WHEN I HAD SOMEONE ELSE IN MY HEAD TO BOUNCE IDEAS OFF OF.

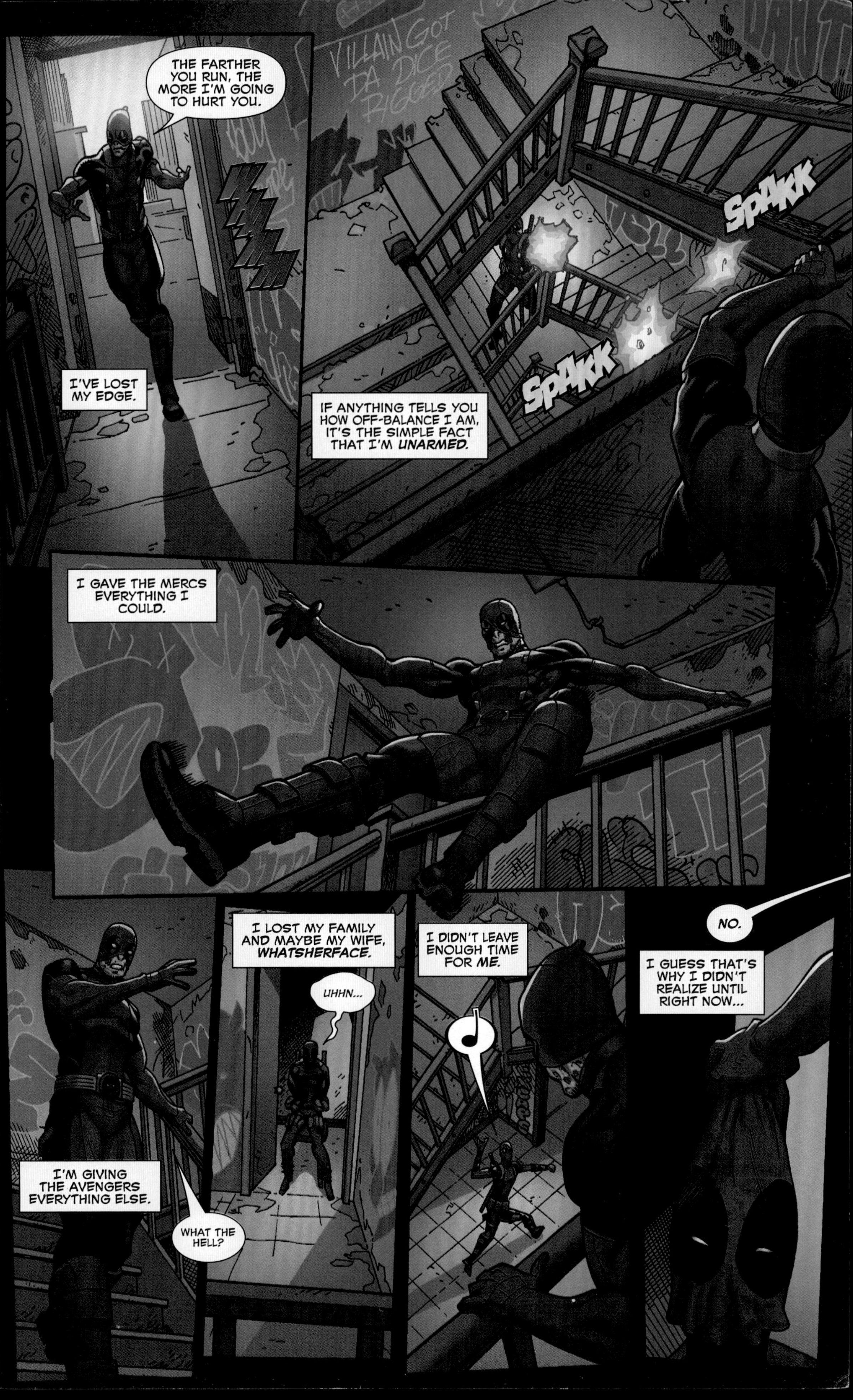

THE FARTHER YOU RUN, THE MORE I'M GOING TO HURT YOU.
VILLAIN GOT DA DICE RIGGED
I'VE LOST MY EDGE.
SPAKK
SPAKK
IF ANYTHING TELLS YOU HOW OFF-BALANCE I AM, IT'S THE SIMPLE FACT THAT I'M UNARMED.
I GAVE THE MERCS EVERYTHING I COULD.
I'M GIVING THE AVENGERS EVERYTHING ELSE.
WHAT THE HELL?
I LOST MY FAMILY AND MAYBE MY WIFE, WHATSHERFACE.
UHHN...
I DIDN'T LEAVE ENOUGH TIME FOR ME.
NO.
I GUESS THAT'S WHY I DIDN'T REALIZE UNTIL RIGHT NOW...

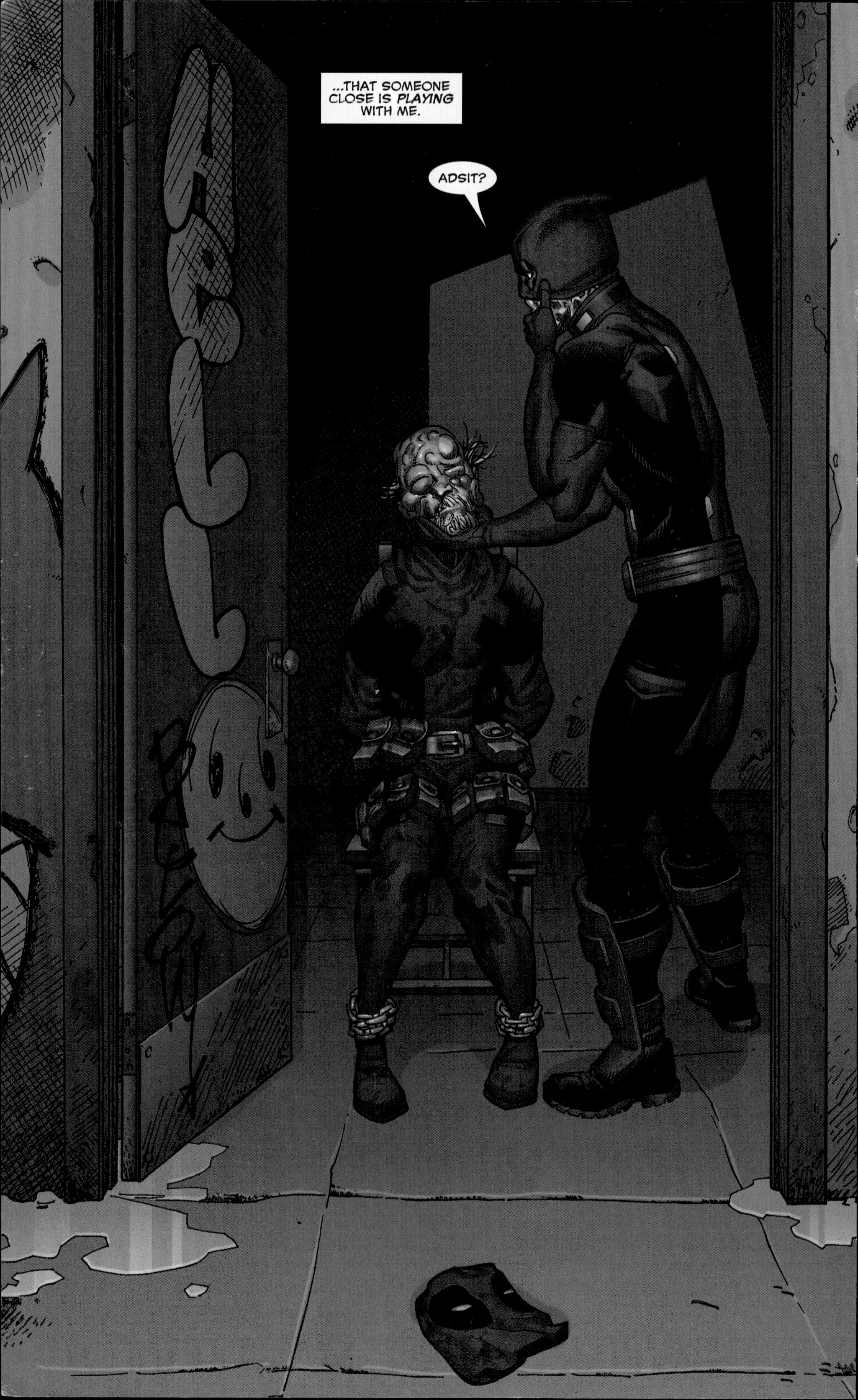
...THAT SOMEONE CLOSE IS *PLAYING* WITH ME.
ADSIT?

DEADPOOL
IS BACK!

THE WORLD'S
GREATEST
COMIC
MAGAZINE!

#2 variant by
KEVIN WADA

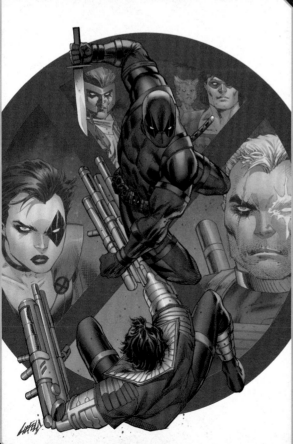

#3 '92 variant by
ROB LIEFELD &
JOHN RAUCH

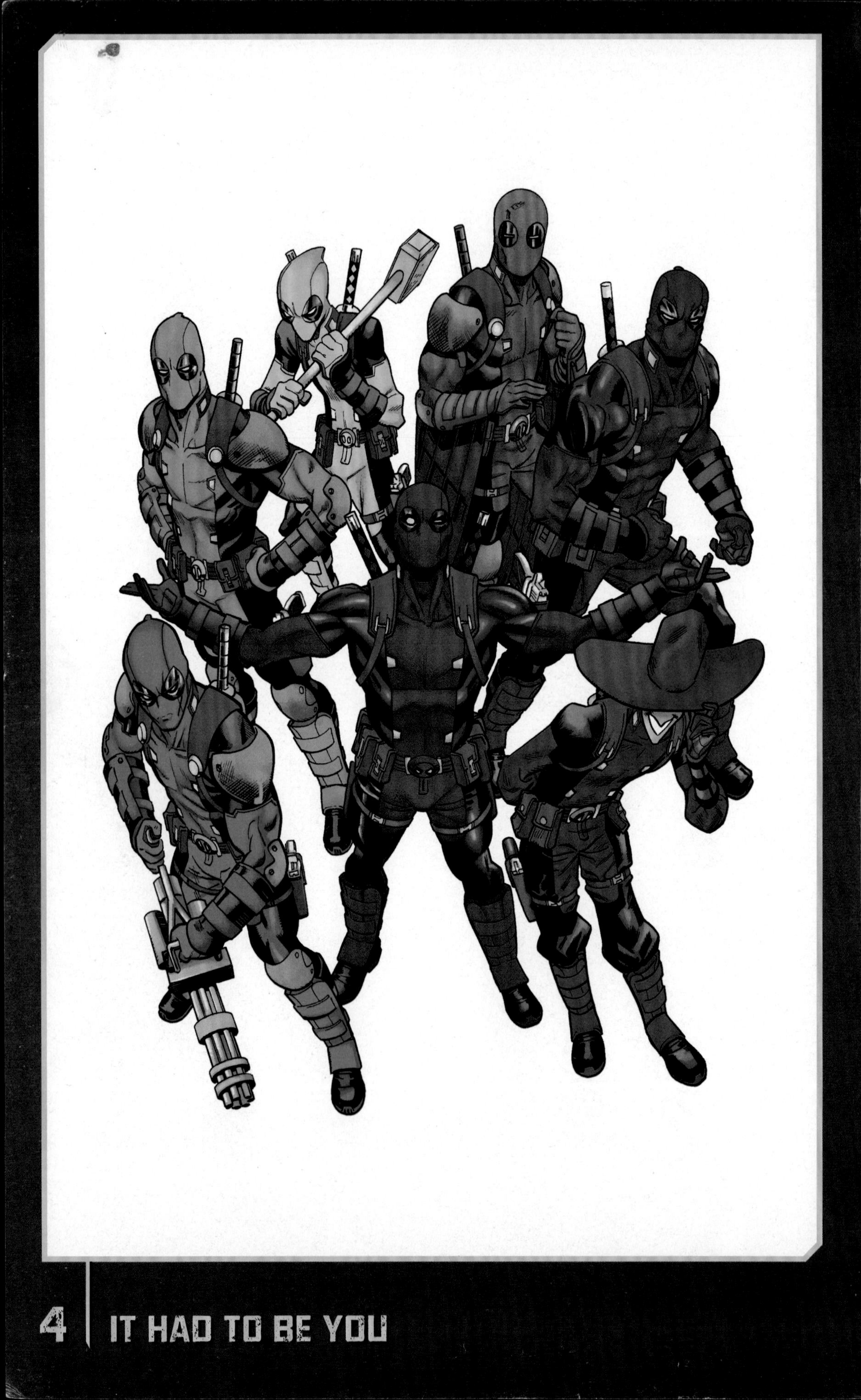

4 IT HAD TO BE YOU

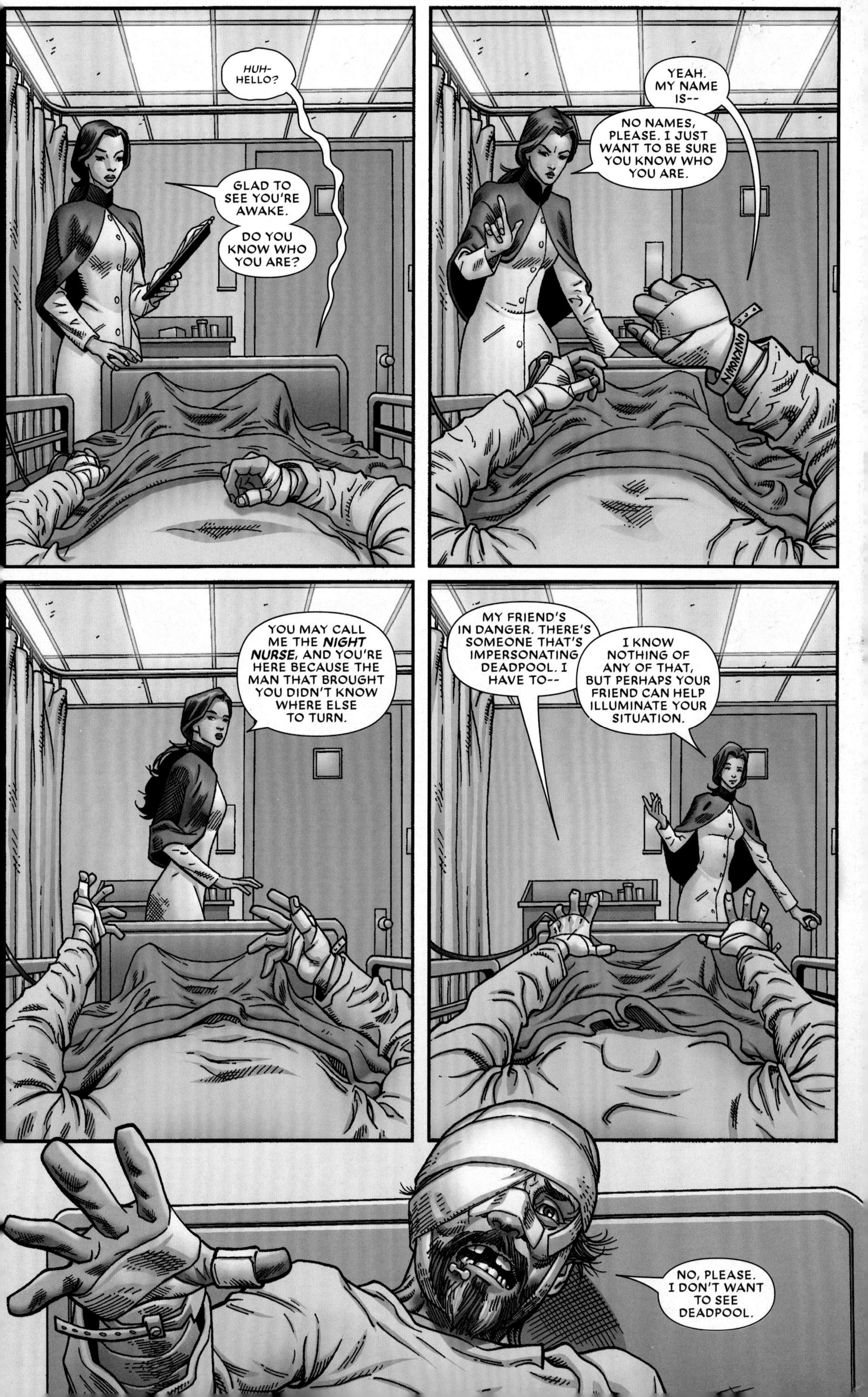
HUH-
HELLO?
GLAD TO SEE YOU'RE AWAKE.
DO YOU KNOW WHO YOU ARE?
YEAH. MY NAME IS--
NO NAMES, PLEASE. I JUST WANT TO BE SURE YOU KNOW WHO YOU ARE.
UNKNOWN
YOU MAY CALL ME THE *NIGHT NURSE,* AND YOU'RE HERE BECAUSE THE MAN THAT BROUGHT YOU DIDN'T KNOW WHERE ELSE TO TURN.
MY FRIEND'S IN DANGER. THERE'S SOMEONE THAT'S IMPERSONATING DEADPOOL. I HAVE TO--
I KNOW NOTHING OF ANY OF THAT, BUT PERHAPS YOUR FRIEND CAN HELP ILLUMINATE YOUR SITUATION.
NO, PLEASE. I DON'T WANT TO SEE DEADPOOL.

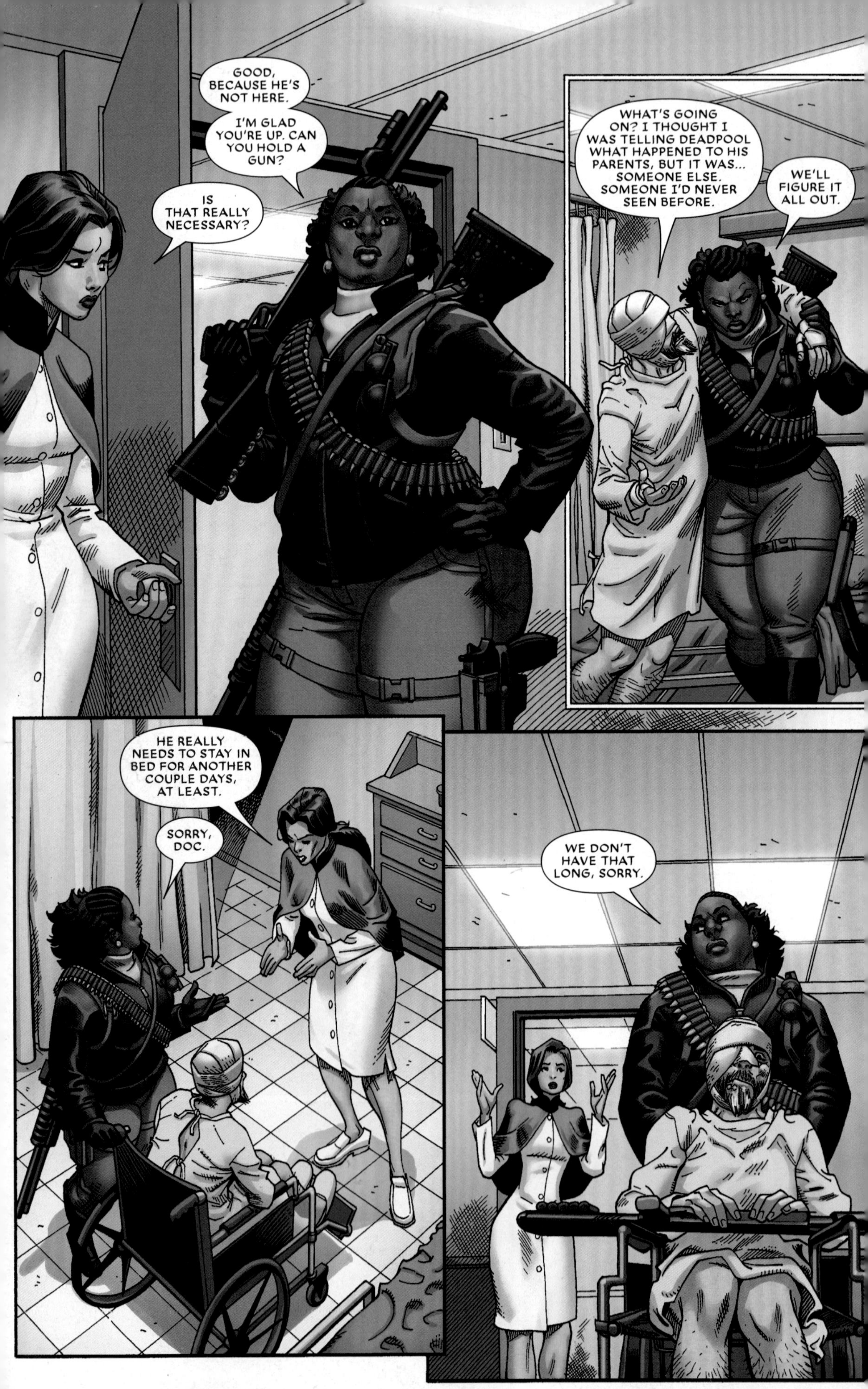
GOOD, BECAUSE HE'S NOT HERE.
I'M GLAD YOU'RE UP. CAN YOU HOLD A GUN?
IS THAT REALLY NECESSARY?
WHAT'S GOING ON? I THOUGHT I WAS TELLING DEADPOOL WHAT HAPPENED TO HIS PARENTS, BUT IT WAS... SOMEONE ELSE. SOMEONE I'D NEVER SEEN BEFORE.
WE'LL FIGURE IT ALL OUT.
HE REALLY NEEDS TO STAY IN BED FOR ANOTHER COUPLE DAYS, AT LEAST.
SORRY, DOC.
WE DON'T HAVE THAT LONG, SORRY.

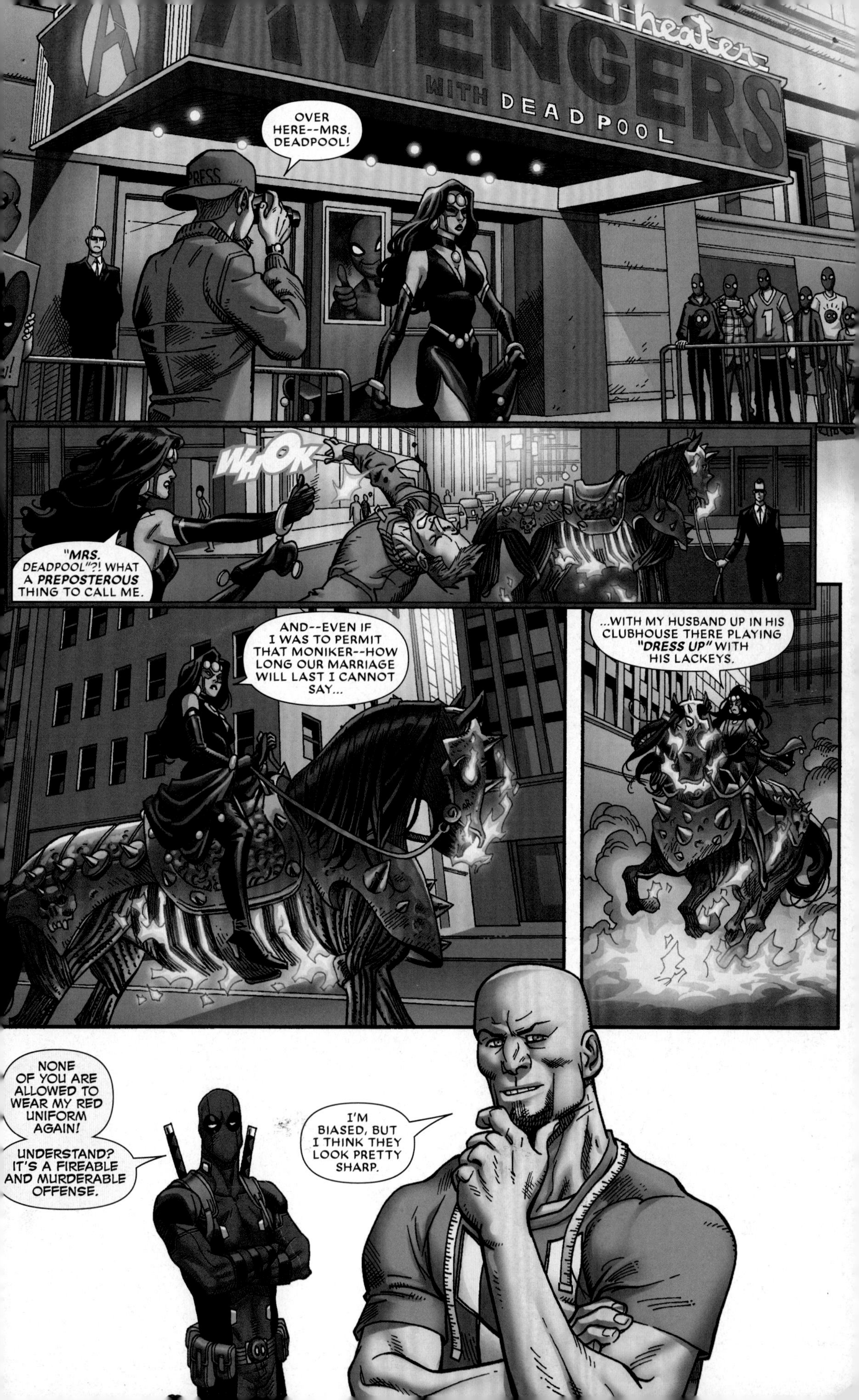
Theater
AVENGERS
WITH DEADPOOL
PRESS
OVER HERE--MRS. DEADPOOL!
WHOK
"MRS. DEADPOOL"?! WHAT A PREPOSTEROUS THING TO CALL ME.
AND--EVEN IF I WAS TO PERMIT THAT MONIKER--HOW LONG OUR MARRIAGE WILL LAST I CANNOT SAY...
...WITH MY HUSBAND UP IN HIS CLUBHOUSE THERE PLAYING "DRESS UP" WITH HIS LACKEYS.
NONE OF YOU ARE ALLOWED TO WEAR MY RED UNIFORM AGAIN!
UNDERSTAND? IT'S A FIREABLE AND MURDERABLE OFFENSE.
I'M BIASED, BUT I THINK THEY LOOK PRETTY SHARP.

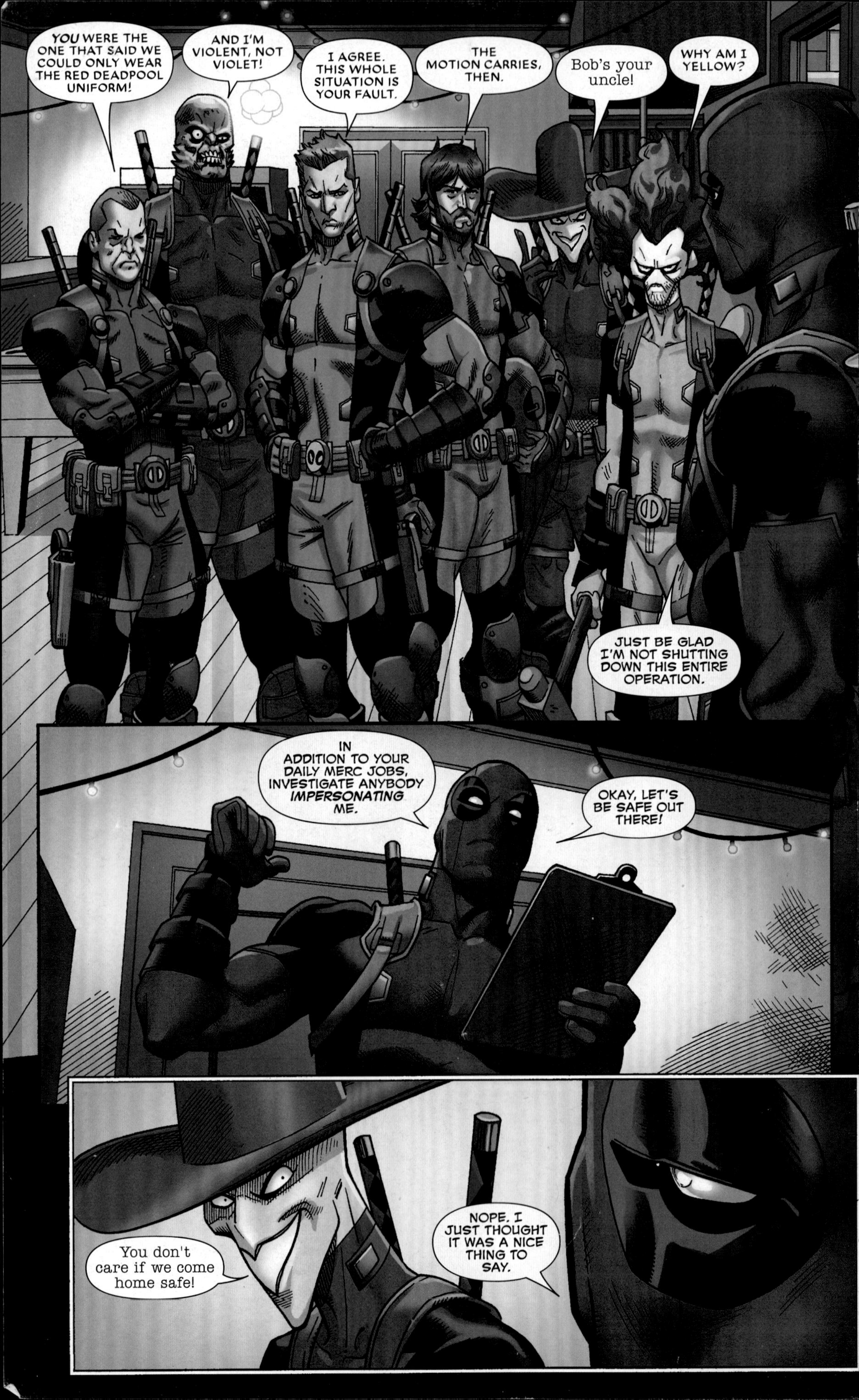
YOU WERE THE ONE THAT SAID WE COULD ONLY WEAR THE RED DEADPOOL UNIFORM!
AND I'M VIOLENT, NOT VIOLET!
I AGREE. THIS WHOLE SITUATION IS YOUR FAULT.
THE MOTION CARRIES, THEN.
Bob's your uncle!
WHY AM I YELLOW?
JUST BE GLAD I'M NOT SHUTTING DOWN THIS ENTIRE OPERATION.
IN ADDITION TO YOUR DAILY MERC JOBS, INVESTIGATE ANYBODY IMPERSONATING ME.
OKAY, LET'S BE SAFE OUT THERE!
You don't care if we come home safe!
NOPE. I JUST THOUGHT IT WAS A NICE THING TO SAY.

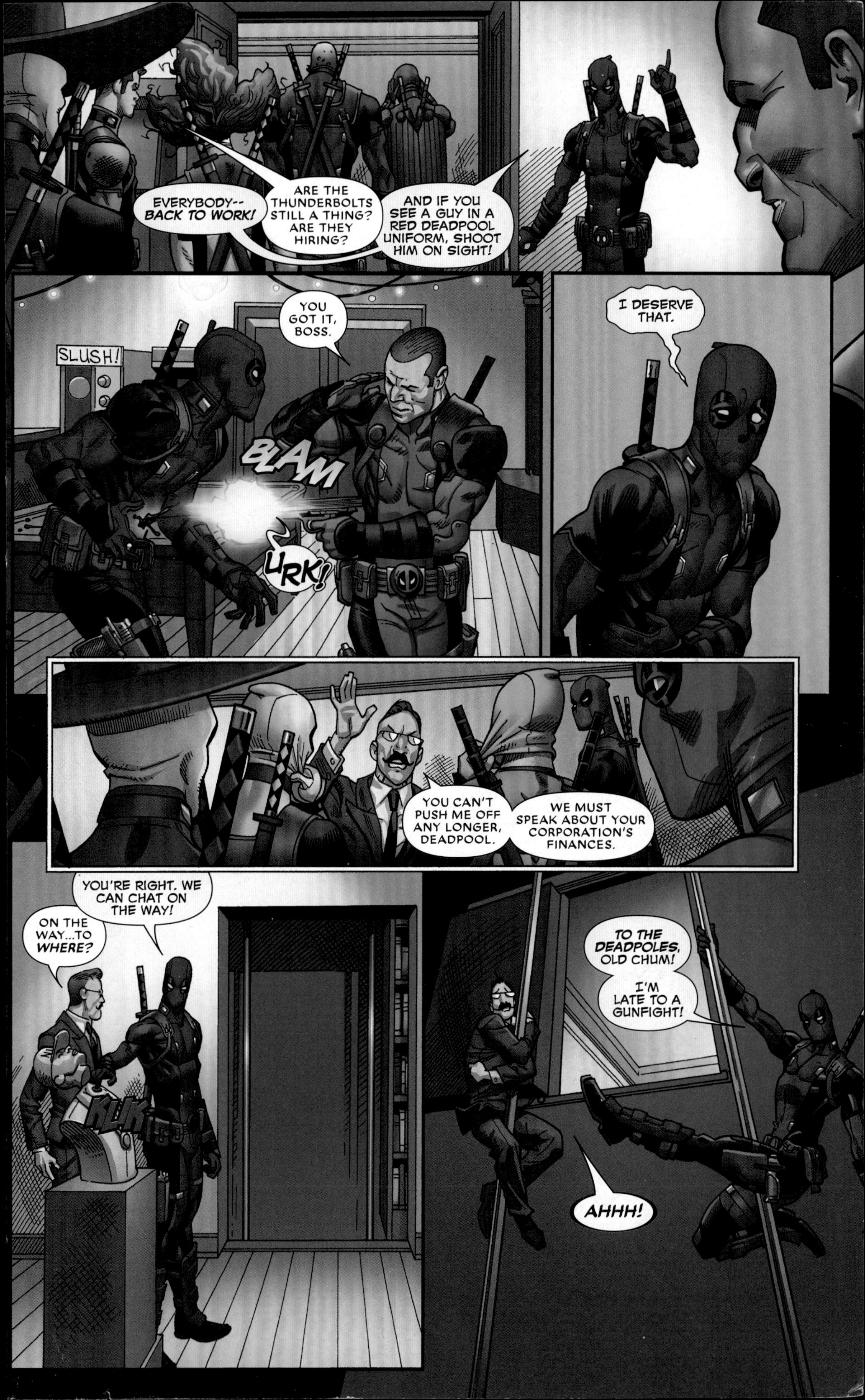
EVERYBODY--
BACK TO WORK!
ARE THE THUNDERBOLTS STILL A THING? ARE THEY HIRING?
AND IF YOU SEE A GUY IN A RED DEADPOOL UNIFORM, SHOOT HIM ON SIGHT!
SLUSH!
YOU GOT IT, BOSS.
BLAM
URK!
I DESERVE THAT.
YOU CAN'T PUSH ME OFF ANY LONGER, DEADPOOL.
WE MUST SPEAK ABOUT YOUR CORPORATION'S FINANCES.
YOU'RE RIGHT. WE CAN CHAT ON THE WAY!
ON THE WAY...TO WHERE?
KLIK
TO THE DEADPOLES, OLD CHUM!
I'M LATE TO A GUNFIGHT!
AHHH!

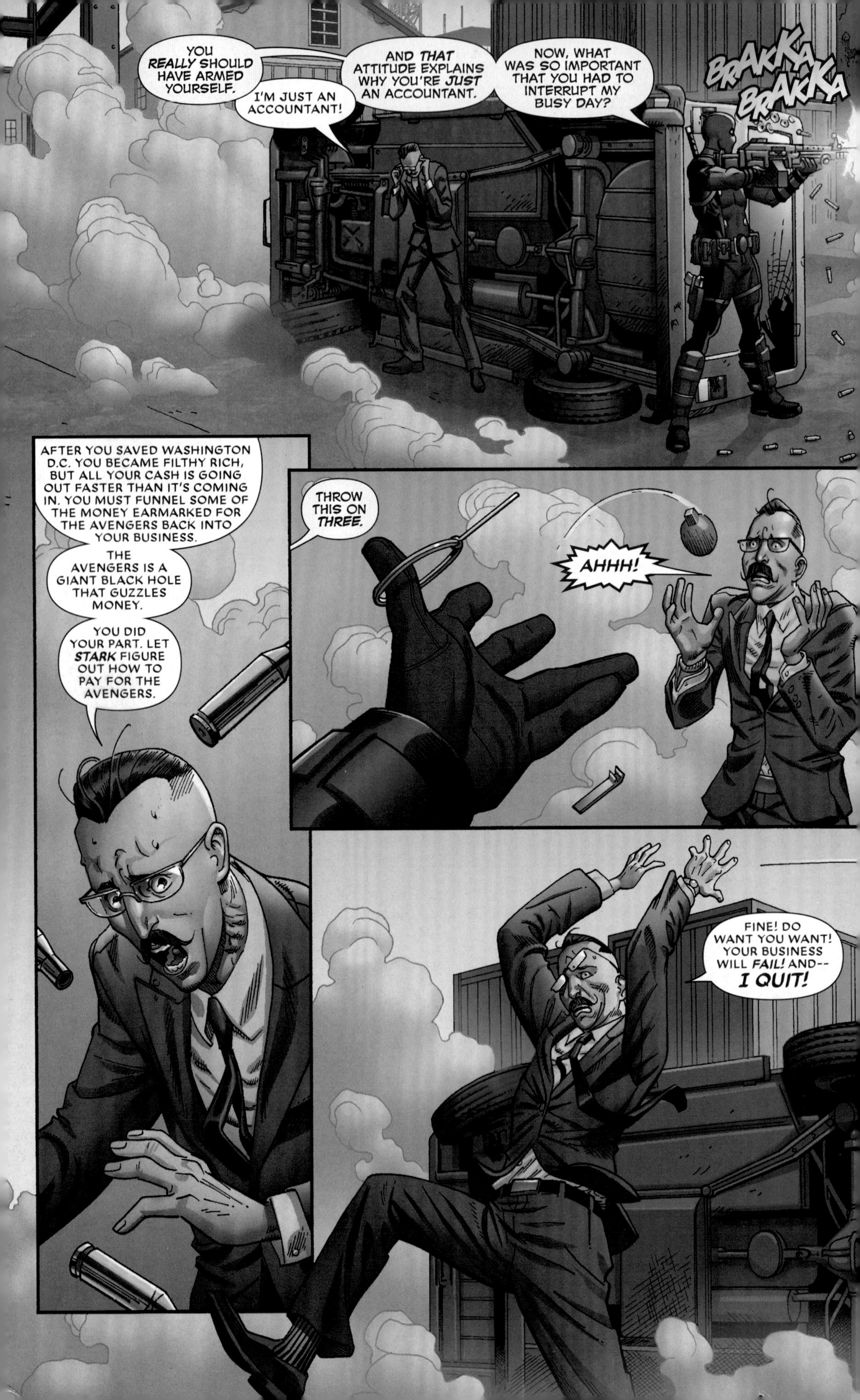
YOU *REALLY* SHOULD HAVE ARMED YOURSELF.
I'M JUST AN ACCOUNTANT!
AND *THAT* ATTITUDE EXPLAINS WHY YOU'RE *JUST* AN ACCOUNTANT.
NOW, WHAT WAS SO IMPORTANT THAT YOU HAD TO INTERRUPT MY BUSY DAY?
BRAKKA BRAKKA
AFTER YOU SAVED WASHINGTON D.C. YOU BECAME FILTHY RICH, BUT ALL YOUR CASH IS GOING OUT FASTER THAN IT'S COMING IN. YOU MUST FUNNEL SOME OF THE MONEY EARMARKED FOR THE AVENGERS BACK INTO YOUR BUSINESS.
THE AVENGERS IS A GIANT BLACK HOLE THAT GUZZLES MONEY.
YOU DID YOUR PART. LET *STARK* FIGURE OUT HOW TO PAY FOR THE AVENGERS.
THROW THIS ON *THREE*.
AHHH!
FINE! DO WANT YOU WANT! YOUR BUSINESS WILL *FAIL!* AND--
I QUIT!

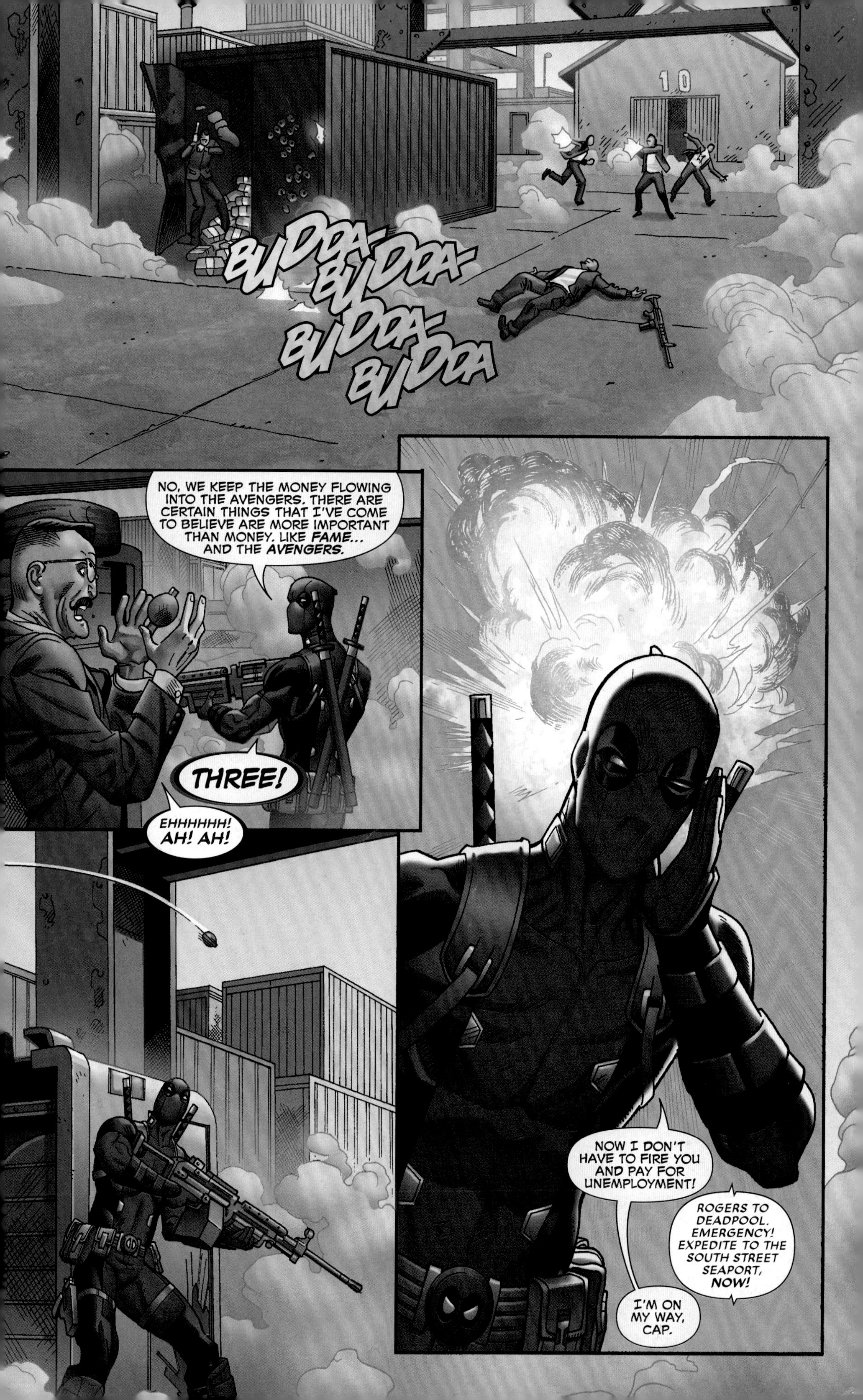
BUDDA-BUDDA-BUDDA-BUDDA
NO, WE KEEP THE MONEY FLOWING INTO THE AVENGERS. THERE ARE CERTAIN THINGS THAT I'VE COME TO BELIEVE ARE MORE IMPORTANT THAN MONEY. LIKE FAME... AND THE AVENGERS.
THREE!
EHHHHHH! AH! AH!
NOW I DON'T HAVE TO FIRE YOU AND PAY FOR UNEMPLOYMENT!
ROGERS TO DEADPOOL. EMERGENCY! EXPEDITE TO THE SOUTH STREET SEAPORT, NOW!
I'M ON MY WAY, CAP.

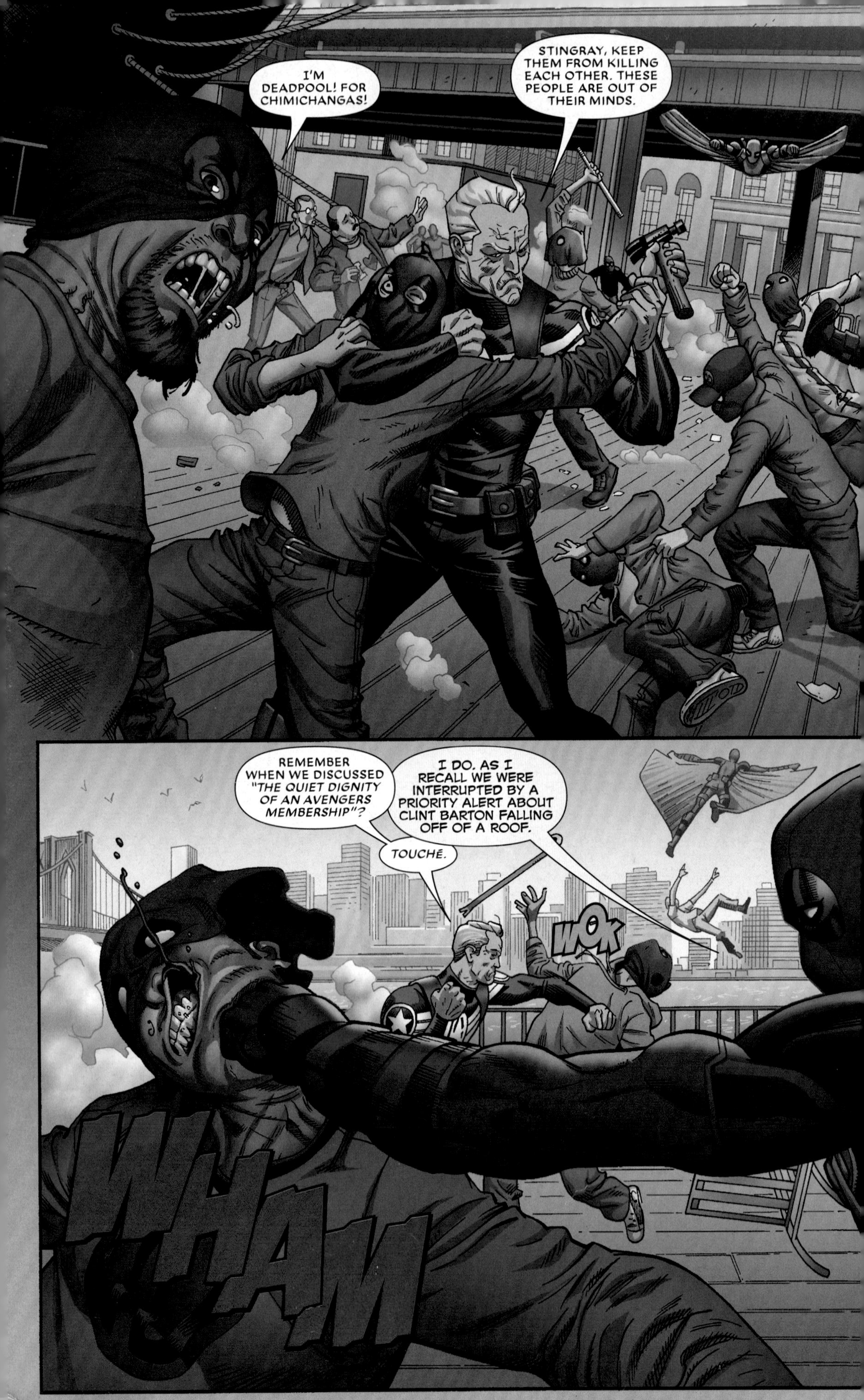
I'M DEADPOOL! FOR CHIMICHANGAS!
STINGRAY, KEEP THEM FROM KILLING EACH OTHER. THESE PEOPLE ARE OUT OF THEIR MINDS.
REMEMBER WHEN WE DISCUSSED "THE QUIET DIGNITY OF AN AVENGERS MEMBERSHIP"?
I DO. AS I RECALL WE WERE INTERRUPTED BY A PRIORITY ALERT ABOUT CLINT BARTON FALLING OFF OF A ROOF.
TOUCHÉ.
WOK
WHAM

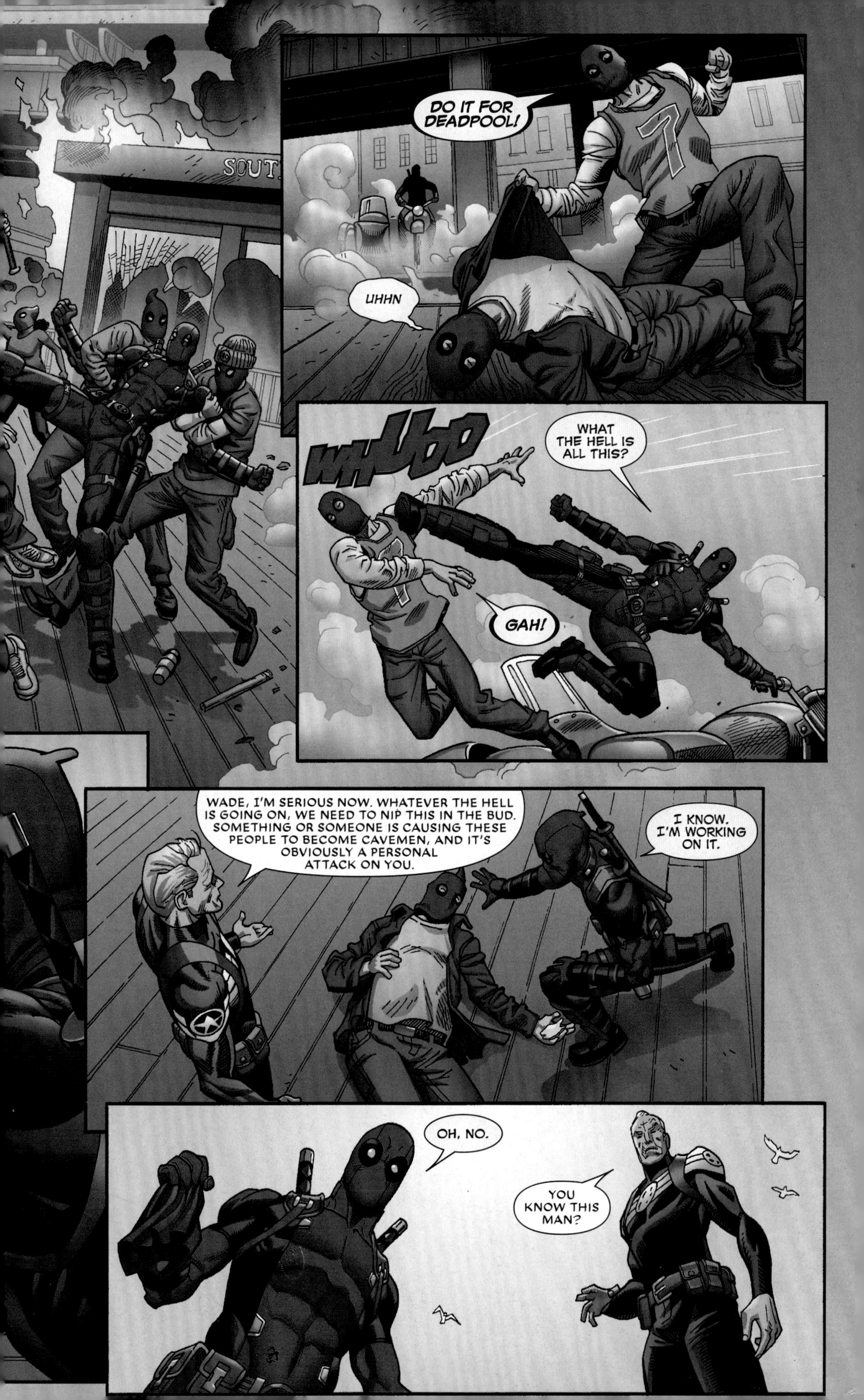
SOUT
DO IT FOR DEADPOOL!
UHHN
WHUDD
WHAT THE HELL IS ALL THIS?
GAH!
WADE, I'M SERIOUS NOW. WHATEVER THE HELL IS GOING ON, WE NEED TO NIP THIS IN THE BUD. SOMETHING OR SOMEONE IS CAUSING THESE PEOPLE TO BECOME CAVEMEN, AND IT'S OBVIOUSLY A PERSONAL ATTACK ON YOU.
I KNOW. I'M WORKING ON IT.
OH, NO.
YOU KNOW THIS MAN?

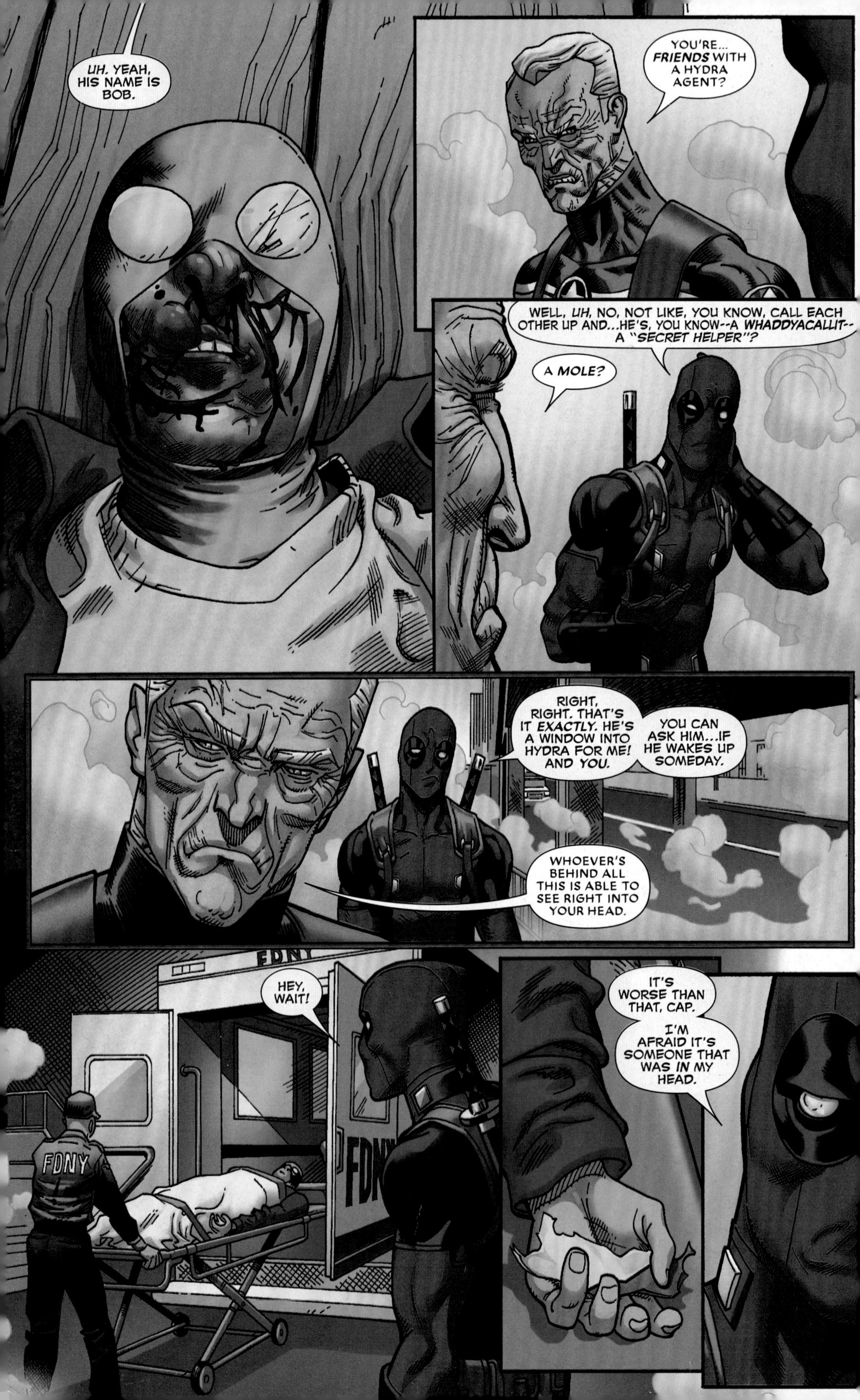
UH. YEAH, HIS NAME IS BOB.
YOU'RE... FRIENDS WITH A HYDRA AGENT?
WELL, UH, NO, NOT LIKE, YOU KNOW, CALL EACH OTHER UP AND...HE'S, YOU KNOW--A WHADDYACALLIT--A "SECRET HELPER"?
A MOLE?
RIGHT, RIGHT. THAT'S IT EXACTLY. HE'S A WINDOW INTO HYDRA FOR ME! AND YOU.
YOU CAN ASK HIM...IF HE WAKES UP SOMEDAY.
WHOEVER'S BEHIND ALL THIS IS ABLE TO SEE RIGHT INTO YOUR HEAD.
FDNY
HEY, WAIT!
FDNY
FDNY
IT'S WORSE THAN THAT, CAP.
I'M AFRAID IT'S SOMEONE THAT WAS IN MY HEAD.

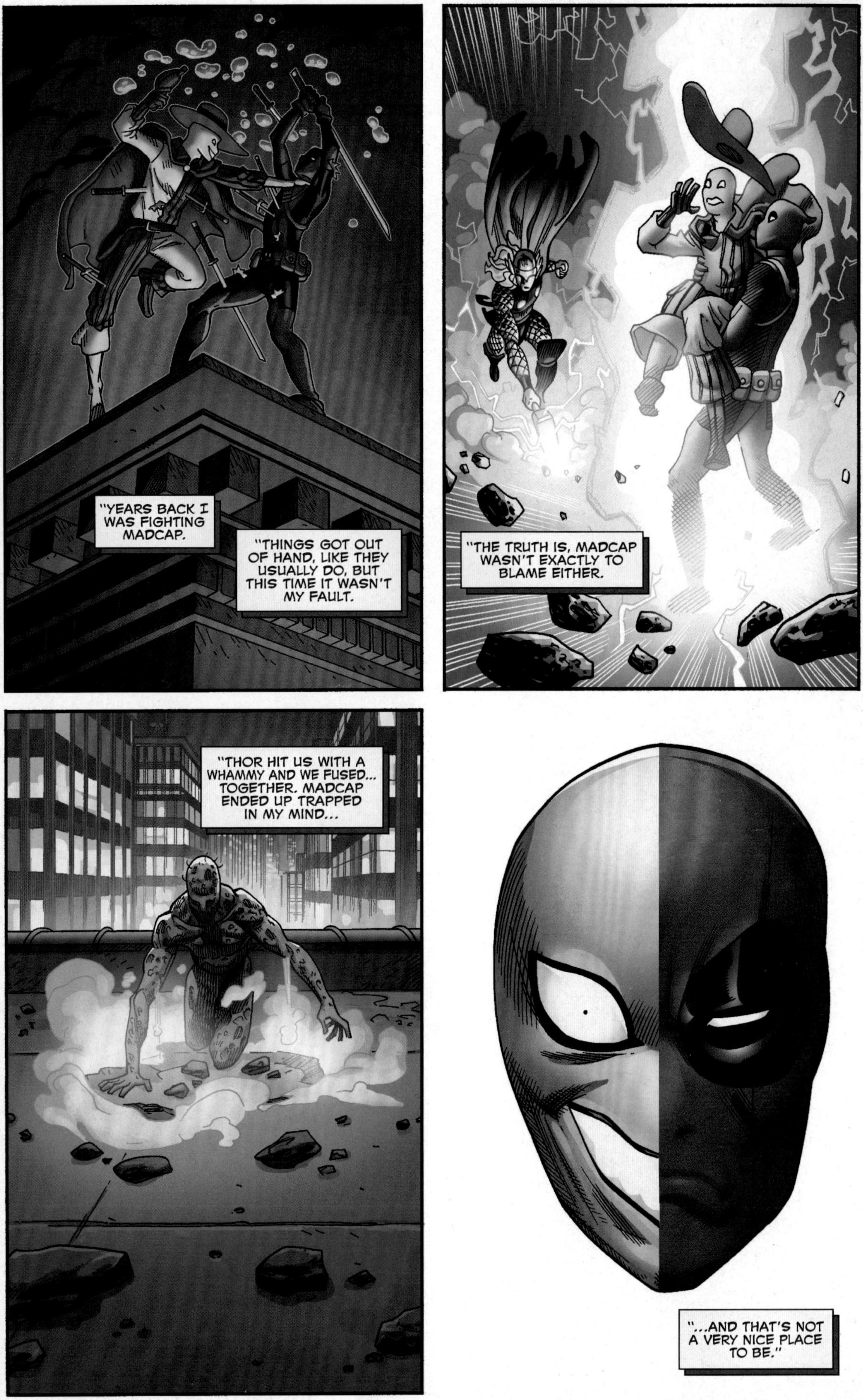
"YEARS BACK I WAS FIGHTING MADCAP.
"THINGS GOT OUT OF HAND, LIKE THEY USUALLY DO, BUT THIS TIME IT WASN'T MY FAULT.
"THE TRUTH IS, MADCAP WASN'T EXACTLY TO BLAME EITHER.
"THOR HIT US WITH A WHAMMY AND WE FUSED... TOGETHER. MADCAP ENDED UP TRAPPED IN MY MIND...
"...AND THAT'S NOT A VERY NICE PLACE TO BE."

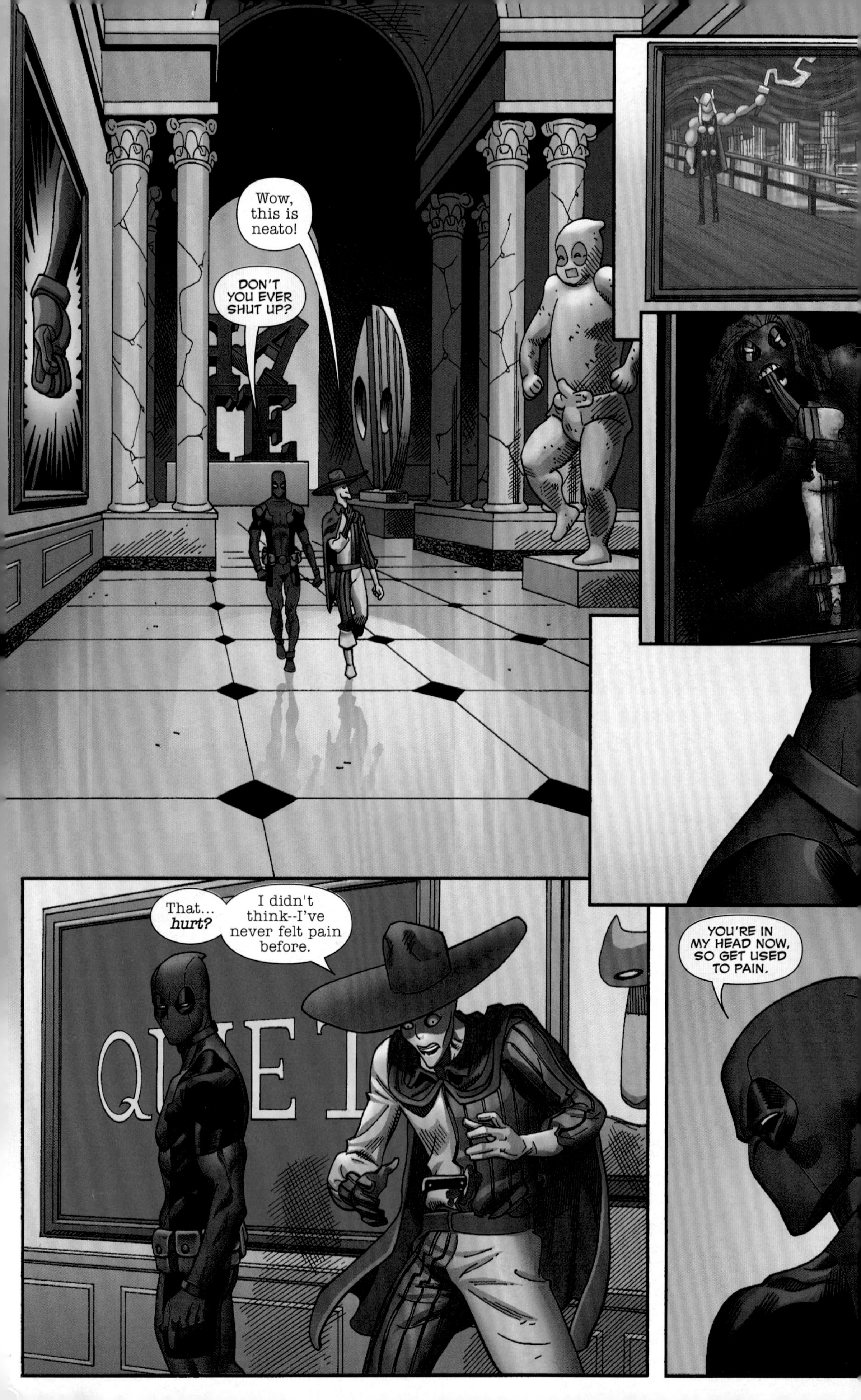

Wow, this is neato!
DON'T YOU EVER SHUT UP?
That... *hurt?*
I didn't think--I've never felt pain before.
YOU'RE IN MY HEAD NOW, SO GET USED TO PAIN.
QUIET

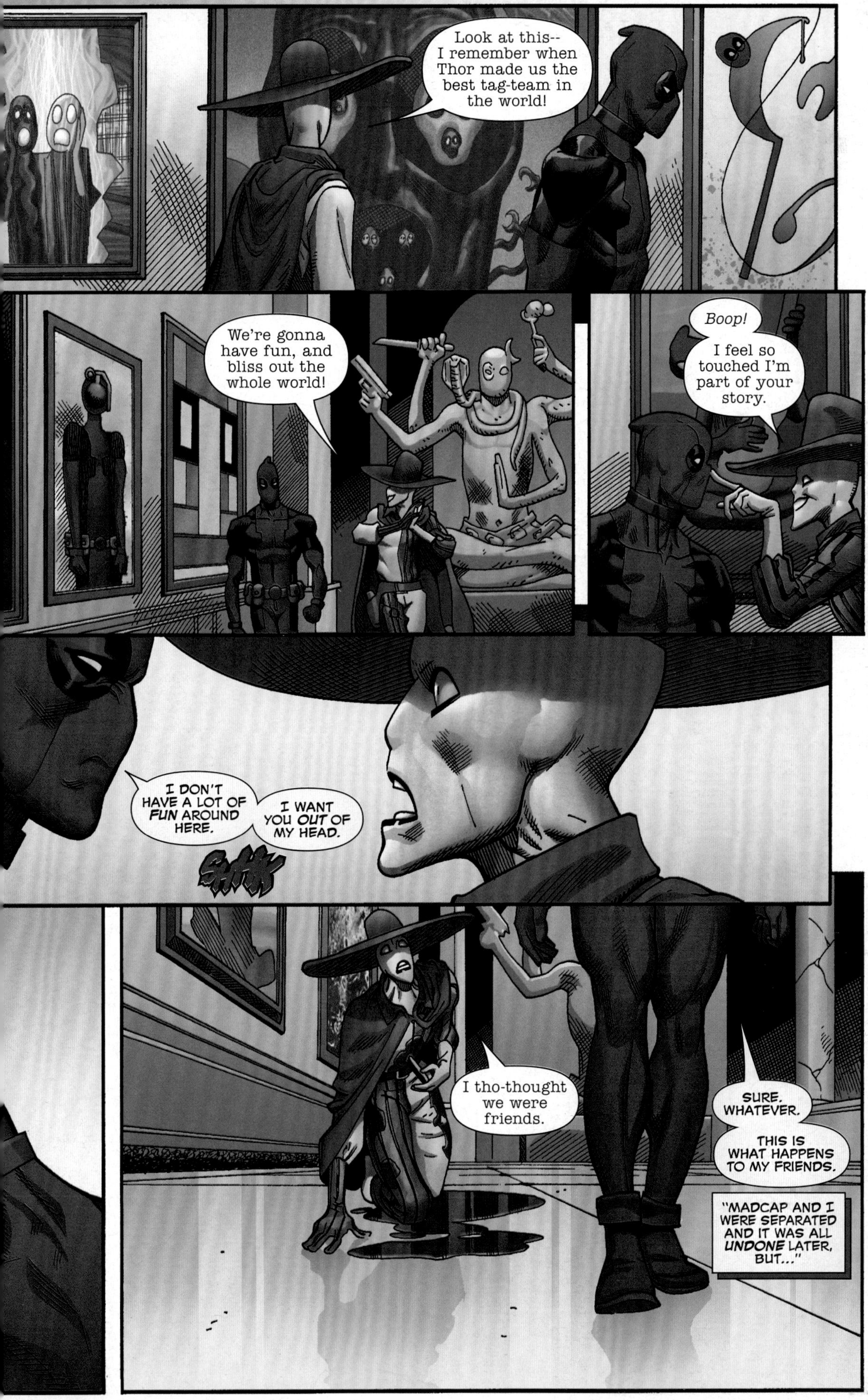
Look at this-- I remember when Thor made us the best tag-team in the world!
We're gonna have fun, and bliss out the whole world!
Boop!
I feel so touched I'm part of your story.
I DON'T HAVE A LOT OF FUN AROUND HERE.
I WANT YOU OUT OF MY HEAD.
I tho-thought we were friends.
SURE. WHATEVER.
THIS IS WHAT HAPPENS TO MY FRIENDS.
"MADCAP AND I WERE SEPARATED AND IT WAS ALL UNDONE LATER, BUT..."

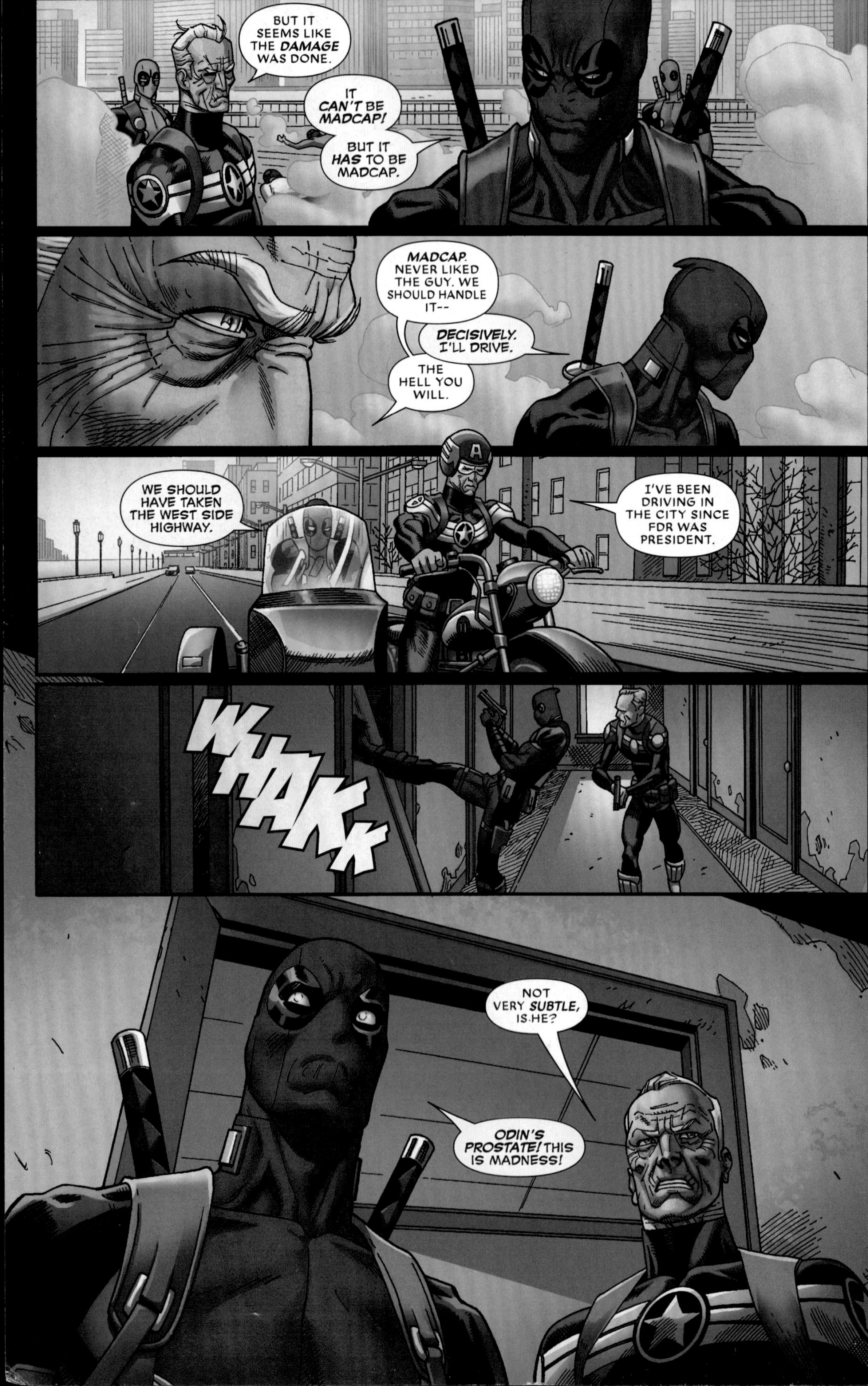
BUT IT SEEMS LIKE THE DAMAGE WAS DONE.
IT CAN'T BE MADCAP!
BUT IT HAS TO BE MADCAP.
MADCAP. NEVER LIKED THE GUY. WE SHOULD HANDLE IT--
DECISIVELY. I'LL DRIVE.
THE HELL YOU WILL.
WE SHOULD HAVE TAKEN THE WEST SIDE HIGHWAY.
I'VE BEEN DRIVING IN THE CITY SINCE FDR WAS PRESIDENT.
WHAKK
NOT VERY SUBTLE, IS HE?
ODIN'S PROSTATE! THIS IS MADNESS!

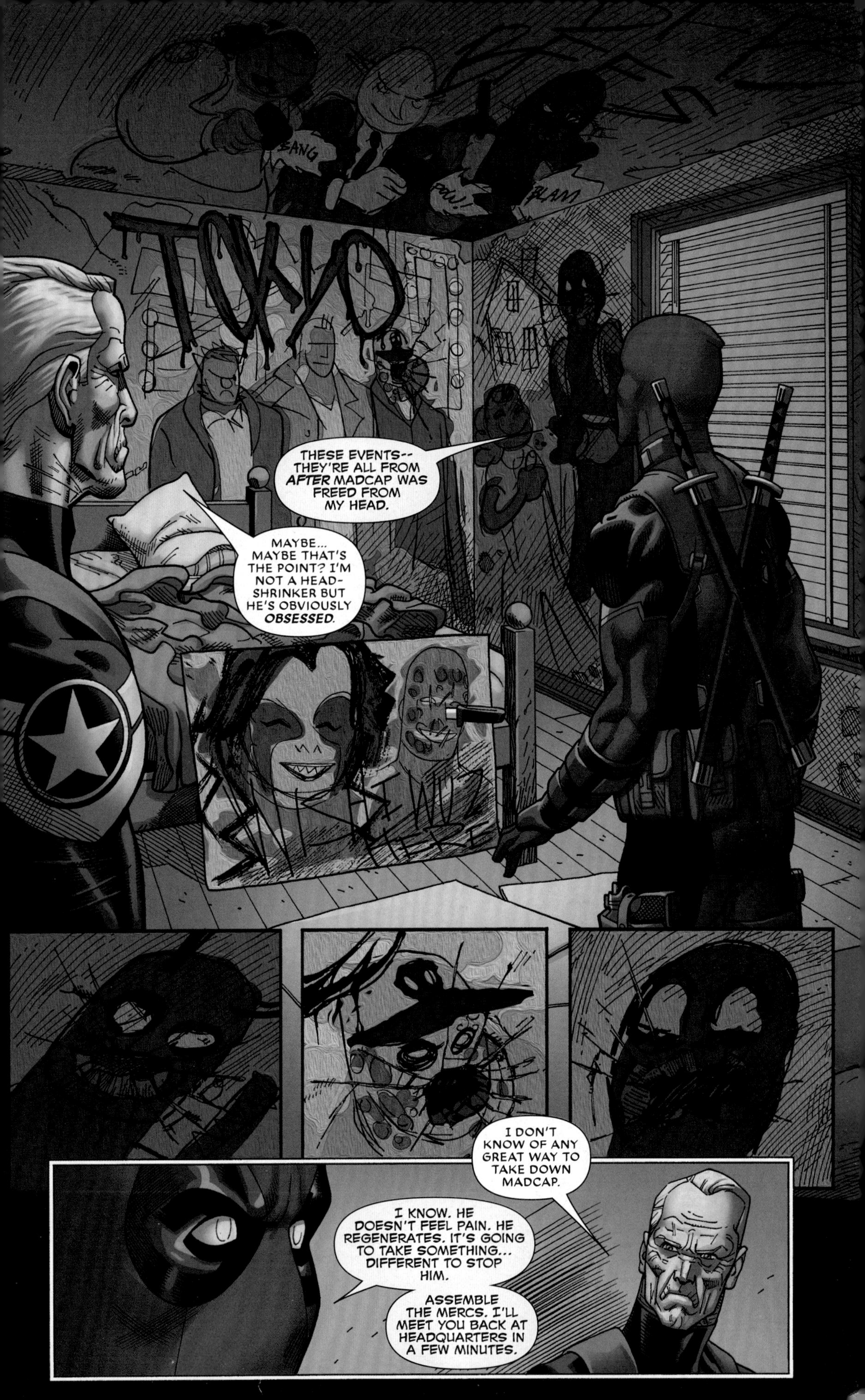
BANG
POW
BLAM
TOKYO
THESE EVENTS--THEY'RE ALL FROM *AFTER* MADCAP WAS FREED FROM MY HEAD.
MAYBE... MAYBE THAT'S THE POINT? I'M NOT A HEAD-SHRINKER BUT HE'S OBVIOUSLY ***OBSESSED***.
I DON'T KNOW OF ANY GREAT WAY TO TAKE DOWN MADCAP.
I KNOW. HE DOESN'T FEEL PAIN. HE REGENERATES. IT'S GOING TO TAKE SOMETHING... DIFFERENT TO STOP HIM.
ASSEMBLE THE MERCS. I'LL MEET YOU BACK AT HEADQUARTERS IN A FEW MINUTES.

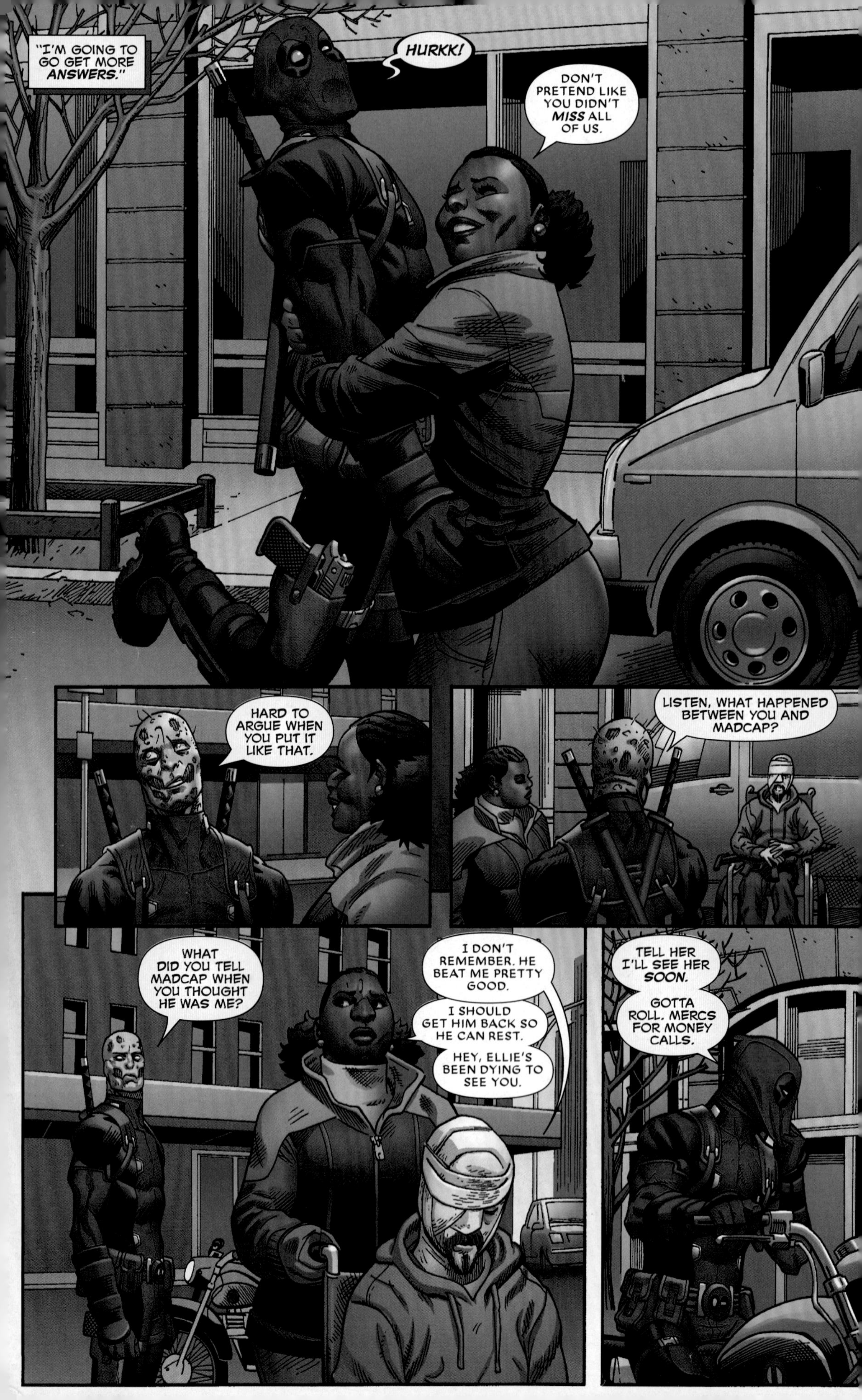
"I'M GOING TO GO GET MORE ANSWERS."
HURKK!
DON'T PRETEND LIKE YOU DIDN'T MISS ALL OF US.
HARD TO ARGUE WHEN YOU PUT IT LIKE THAT.
LISTEN, WHAT HAPPENED BETWEEN YOU AND MADCAP?
WHAT DID YOU TELL MADCAP WHEN YOU THOUGHT HE WAS ME?
I DON'T REMEMBER. HE BEAT ME PRETTY GOOD.
I SHOULD GET HIM BACK SO HE CAN REST.
HEY, ELLIE'S BEEN DYING TO SEE YOU.
TELL HER I'LL SEE HER SOON.
GOTTA ROLL. MERCS FOR MONEY CALLS.

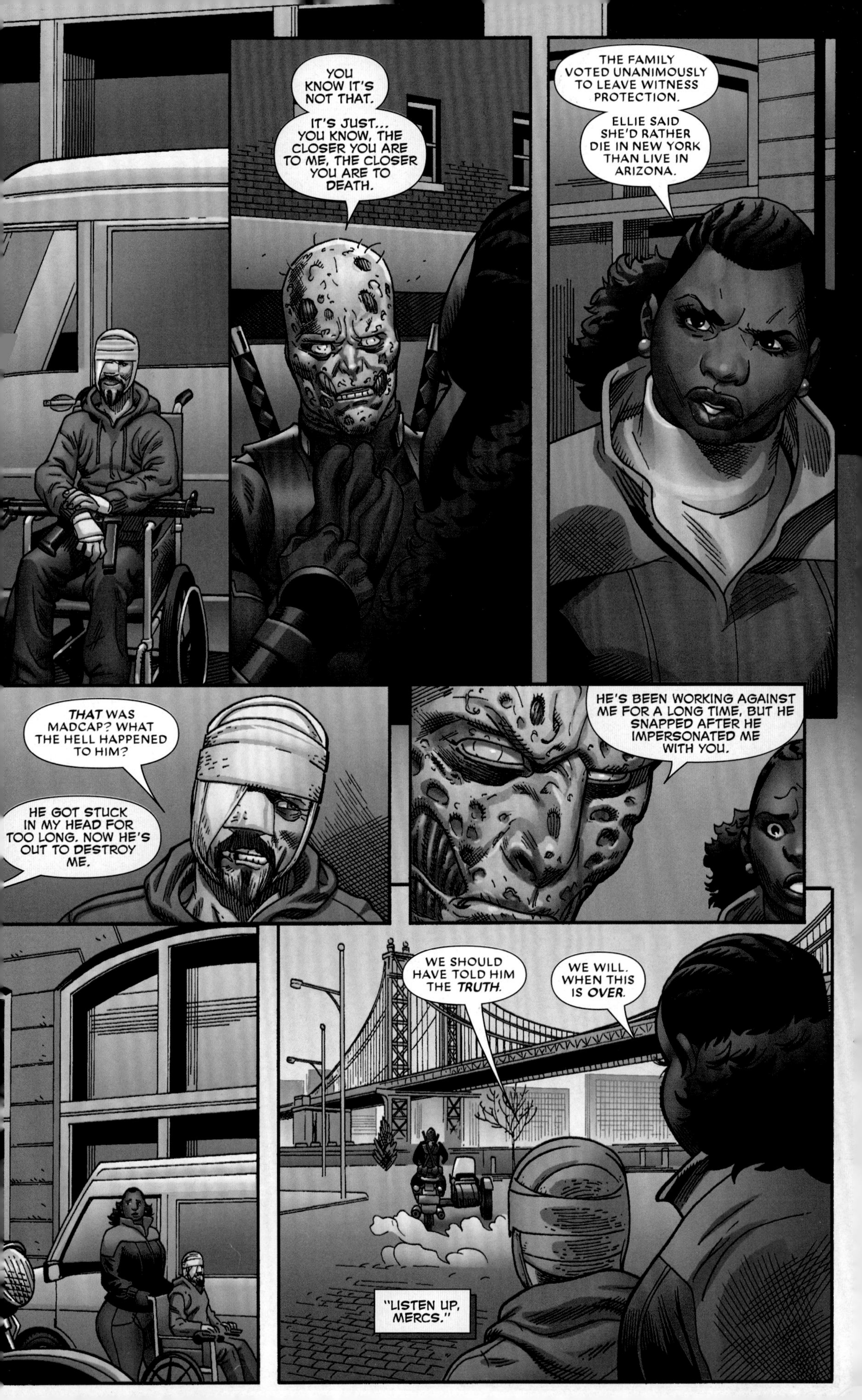
YOU KNOW IT'S NOT THAT.
IT'S JUST... YOU KNOW, THE CLOSER YOU ARE TO ME, THE CLOSER YOU ARE TO DEATH.
THE FAMILY VOTED UNANIMOUSLY TO LEAVE WITNESS PROTECTION.
ELLIE SAID SHE'D RATHER DIE IN NEW YORK THAN LIVE IN ARIZONA.
THAT WAS MADCAP? WHAT THE HELL HAPPENED TO HIM?
HE GOT STUCK IN MY HEAD FOR TOO LONG. NOW HE'S OUT TO DESTROY ME.
HE'S BEEN WORKING AGAINST ME FOR A LONG TIME, BUT HE SNAPPED AFTER HE IMPERSONATED ME WITH YOU.
WE SHOULD HAVE TOLD HIM THE *TRUTH*.
WE WILL. WHEN THIS IS *OVER*.
"LISTEN UP, MERCS."

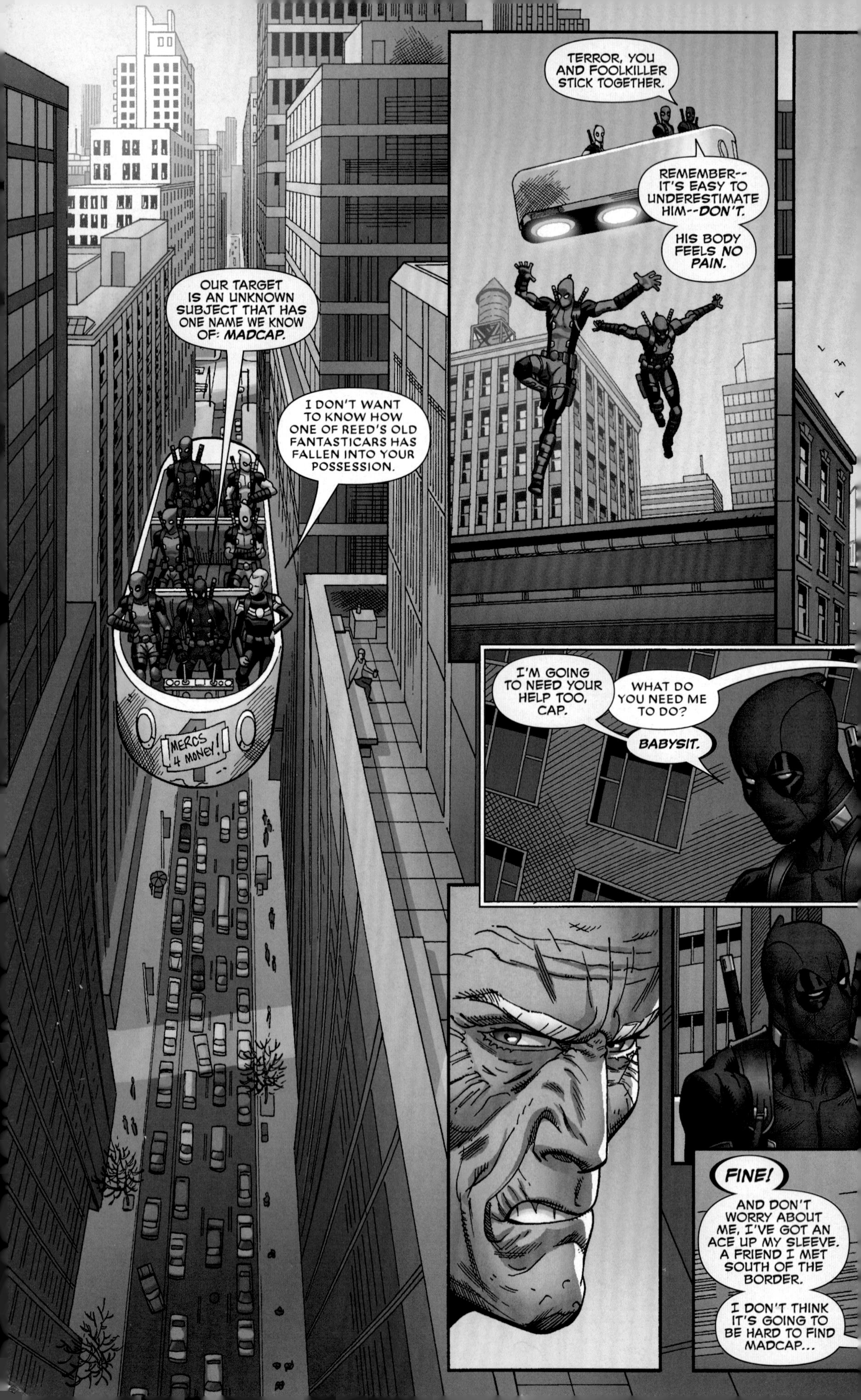
OUR TARGET IS AN UNKNOWN SUBJECT THAT HAS ONE NAME WE KNOW OF: MADCAP.
I DON'T WANT TO KNOW HOW ONE OF REED'S OLD FANTASTICARS HAS FALLEN INTO YOUR POSSESSION.
MERCS 4 MONEY!
TERROR, YOU AND FOOLKILLER STICK TOGETHER.
REMEMBER-- IT'S EASY TO UNDERESTIMATE HIM--DON'T.
HIS BODY FEELS NO PAIN.
I'M GOING TO NEED YOUR HELP TOO, CAP.
WHAT DO YOU NEED ME TO DO?
BABYSIT.
FINE!
AND DON'T WORRY ABOUT ME, I'VE GOT AN ACE UP MY SLEEVE. A FRIEND I MET SOUTH OF THE BORDER.
I DON'T THINK IT'S GOING TO BE HARD TO FIND MADCAP...

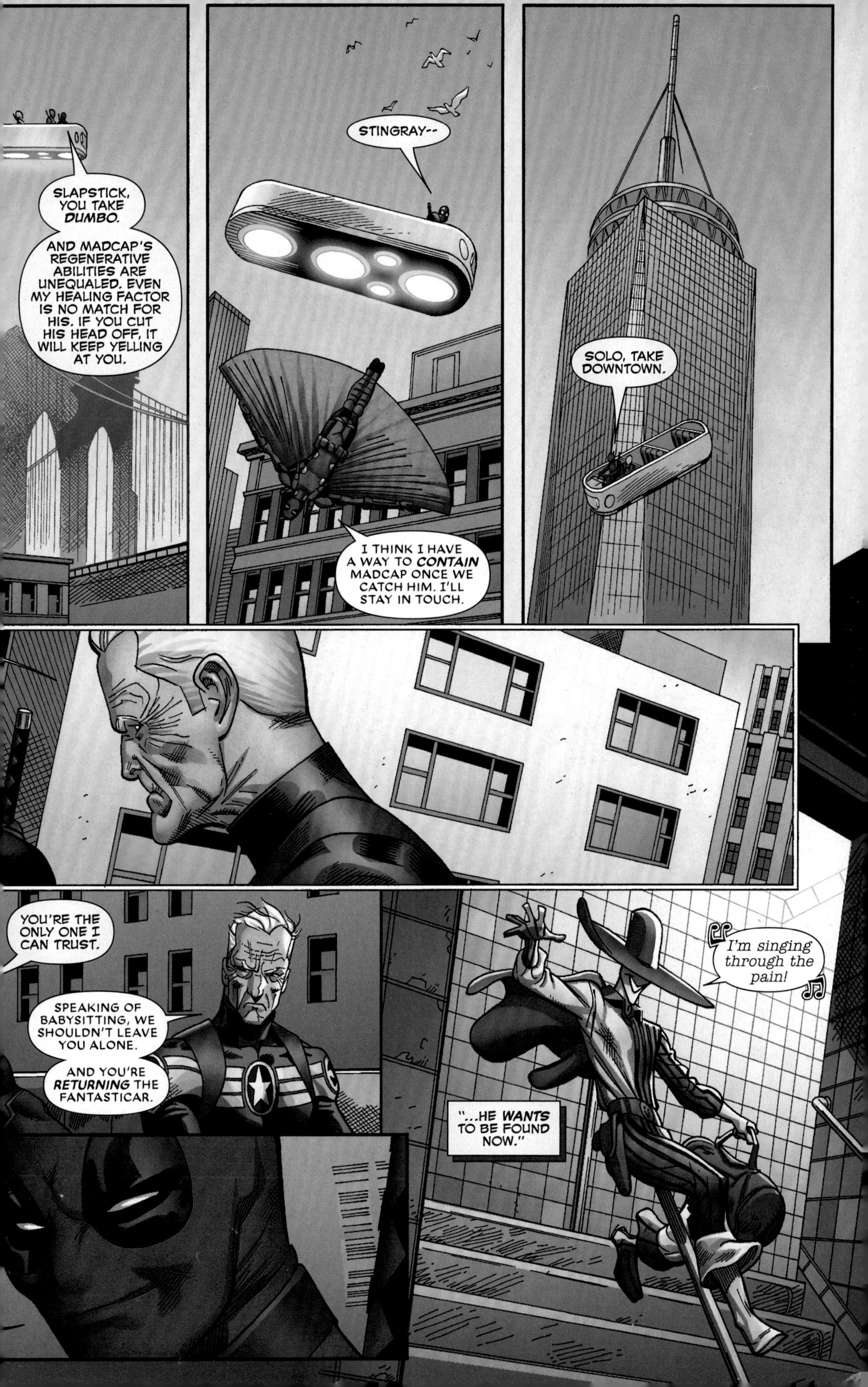
SLAPSTICK, YOU TAKE DUMBO.
AND MADCAP'S REGENERATIVE ABILITIES ARE UNEQUALED. EVEN MY HEALING FACTOR IS NO MATCH FOR HIS. IF YOU CUT HIS HEAD OFF, IT WILL KEEP YELLING AT YOU.
STINGRAY--
I THINK I HAVE A WAY TO CONTAIN MADCAP ONCE WE CATCH HIM. I'LL STAY IN TOUCH.
SOLO, TAKE DOWNTOWN.
YOU'RE THE ONLY ONE I CAN TRUST.
SPEAKING OF BABYSITTING, WE SHOULDN'T LEAVE YOU ALONE.
AND YOU'RE RETURNING THE FANTASTICAR.
"...HE WANTS TO BE FOUND NOW."
I'm singing through the pain!

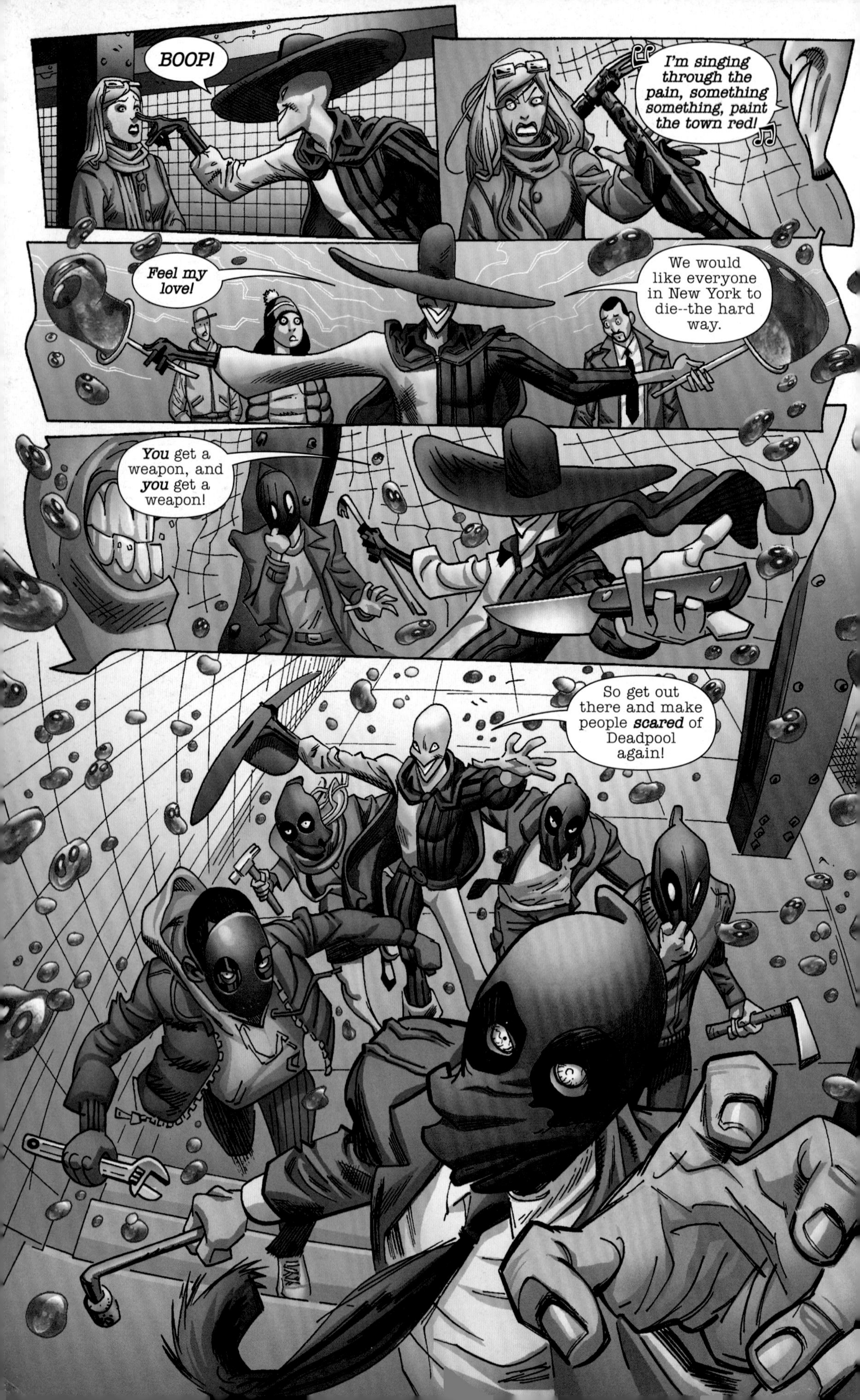
BOOP!
I'm singing through the pain, something something, paint the town red!
Feel my love!
We would like everyone in New York to die--the hard way.
You get a weapon, and you get a weapon!
So get out there and make people scared of Deadpool again!

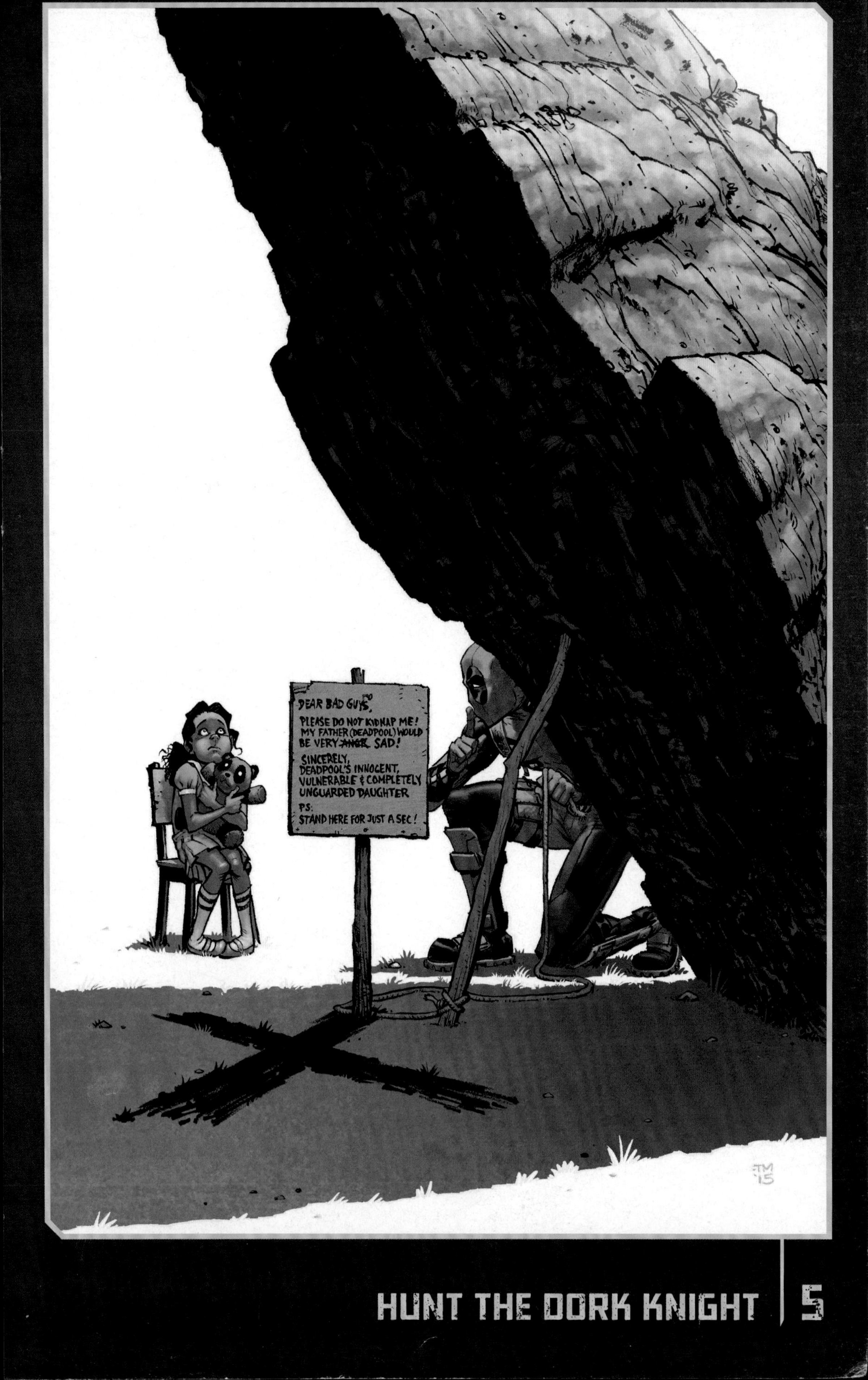
DEAR BAD GUYS,
PLEASE DO NOT KIDNAP ME! MY FATHER (DEADPOOL) WOULD BE VERY ~~ANGR~~ SAD!
SINCERELY, DEADPOOL'S INNOCENT, VULNERABLE & COMPLETELY UNGUARDED DAUGHTER
PS: STAND HERE FOR JUST A SEC!

HUNT THE DORK KNIGHT | 5

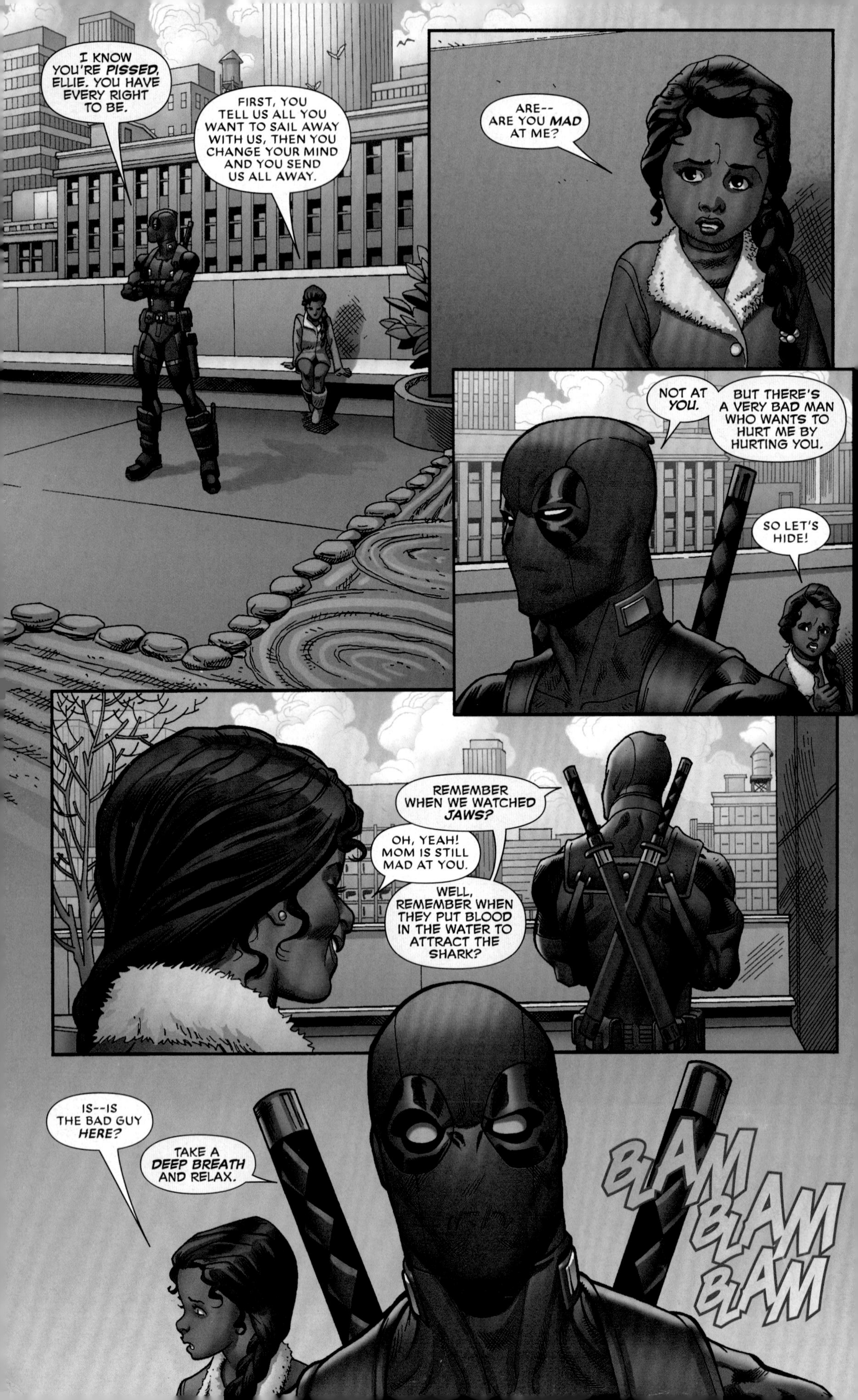
I KNOW YOU'RE PISSED, ELLIE. YOU HAVE EVERY RIGHT TO BE.
FIRST, YOU TELL US ALL YOU WANT TO SAIL AWAY WITH US, THEN YOU CHANGE YOUR MIND AND YOU SEND US ALL AWAY.
ARE-- ARE YOU MAD AT ME?
NOT AT YOU.
BUT THERE'S A VERY BAD MAN WHO WANTS TO HURT ME BY HURTING YOU.
SO LET'S HIDE!
REMEMBER WHEN WE WATCHED JAWS?
OH, YEAH! MOM IS STILL MAD AT YOU.
WELL, REMEMBER WHEN THEY PUT BLOOD IN THE WATER TO ATTRACT THE SHARK?
IS--IS THE BAD GUY HERE?
TAKE A DEEP BREATH AND RELAX.
BLAM
BLAM
BLAM

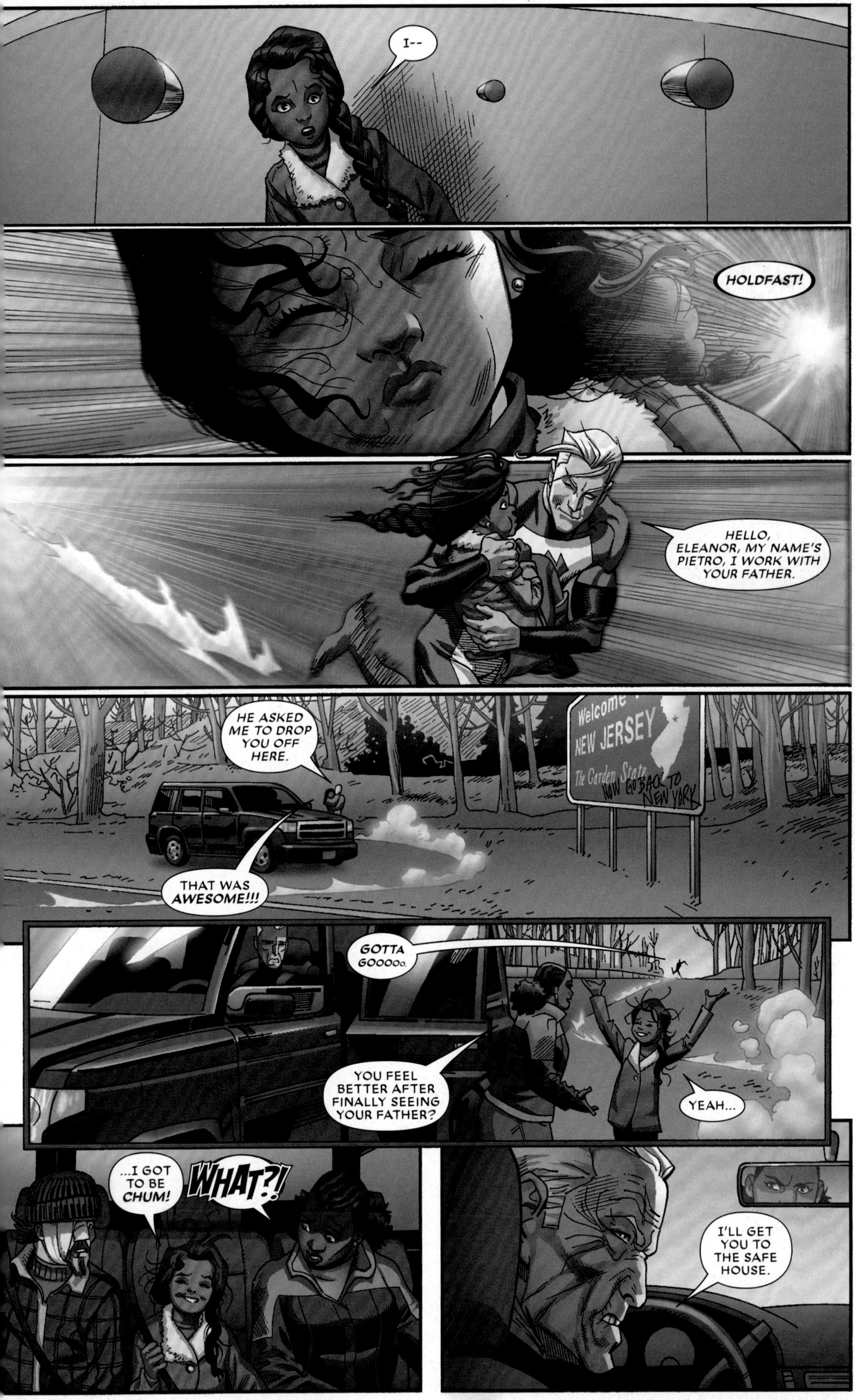
I--
HOLDFAST!
HELLO, ELEANOR, MY NAME'S PIETRO, I WORK WITH YOUR FATHER.
HE ASKED ME TO DROP YOU OFF HERE.
Welcome
NEW JERSEY
The Garden State
NOW GO BACK TO NEW YORK
THAT WAS AWESOME!!!
GOTTA GOOOOo.
YOU FEEL BETTER AFTER FINALLY SEEING YOUR FATHER?
YEAH...
...I GOT TO BE CHUM!
WHAT?!
I'LL GET YOU TO THE SAFE HOUSE.

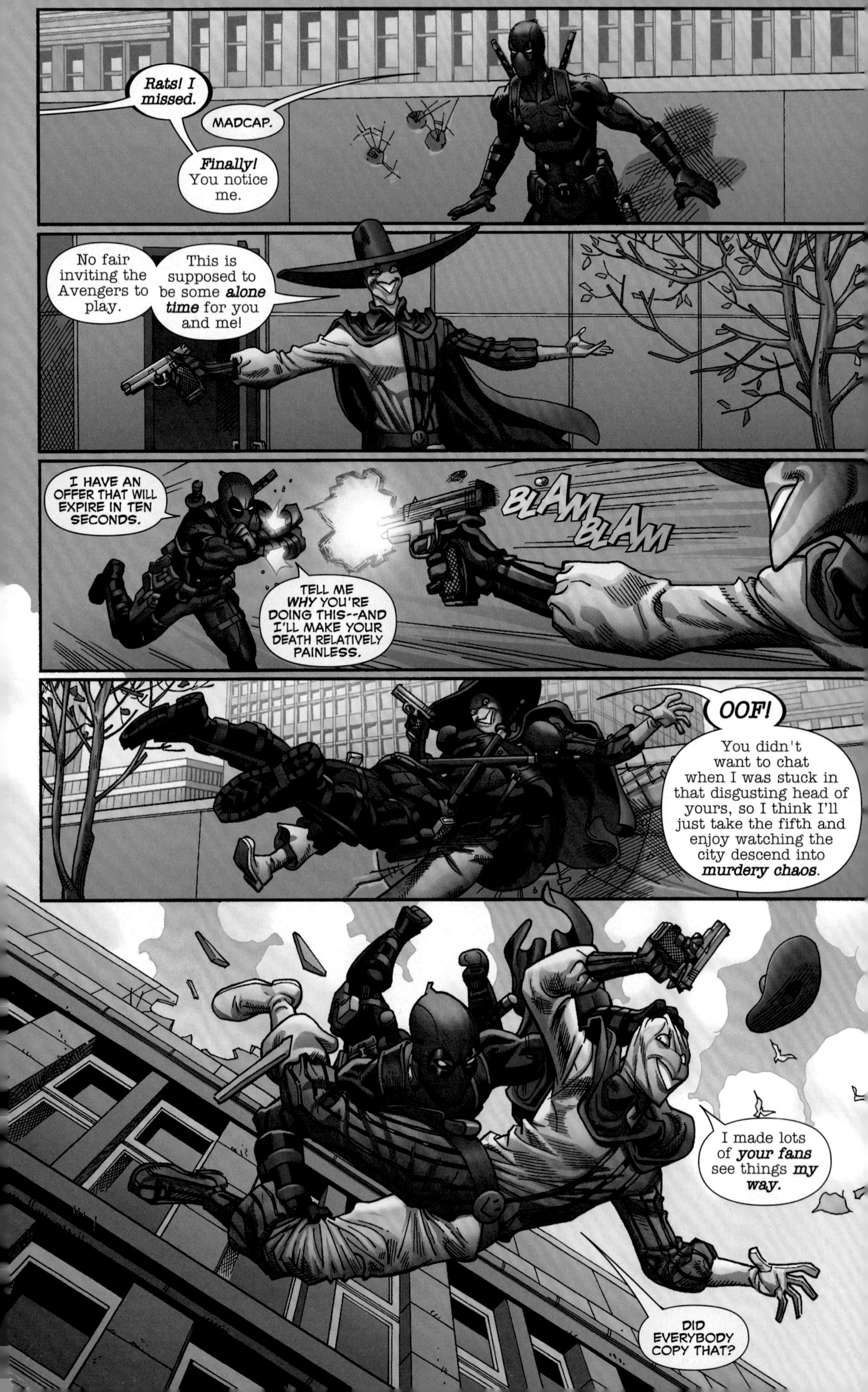
Rats! I missed.
MADCAP.
Finally! You notice me.
No fair inviting the Avengers to play.
This is supposed to be some alone time for you and me!
I HAVE AN OFFER THAT WILL EXPIRE IN TEN SECONDS.
BLAM BLAM
TELL ME WHY YOU'RE DOING THIS--AND I'LL MAKE YOUR DEATH RELATIVELY PAINLESS.
OOF!
You didn't want to chat when I was stuck in that disgusting head of yours, so I think I'll just take the fifth and enjoy watching the city descend into murdery chaos.
I made lots of your fans see things my way.
DID EVERYBODY COPY THAT?

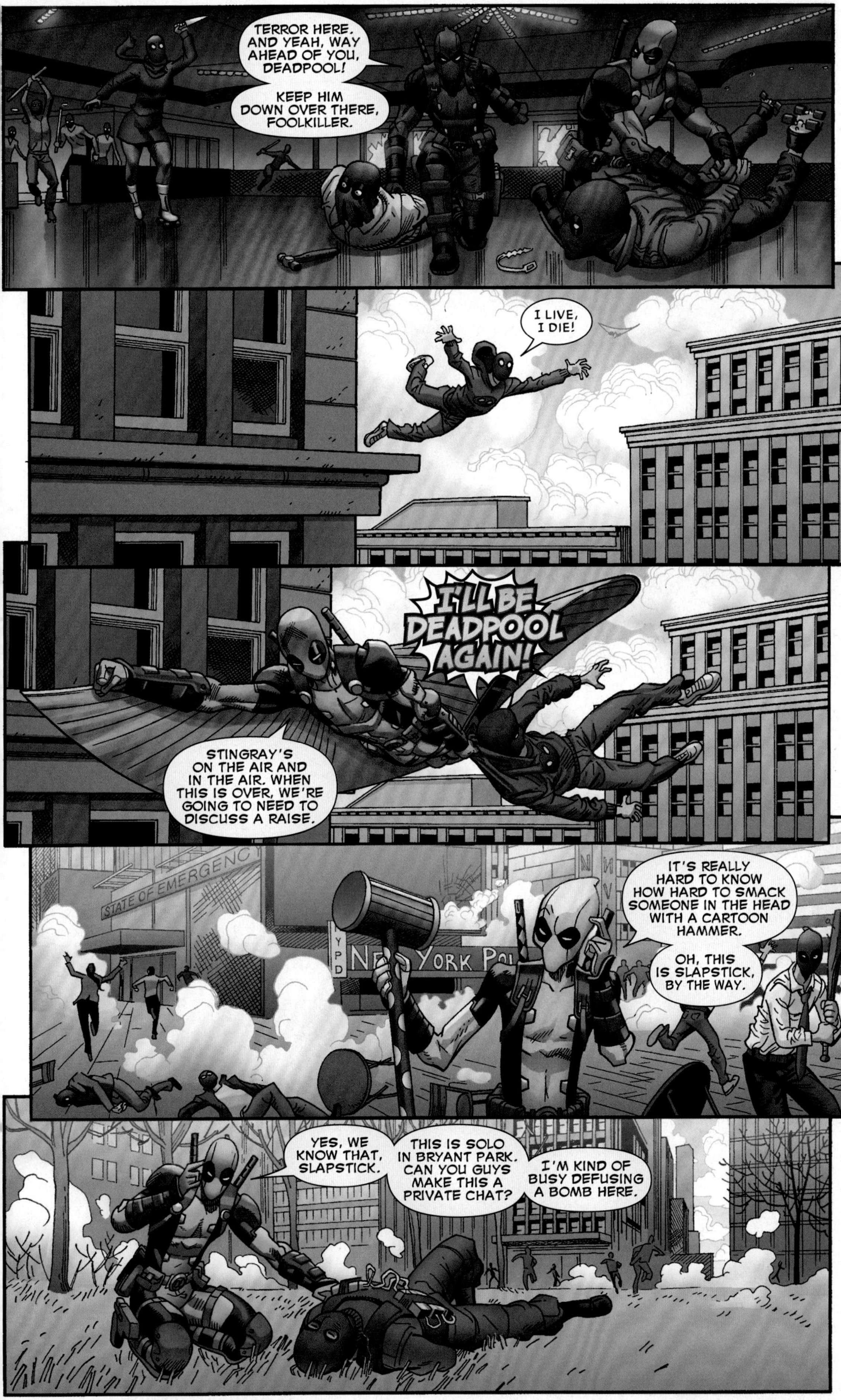
TERROR HERE. AND YEAH, WAY AHEAD OF YOU, DEADPOOL!
KEEP HIM DOWN OVER THERE, FOOLKILLER.
I LIVE, I DIE!
I'LL BE DEADPOOL AGAIN!
STINGRAY'S ON THE AIR AND IN THE AIR. WHEN THIS IS OVER, WE'RE GOING TO NEED TO DISCUSS A RAISE.
STATE OF EMERGENCY
NEW YORK POL
IT'S REALLY HARD TO KNOW HOW HARD TO SMACK SOMEONE IN THE HEAD WITH A CARTOON HAMMER.
OH, THIS IS SLAPSTICK, BY THE WAY.
YES, WE KNOW THAT, SLAPSTICK.
THIS IS SOLO IN BRYANT PARK. CAN YOU GUYS MAKE THIS A PRIVATE CHAT?
I'M KIND OF BUSY DEFUSING A BOMB HERE.

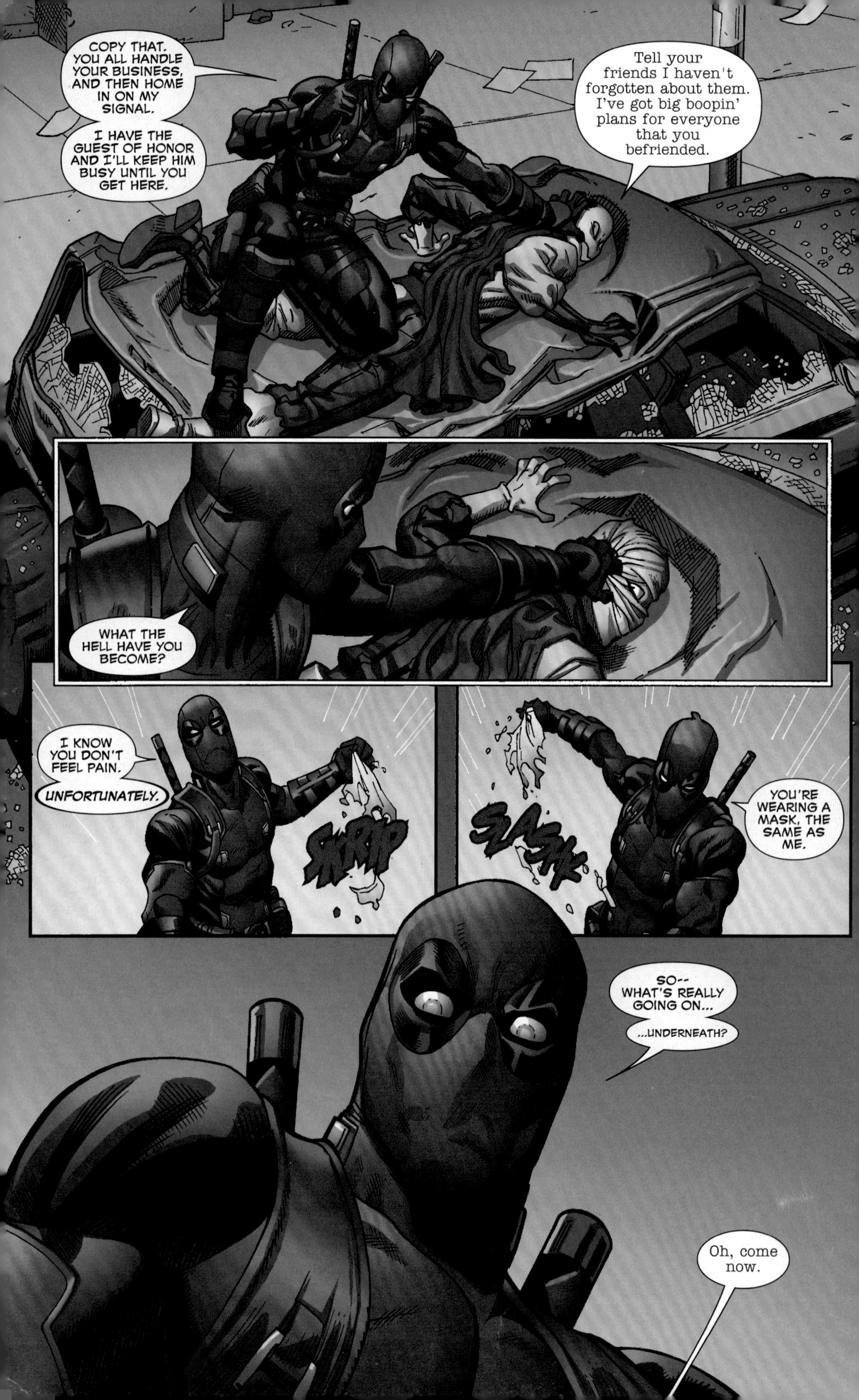
COPY THAT. YOU ALL HANDLE YOUR BUSINESS, AND THEN HOME IN ON MY SIGNAL.
I HAVE THE GUEST OF HONOR AND I'LL KEEP HIM BUSY UNTIL YOU GET HERE.
Tell your friends I haven't forgotten about them. I've got big boopin' plans for everyone that you befriended.
WHAT THE HELL HAVE YOU BECOME?
I KNOW YOU DON'T FEEL PAIN.
UNFORTUNATELY.
SKRIP
SLASHK
YOU'RE WEARING A MASK, THE SAME AS ME.
SO-- WHAT'S REALLY GOING ON...
...UNDERNEATH?
Oh, come now.

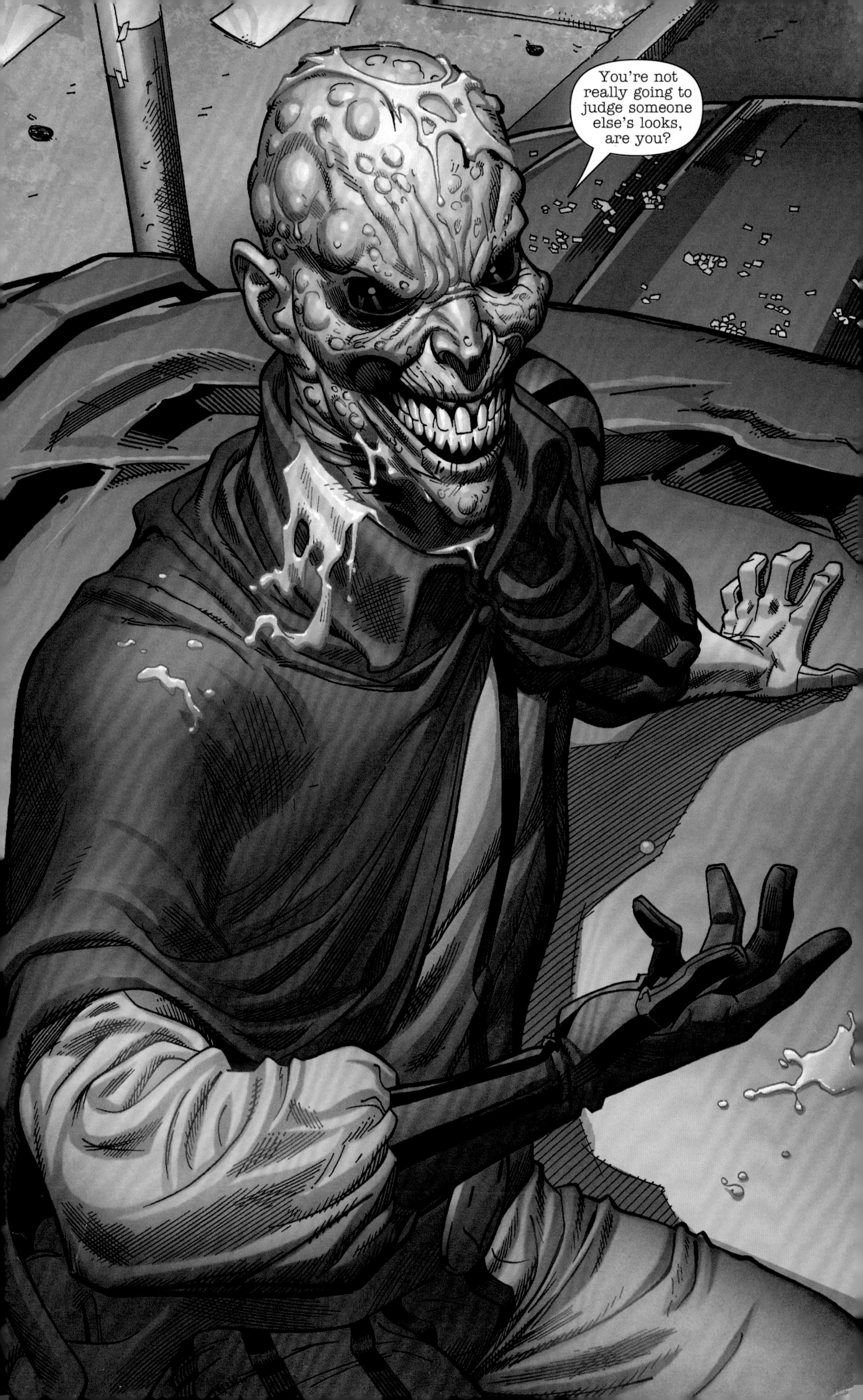
You're not really going to judge someone else's looks, are you?

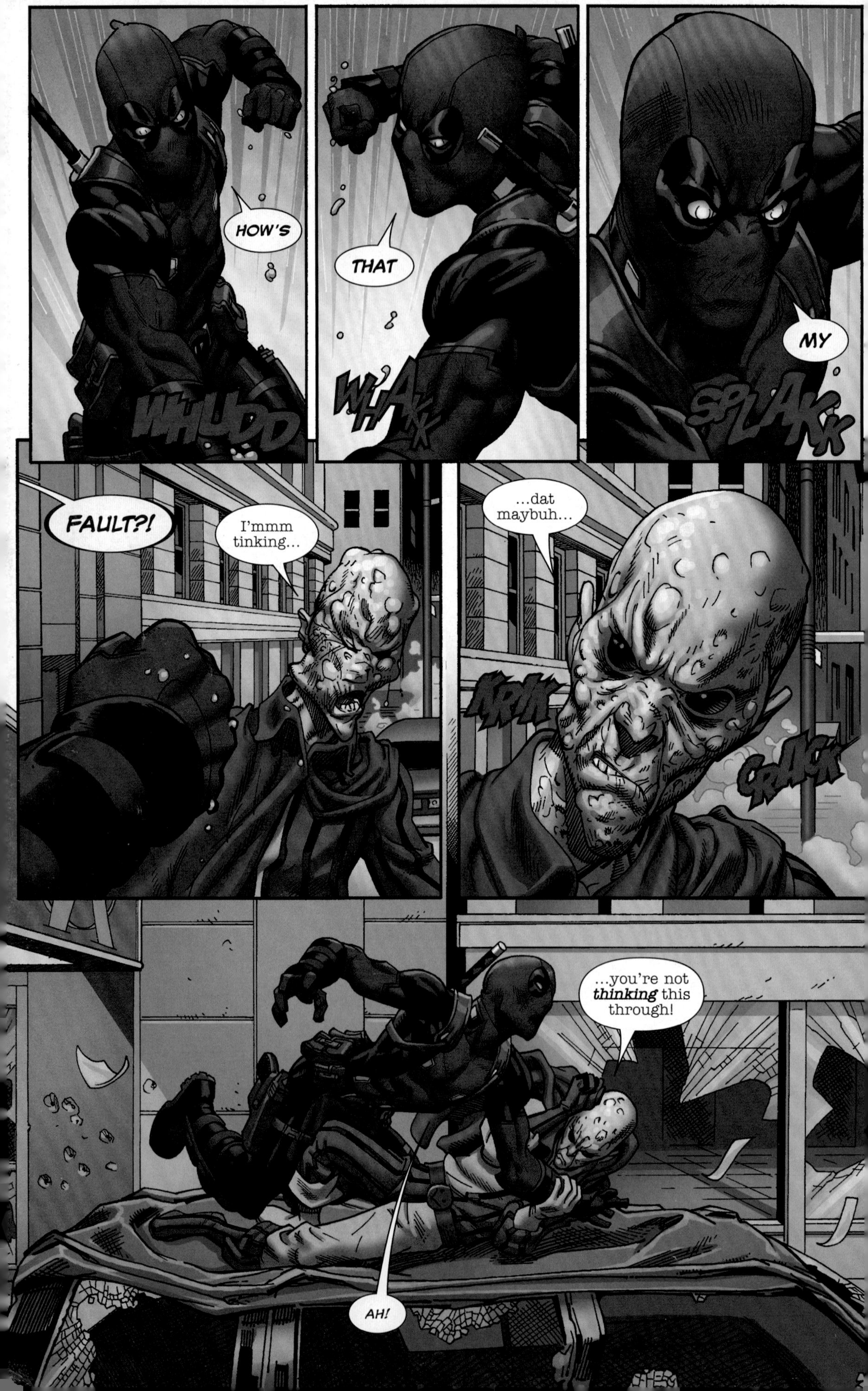
HOW'S
WHUDD
THAT
WHAKK
MY
SPLAKKK
FAULT?!
I'mmm tinking...
...dat maybuh...
KRIK
CRACK
...you're not *thinking* this through!
AH!

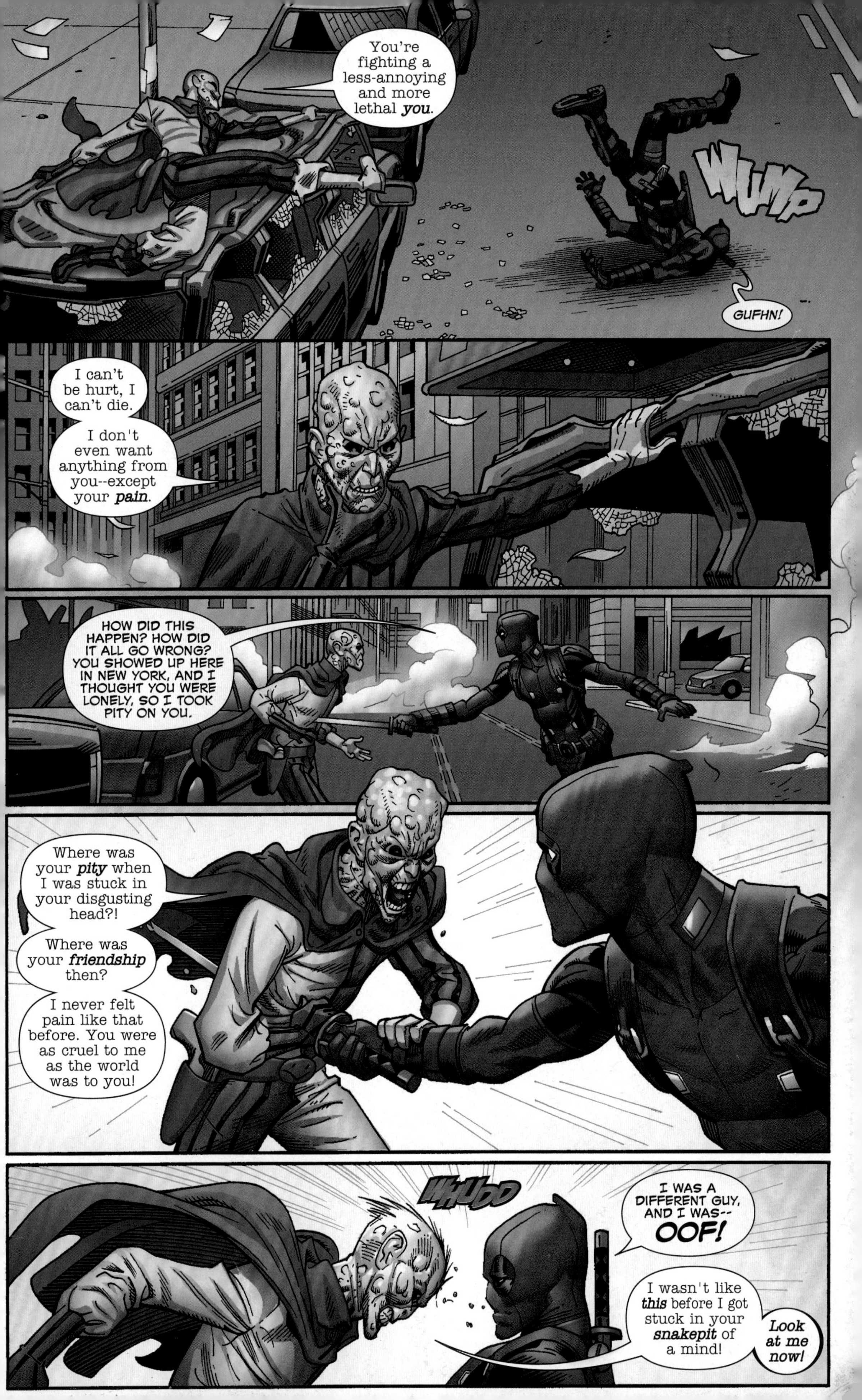
You're fighting a less-annoying and more lethal *you*.
WUMP
GUFHN!
I can't be hurt, I can't die.
I don't even want anything from you--except your *pain*.
HOW DID THIS HAPPEN? HOW DID IT ALL GO WRONG? YOU SHOWED UP HERE IN NEW YORK, AND I THOUGHT YOU WERE LONELY, SO I TOOK PITY ON YOU.
Where was your *pity* when I was stuck in your disgusting head?!
Where was your *friendship* then?
I never felt pain like that before. You were as cruel to me as the world was to you!
WHUDD
I WAS A DIFFERENT GUY, AND I WAS-- OOF!
I wasn't like *this* before I got stuck in your *snakepit* of a mind!
Look at me now!

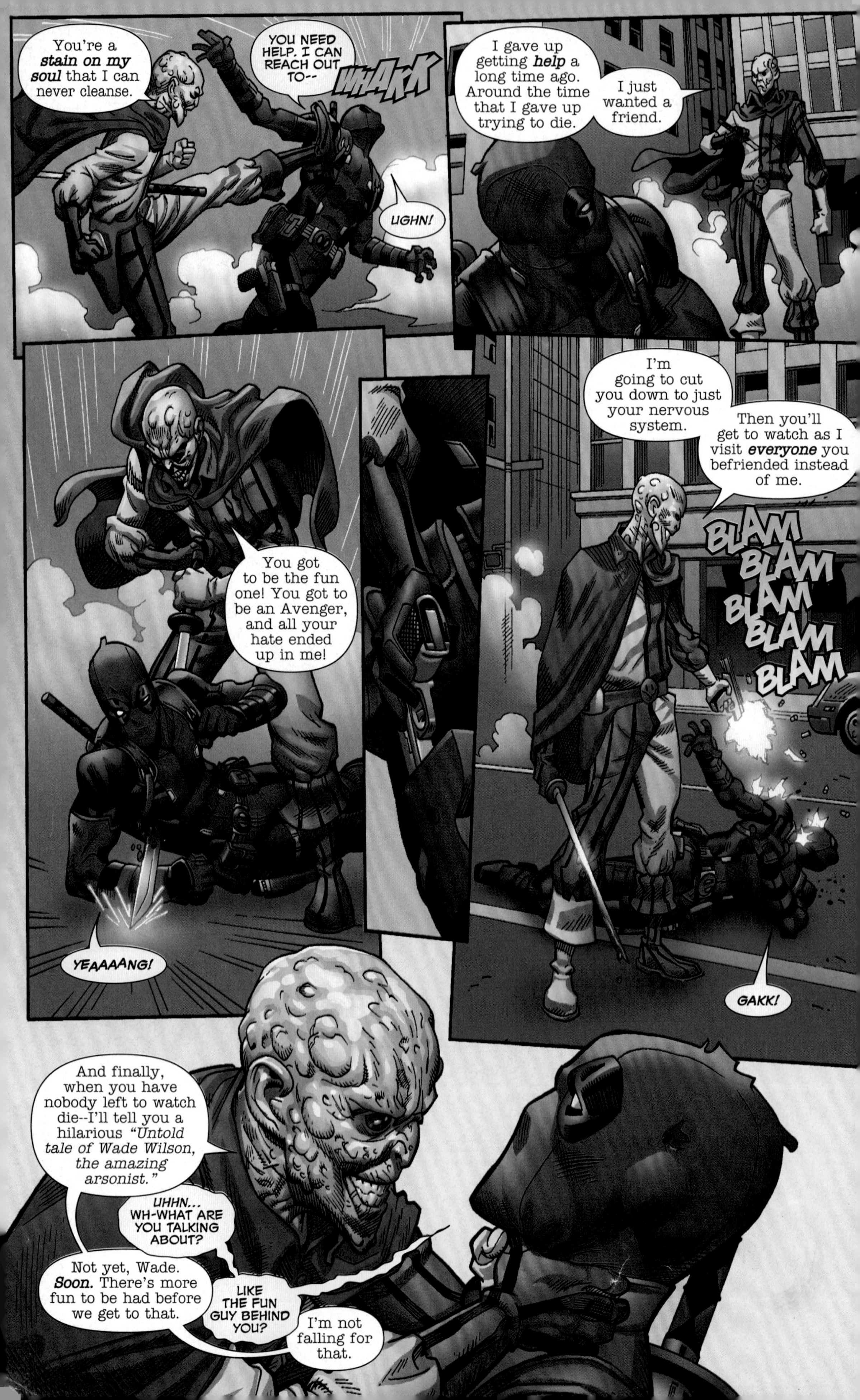
You're a ***stain on my soul*** that I can never cleanse.
YOU NEED HELP. I CAN REACH OUT TO--
WHAKK
UGHN!
I gave up getting ***help*** a long time ago. Around the time that I gave up trying to die.
I just wanted a friend.
You got to be the fun one! You got to be an Avenger, and all your hate ended up in me!
YEAAAANG!
I'm going to cut you down to just your nervous system.
Then you'll get to watch as I visit ***everyone*** you befriended instead of me.
BLAM BLAM BLAM BLAM BLAM
GAKK!
And finally, when you have nobody left to watch die--I'll tell you a hilarious *"Untold tale of Wade Wilson, the amazing arsonist."*
UHHN... WH-WHAT ARE YOU TALKING ABOUT?
Not yet, Wade. ***Soon.*** There's more fun to be had before we get to that.
LIKE THE FUN GUY BEHIND YOU?
I'm not falling for that.

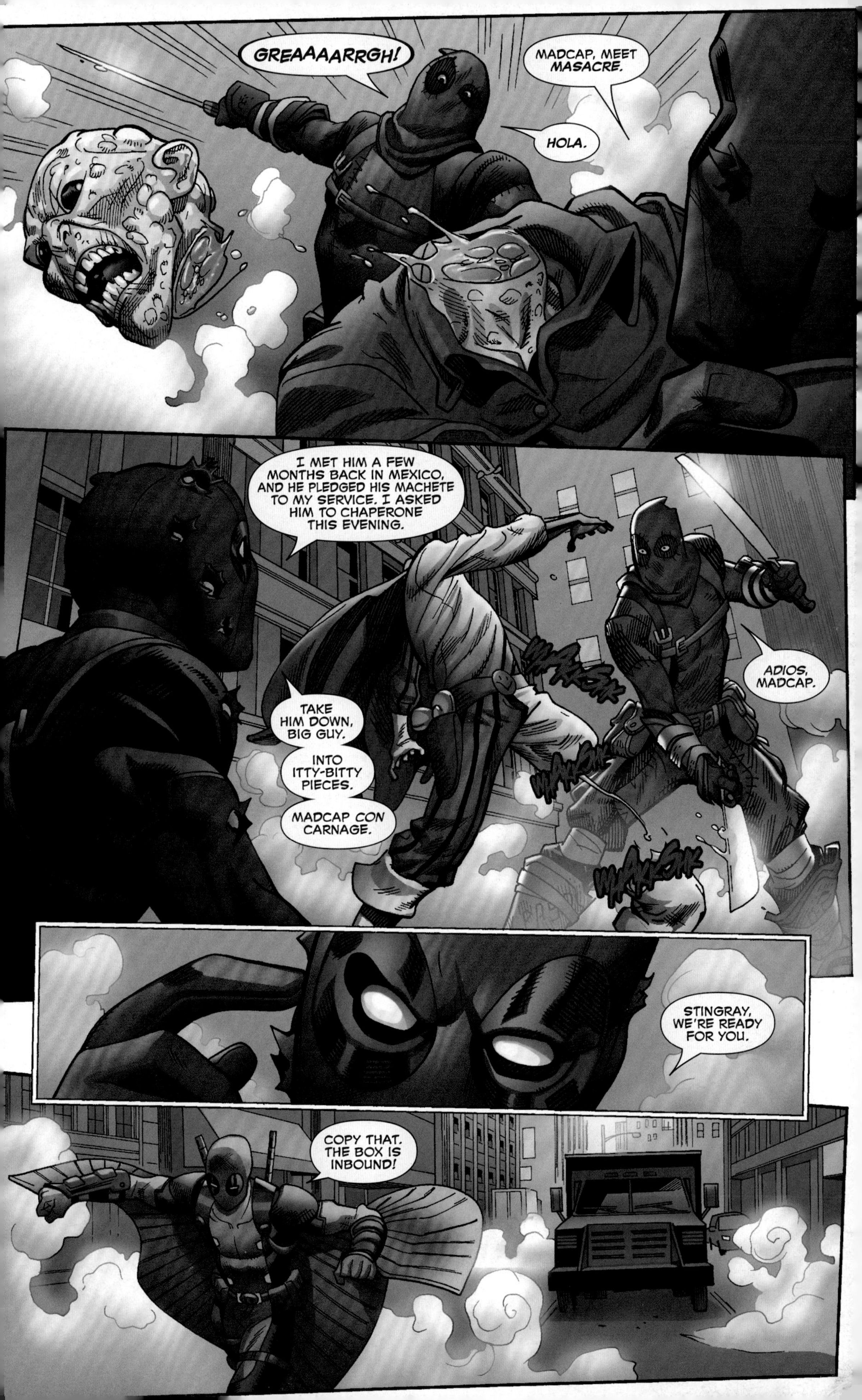
GREAAAARRGH!
MADCAP, MEET MASACRE.
HOLA.
I MET HIM A FEW MONTHS BACK IN MEXICO, AND HE PLEDGED HIS MACHETE TO MY SERVICE. I ASKED HIM TO CHAPERONE THIS EVENING.
TAKE HIM DOWN, BIG GUY.
INTO ITTY-BITTY PIECES.
MADCAP CON CARNAGE.
ADIOS, MADCAP.
STINGRAY, WE'RE READY FOR YOU.
COPY THAT. THE BOX IS INBOUND!

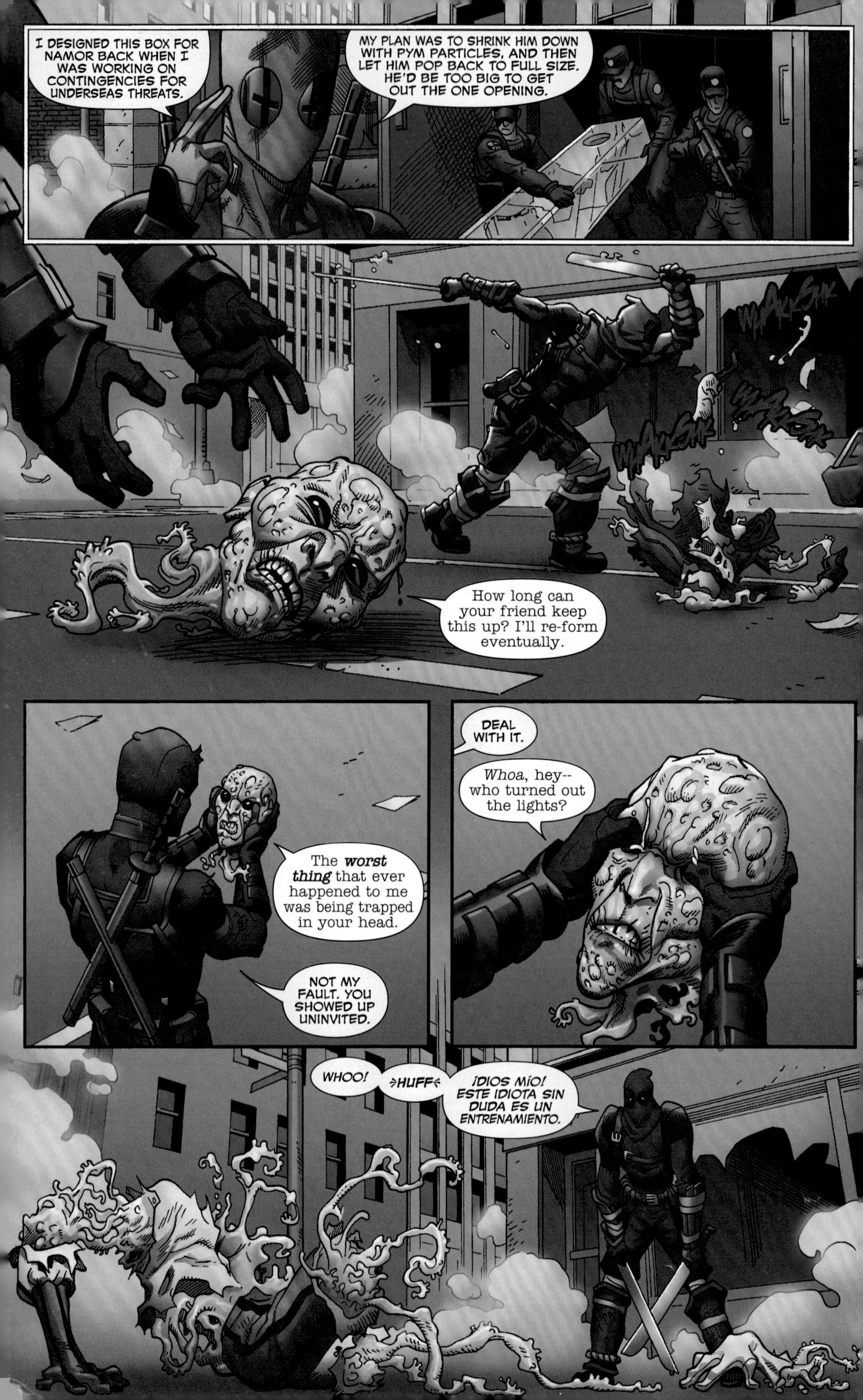

I DESIGNED THIS BOX FOR NAMOR BACK WHEN I WAS WORKING ON CONTINGENCIES FOR UNDERSEAS THREATS.
MY PLAN WAS TO SHRINK HIM DOWN WITH PYM PARTICLES, AND THEN LET HIM POP BACK TO FULL SIZE. HE'D BE TOO BIG TO GET OUT THE ONE OPENING.
WHAKKSHK
WHAKKSHK
WHAKKSHK
WHAKKSHK
How long can your friend keep this up? I'll re-form eventually.
The *worst thing* that ever happened to me was being trapped in your head.
NOT MY FAULT. YOU SHOWED UP UNINVITED.
DEAL WITH IT.
Whoa, hey-- who turned out the lights?
WHOO!
HUFF
¡DIOS MÍO! ESTE IDIOTA SIN DUDA ES UN ENTRENAMIENTO.

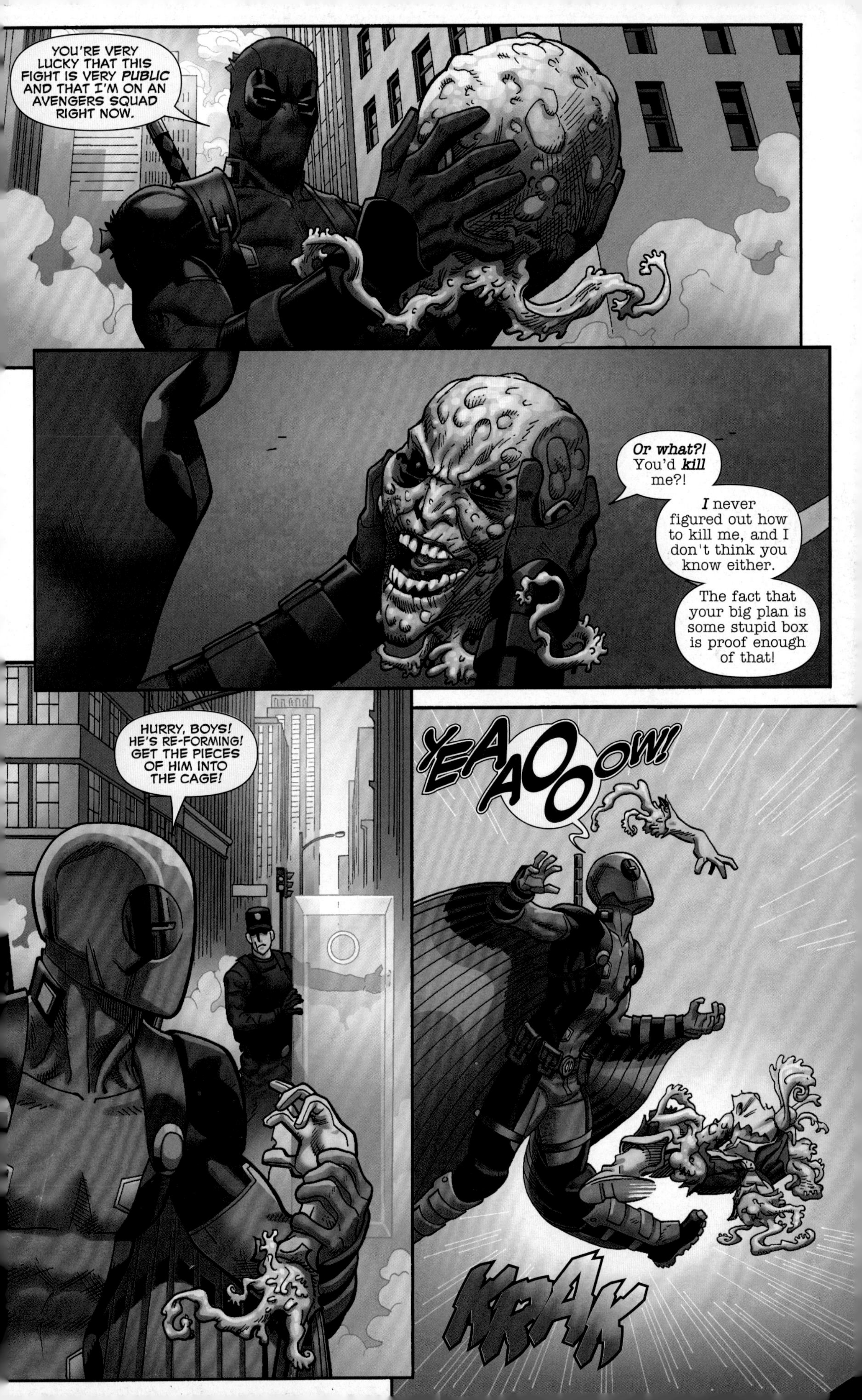
YOU'RE VERY LUCKY THAT THIS FIGHT IS VERY *PUBLIC* AND THAT I'M ON AN AVENGERS SQUAD RIGHT NOW.
Or what?! You'd ***kill*** me?!
I never figured out how to kill me, and I don't think you know either.
The fact that your big plan is some stupid box is proof enough of that!
HURRY, BOYS! HE'S RE-FORMING! GET THE PIECES OF HIM INTO THE CAGE!
YEAAOOOOW!
KRAK

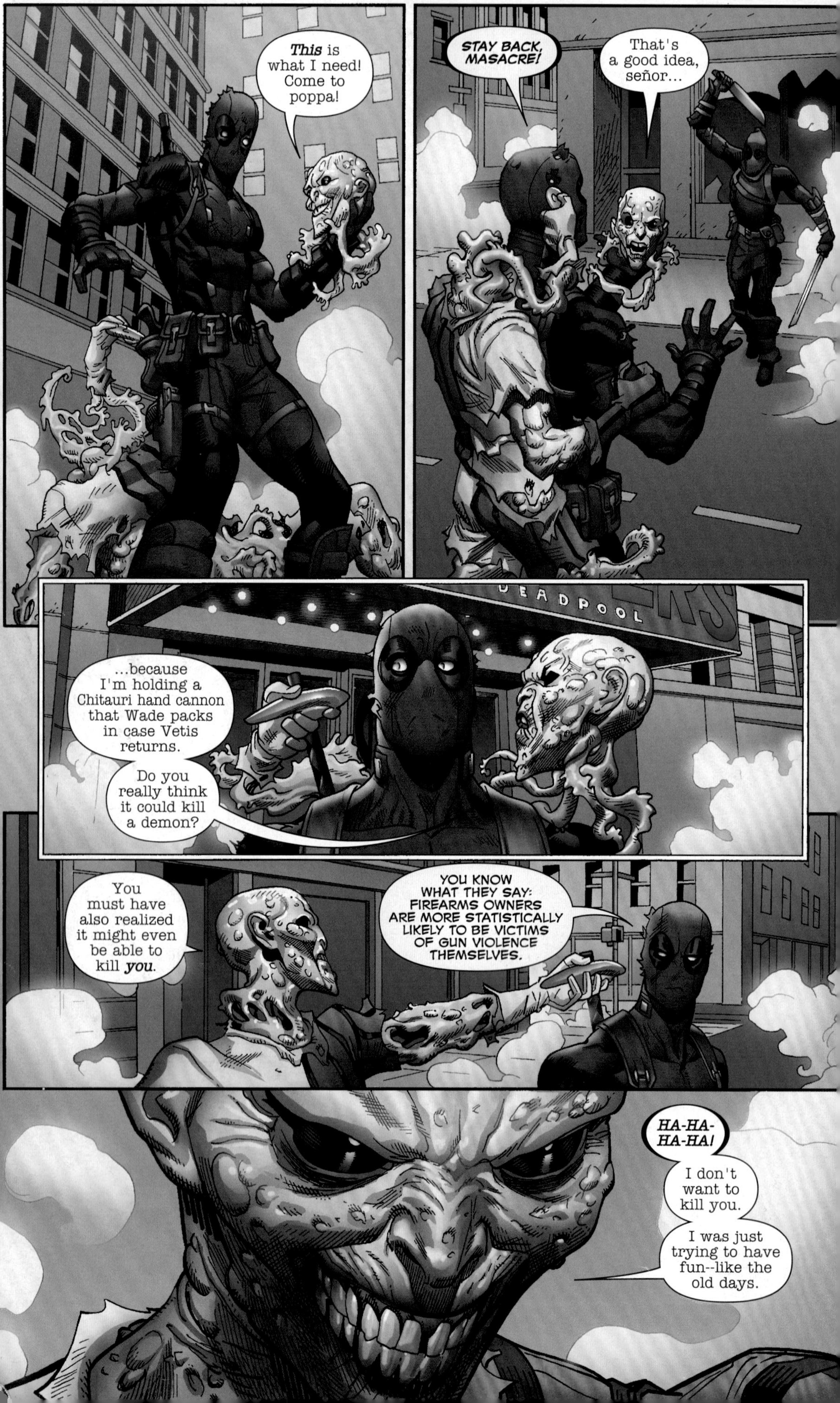
This is what I need! Come to poppa!
STAY BACK, MASACRE!
That's a good idea, señor...
DEADPOOL
...because I'm holding a Chitauri hand cannon that Wade packs in case Vetis returns.
Do you really think it could kill a demon?
You must have also realized it might even be able to kill you.
YOU KNOW WHAT THEY SAY: FIREARMS OWNERS ARE MORE STATISTICALLY LIKELY TO BE VICTIMS OF GUN VIOLENCE THEMSELVES.
HA-HA-HA-HA!
I don't want to kill you.
I was just trying to have fun--like the old days.

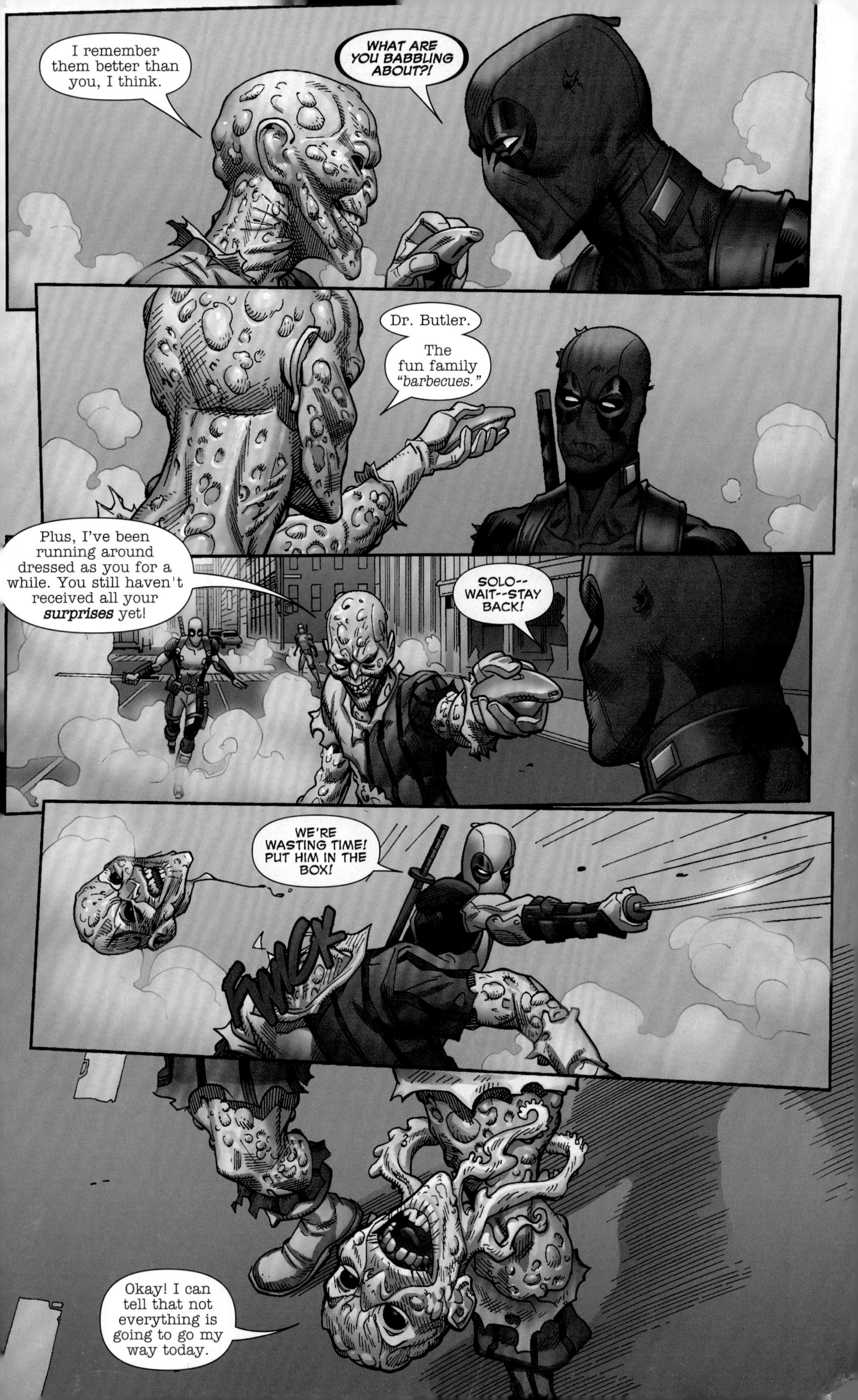
I remember them better than you, I think.
WHAT ARE YOU BABBLING ABOUT?!
Dr. Butler.
The fun family "barbecues."
Plus, I've been running around dressed as you for a while. You still haven't received all your surprises yet!
SOLO-- WAIT--STAY BACK!
WE'RE WASTING TIME! PUT HIM IN THE BOX!
FWICK
Okay! I can tell that not everything is going to go my way today.

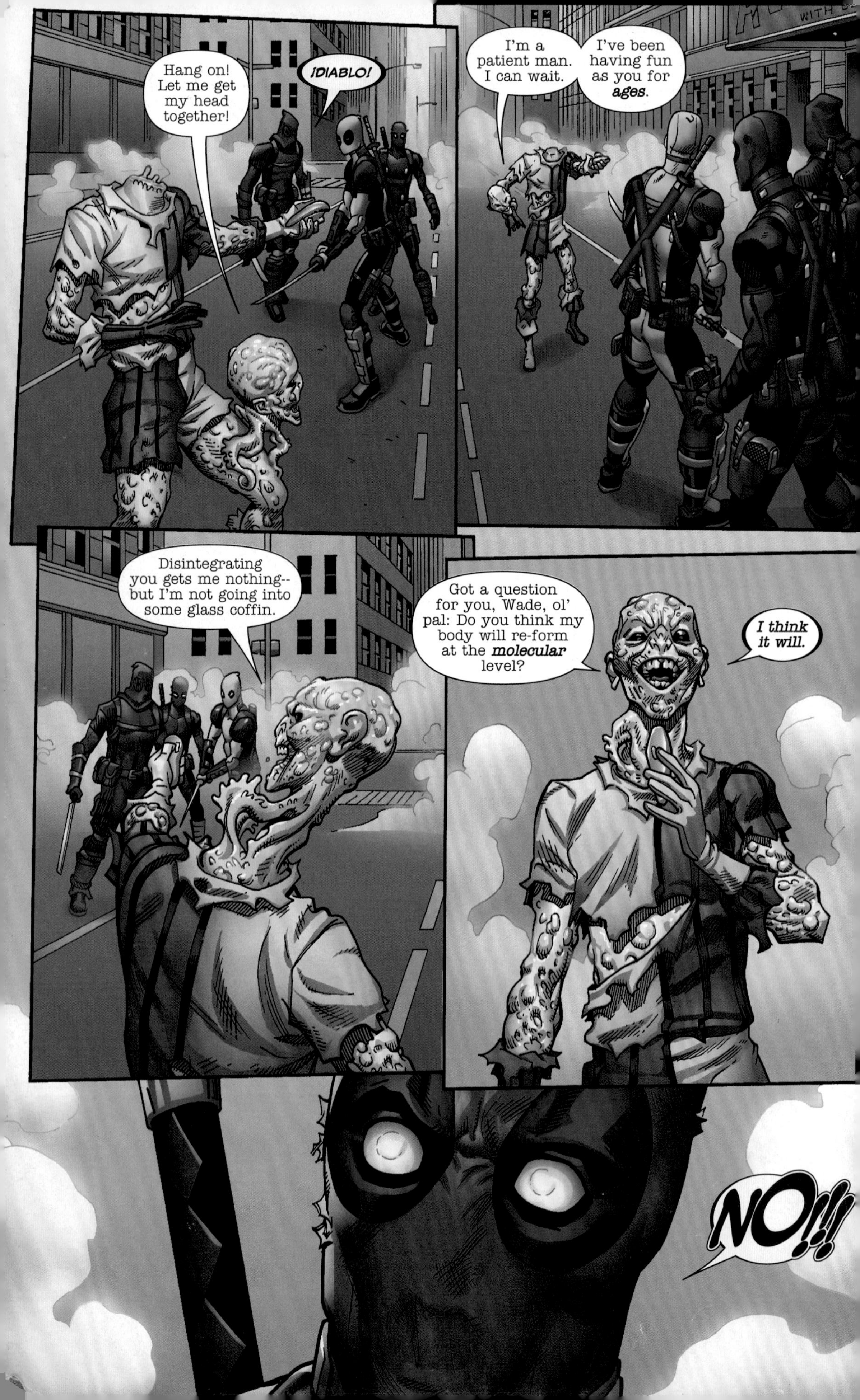
Hang on! Let me get my head together!
¡DIABLO!
I'm a patient man. I can wait.
I've been having fun as you for *ages*.
Disintegrating you gets me nothing-- but I'm not going into some glass coffin.
Got a question for you, Wade, ol' pal: Do you think my body will re-form at the *molecular* level?
I think it will.
NO!!!

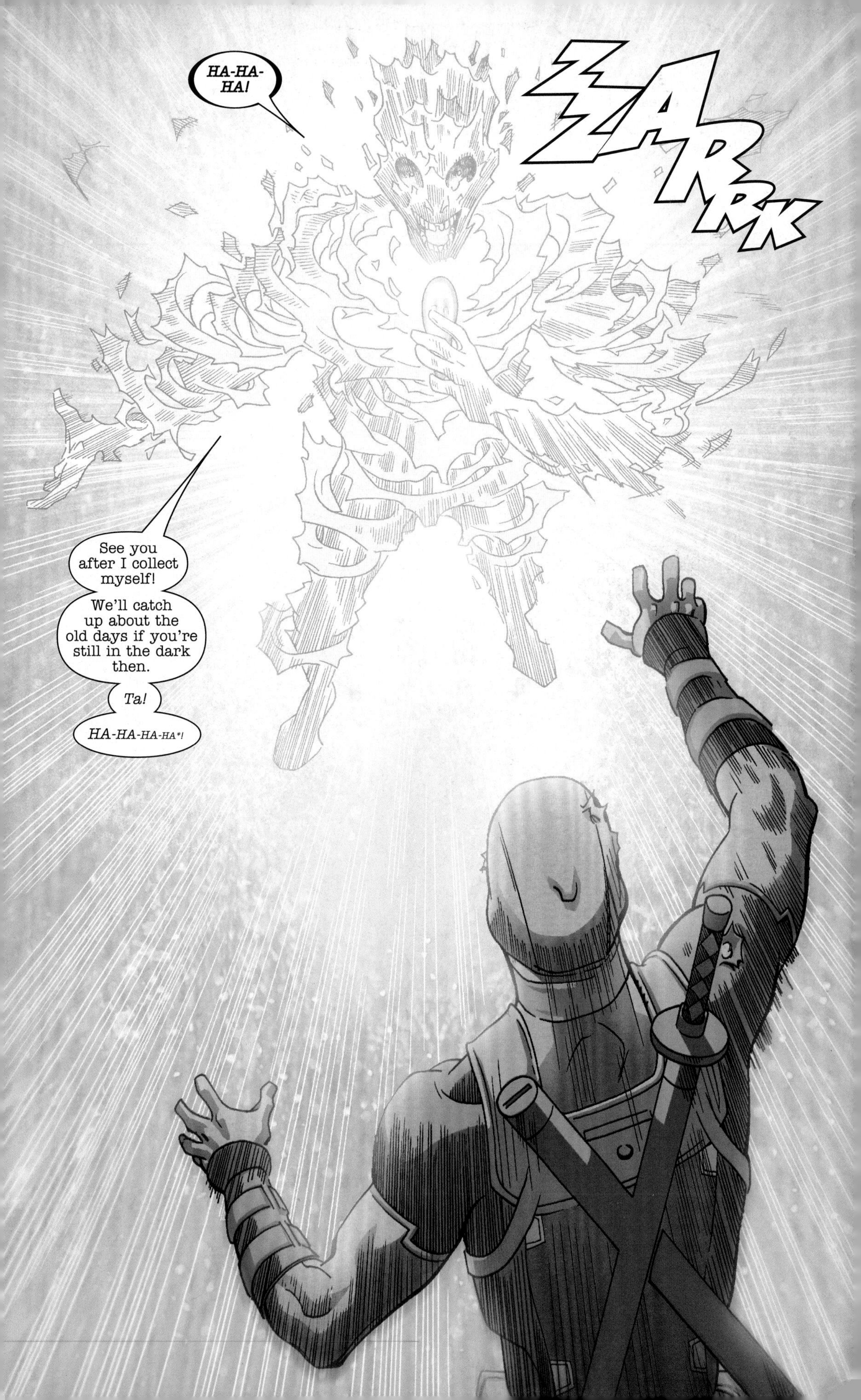

HA-HA-HA!
ZZARRRK
See you after I collect myself!
We'll catch up about the old days if you're still in the dark then.
Ta!
HA-HA-HA-HA*!

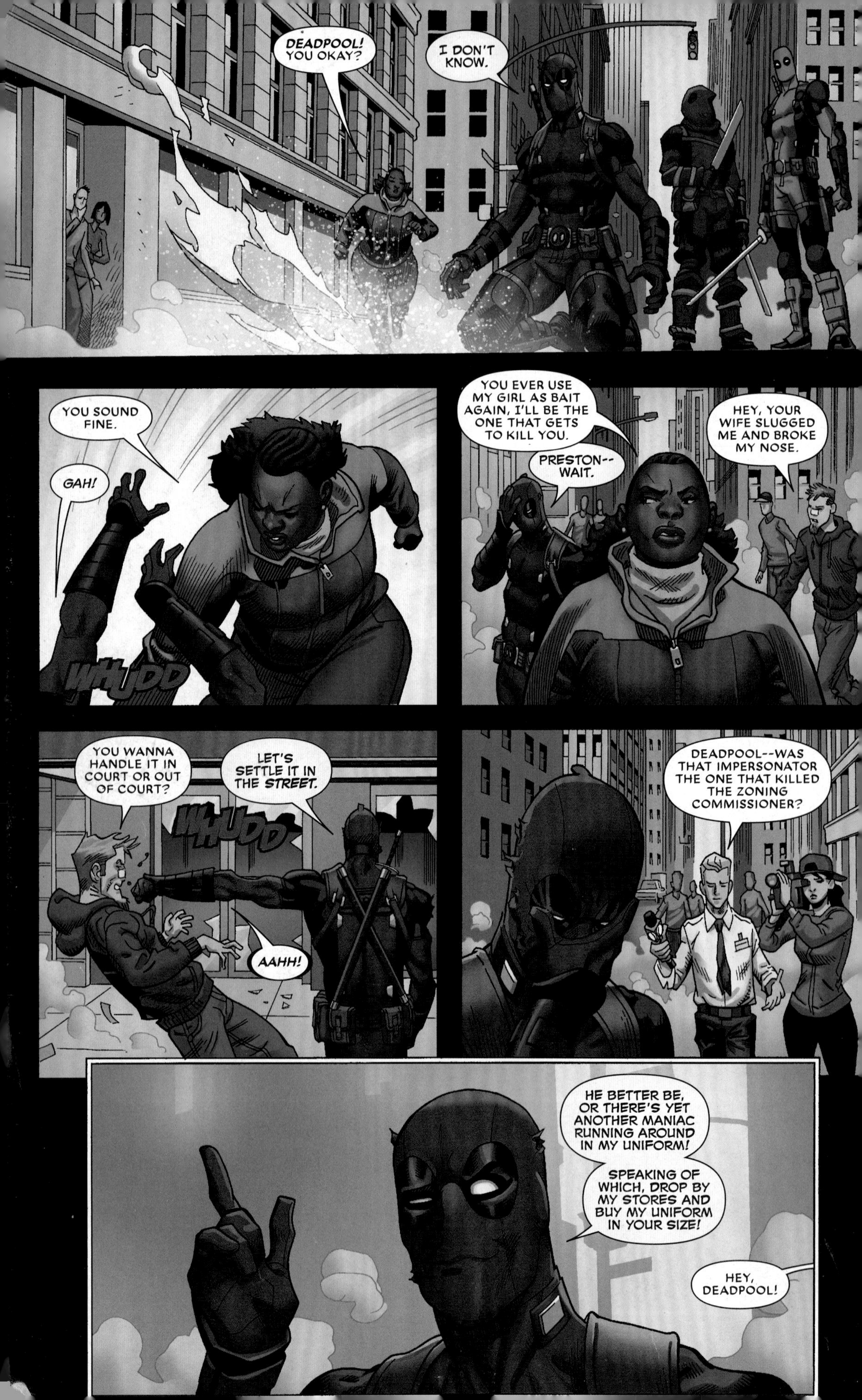
DEADPOOL! YOU OKAY?
I DON'T KNOW.
YOU SOUND FINE.
GAH!
WHUDD
YOU EVER USE MY GIRL AS BAIT AGAIN, I'LL BE THE ONE THAT GETS TO KILL YOU.
PRESTON--WAIT.
HEY, YOUR WIFE SLUGGED ME AND BROKE MY NOSE.
YOU WANNA HANDLE IT IN COURT OR OUT OF COURT?
LET'S SETTLE IT IN THE STREET.
WHUDD
AAHH!
DEADPOOL--WAS THAT IMPERSONATOR THE ONE THAT KILLED THE ZONING COMMISSIONER?
HE BETTER BE, OR THERE'S YET ANOTHER MANIAC RUNNING AROUND IN MY UNIFORM!
SPEAKING OF WHICH, DROP BY MY STORES AND BUY MY UNIFORM IN YOUR SIZE!
HEY, DEADPOOL!

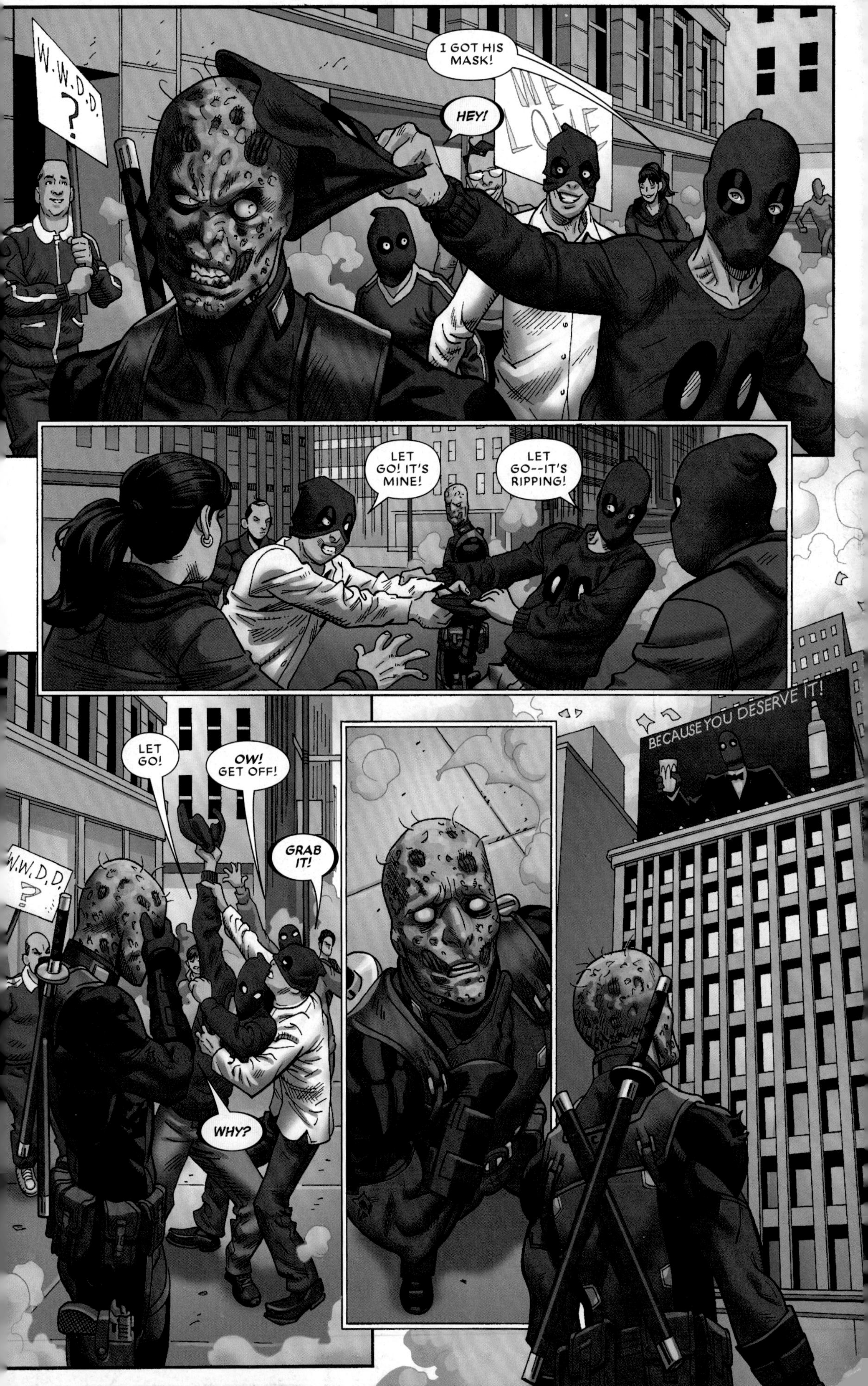
W.W.D.D. ?
I GOT HIS MASK!
HEY!
LET GO! IT'S MINE!
LET GO--IT'S RIPPING!
BECAUSE YOU DESERVE IT!
LET GO!
OW! GET OFF!
GRAB IT!
W.W.D.D. ?
WHY?

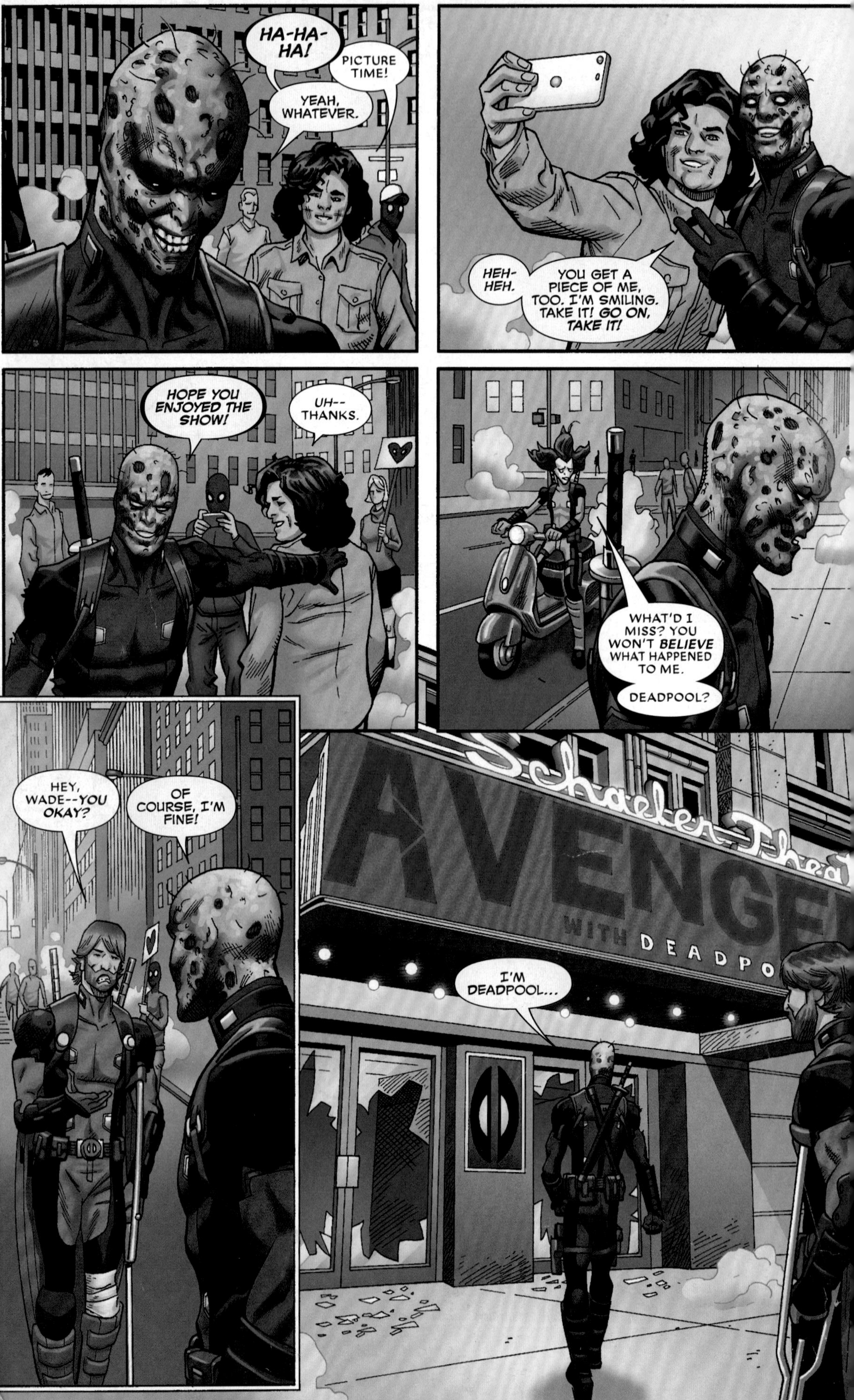
HA-HA-HA!
PICTURE TIME!
YEAH, WHATEVER.
HEH-HEH.
YOU GET A PIECE OF ME, TOO. I'M SMILING. TAKE IT! GO ON, TAKE IT!
HOPE YOU ENJOYED THE SHOW!
UH-- THANKS.
WHAT'D I MISS? YOU WON'T BELIEVE WHAT HAPPENED TO ME.
DEADPOOL?
HEY, WADE--YOU OKAY?
OF COURSE, I'M FINE!
Schaefer Theat
AVENGE
WITH DEADPO
I'M DEADPOOL...

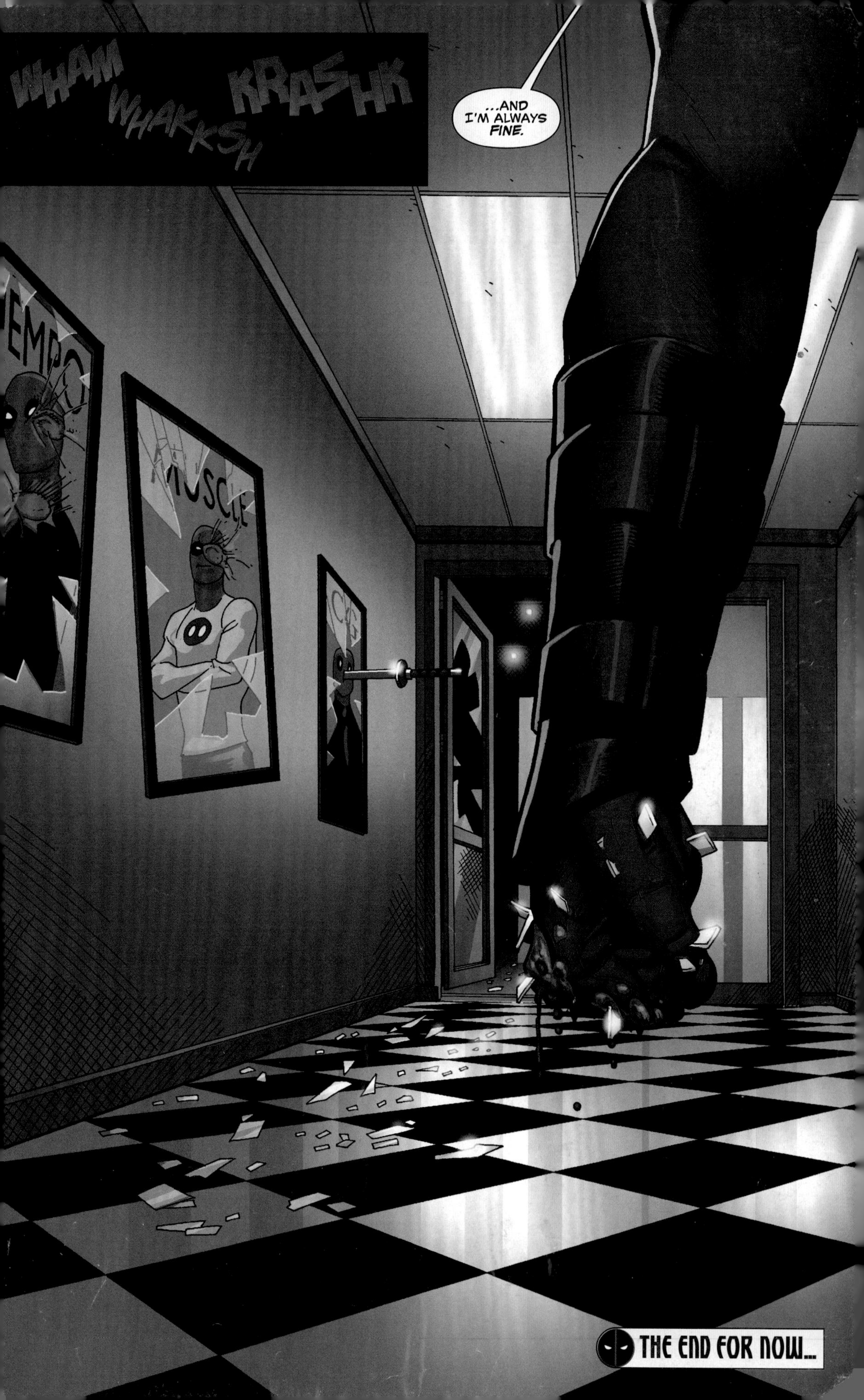
WHAM
WHAKKSH
KRASHK
...AND I'M ALWAYS FINE.
VEMPO
MUSCLE
THE END FOR NOW...

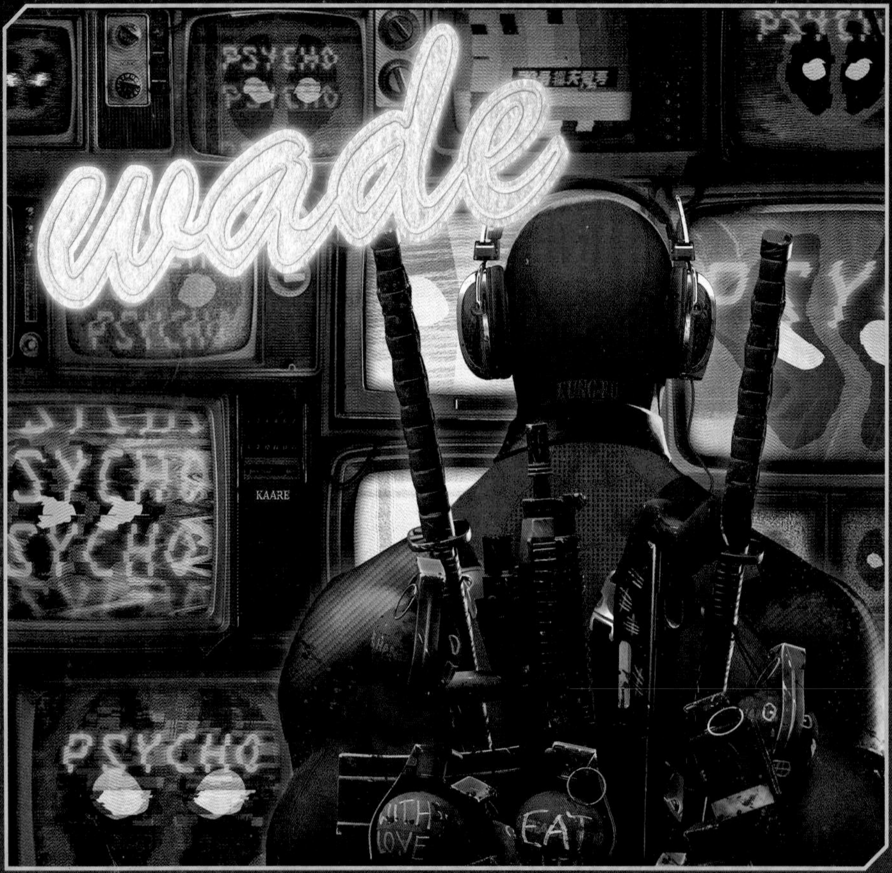
wade
PSYCHO
PSYCHO
KAARE
WITH LOVE
EAT

#1 hip-hop variant by KAARE ANDREWS

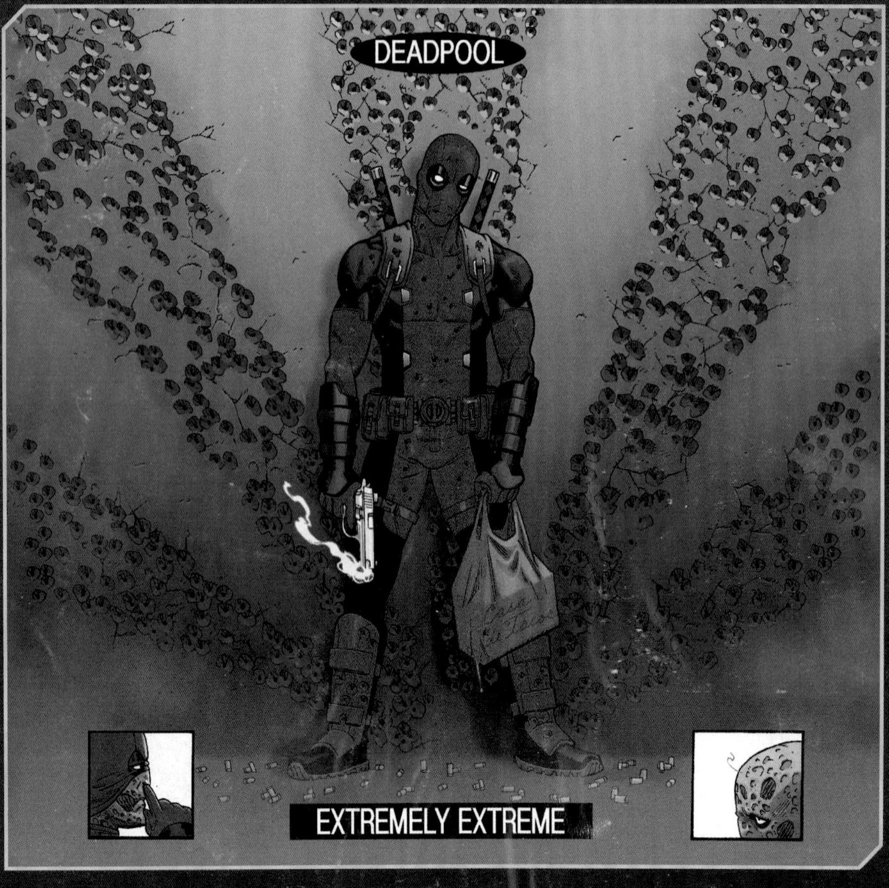
DEADPOOL
EXTREMELY EXTREME

#2 hip-hop variant by MIKE HAWTHORNE